D0346896

British Po

Also available from Continuum:

Roger Eatwell and Anthony Wright (eds), *Contemporary Political Ideologies*
Peter John, *Analysing Public Policy*
Sandra Joireman, *Nationalism and Political Identity*
Stephen Parsons, *Rational Choice and Politics*
Guy Peters, *Institutional Theory in Political Science*
Geoffrey Stern, *The Structure of International Society*
Alison Watson, *An Introduction to International Political Economy*

British Politics

A Critical Introduction

Stuart McAnulla
Series Editor: Jules Townshend

PARK LEARNING CENTRE
UNIVERSITY OF GLOUCESTERSHIRE
PO Box 220, The Park
Cheltenham GL50 2RH
Tel: 01242 714333

Continuum International Publishing Group
The Tower Building
11 York Road
London SE1 7NX

15 East 26th Street
New York
NY 10010

www.continuumbooks.com

© Stuart McAnulla 2006

All rights reserved. No part of this publication may be reproduced or transmitted in any form or by any means, electronic or mechanical, including photocopying, recording, or any information storage or retrieval system, without prior permission in writing from the publishers.

British Library Cataloguing-in-Publication Data
A catalogue record for this book is available from The British Library.

ISBN 0 8264 6155 7 (hardback)
0 8264 6156 5 (paperback)

Typeset by YHT Ltd, London
Printed and bound in Great Britain by MPG Books Ltd, Bodmin, Cornwall

DETAILED CONTENTS

List of Boxes

Acknowledgements

I wish to thank current colleagues at the University of Leeds for their consistent encouragement and advice over recent years, in particular David Seawright, Kevin Theakston and Nick Robinson. I also owe thanks to former colleagues at the University of Central England, Chris Painter and John Rouse, for numerous influential conversations on public sector reform. Not for the first time I am very much indebted to David Marsh from the University of Birmingham; although he has had no direct input into this book, his views have had strong (and self-evident) impact on a number of the arguments advanced. I would also like to thank Ian Price and Christina Parkinson at Continuum for their strong support for this project.

I must pay special tribute to Peter Kerr from the University of Birmingham, whose influence on this project has been immense. It was Peter who originally identified the need for a book of this nature and persuaded me to embark on its writing. Not only has Peter provided invaluable feedback on drafts on much of this work, he has also offered excellent advice regarding the scope, purpose and arguments of the book. Without Peter's enduring support for this project, it would not have got off the ground, let alone reached completion. My deepest gratitude is also extended to Jules Townshend (editor of the *Critical Political Studies* series) whose patience, unstinting support and editorial expertise have been of enormous importance. I am extremely grateful for the faith and encouragement he has provided throughout. Furthermore, it is a privilege to contribute to the excellent book series Jules has nurtured over recent years.

Finally, I thank Faye, to whom this volume is dedicated.

Introduction

PURPOSE AND AIMS

British politics has been studied from a wide variety of perspectives. Even a cursory review of the literature reveals extensive controversy as to the nature and key characteristics of British politics. Debates have rarely been more intense than during the last three decades, when scholars have grappled with topics such as political and industrial crises in the 1970s, the emergence of Thatcherism in the 1980s and triumph of new Labour in the 1990s. However, at the same time, many accounts of British politics are highly descriptive in content. For example, it is common for textbooks to focus on outlining key institutions such as parliament and other features such as the electoral system, or general trends in public policy. Too often the importance of *interpretation*, necessary for any understanding of British politics, is neglected. Attention to conveying factual information takes precedence over developing theoretical understandings.

The approach of this book is different. The overall aim is to provide an account of British politics that is *conceptually* and *theoretically* driven. The goal is to offer an account which not only outlines the key features of British politics but which also provides critical perspectives on them. Consequently the content, style and structure differ somewhat from conventional formats. Textbooks are often structured to devote individual chapters to examining particular institutions in detail, with other chapters devoted to important areas such as public policy, the electoral system and the constitution. In contrast, this book uses particular concepts and theories to illuminate the key dynamics of British politics, i.e. the ideas, practices and relationships that sustain the political system. Particular attention is devoted to understanding *contemporary* developments through an appreciation of the *traditional* dynamics of British politics.

The 'end' of British politics?

Yet in some ways it may be considered a peculiar time to produce a new textbook on British politics. For in recent years, a number of authors have questioned whether British politics even has a future. Book titles abound such *The Death of Britain*, *After Britain*, *The Break-up of Britain* and *The Day Britain Died*. More generally, it has become common for people to use terms such as 'the end of history', 'the end of ideology' and the 'post-political era'. Yet why have such epochal, even apocalyptic, theories become commonplace? A number of alleged economic, political and cultural trends are cited in support of these 'endist' theories, including:

- *Globalization* – global economic and political integration is making nation-state governments, such as Britain, increasingly irrelevant.
- *Europeanization* – European integration means that sovereignty is increasingly shared between European countries, making individual state governments less significant.
- *Governance* – public policy is increasingly delivered by a complex mix of public, private and voluntary bodies which 'govern without government'.
- *Devolution* – the devolution of power to the constituent nations of Britain means that it is becoming less meaningful to speak of 'British politics' in a holistic sense.
- *The 'end of ideology'* – following the defeat of Communism there is now no major conflict of political ideas in Britain. There is agreement between the main parties on all fundamental issues.

Each of these arguments highlights important issues. Most contain at least a kernel of truth. British politics has indeed been subject to far-reaching change in recent decades and a range of both external and internal pressures has contributed to this. However, arguments that British politics is coming to an end, or is being transformed beyond recognition, are overblown. Many of the traditional dynamics of British politics, including key ideas and institutional relationships, remain in place. Moreover, there are strong patterns of both continuity *and* change in the structure of British politics. In contrast to 'endist' theories, this book affirms a number of points:

- *The British state remains powerful* – British government is still strong government. External and internal factors (such as Europeanization and privatization) have altered its role but it remains the key to shaping public policy in Britain.
- *Traditional political ideas remain important* – despite the impact of notions of globalization, new right and 'third way' perspectives on British politics, many traditional ideas remain important to the function of British politics. In particular, notions of British democracy and British nationalism play a key role.
- *Traditional institutional relationships remain important* – despite numerous reforms such as privatization, devolution and decentralization, many traditional institutional relationships remain important. In general, the British state retains a highly centralized, elitist character.
- *Significant political/ideological conflict persists* – despite the domination of neo-liberalism, there are still significant clashes of political ideas. In particular, important conflicts persist over British identity and Britain's role in Europe.

The book has three main aims:

(1) To compare, contrast and evaluate rival models and perspectives on British politics.
(2) To account for the traditional dynamics of British politics, in particular key ideas and institutional relationships.
(3) To evaluate contemporary developments in British politics, including the politics of new Labour, the 'modernization' of British government and constitutional reform.

ASSUMPTIONS AND CONTRIBUTIONS OF THIS BOOK

Points of departure: the role of theory

The Poverty of theory on British politics

One of the weaknesses of the literature on British politics is the lack of theoretical models or general perspectives on the nature of the British political system. Historically, much work has neglected theory, with authors preferring to focus on describing institutions and processes in detail rather than producing general conceptualizations (Rhodes 1995). Greenleaf (1983:7) argues many scholars tended to get entrapped in a 'mass of detail', meaning they lack 'an explicit organising perspective ...'. Often, theoretical assumptions of authors are implicit rather than explicit. Moreover, in the postwar period many analysts have become specialists in *particular* aspects of the system (e.g. voting behaviour or pressure groups) and have been less interested in theorizing about British politics in a holistic way. The problems created by a lack of theory are compounded by the lack of attention given to the models of British politics that do exist. Many textbooks present important perspectives such as pluralism or Marxism in a very brief, cursory manner, making little attempt to link these to their discussion of concrete political events and institutions. Often theory is regarded as something of a side-show, to be picked up where useful but non-essential next to the study of actual political events and processes. Even advanced research monographs on British politics often make limited reference to theory, with influential concepts such as the 'Westminster model' used in loose and vaguely defined ways. Some of the reasons for this lack of theory are discussed below. However, should this neglect of theory be a cause for concern? Is it not better to focus on real events and processes rather than bothering with abstract theories? Theory can have a number of uses, including:

- *Acting as a starting point* – in a subject as dense as politics there is a wealth of historical facts, institutions and ideas to come to grips with. Theory can provide a starting point, an organizing perspective which outlines the key features or dynamics of political processes.
- *Acting as a simplifying device* – the purpose of most theory is to *simplify* a highly complex reality and to draw attention to the most significant factors or ideas relevant to understanding a political

context. On occasions, theory may seem to students like a conspiracy to make life harder! However, the aim is (or should be) the opposite.

- *Assisting explanation of political events* – the aim of much theory is to help explain *why* events happen rather than just describe what does happen. Theories often attempt to identify the key reasons why things are the way they are, reasons that may not be apparent to us in daily life.

Thus theory can be an important tool for scholars of politics, aiding both understanding and explanation. Furthermore, it can be argued that it is impossible fully to avoid theory when approaching the study of politics. Each of us approaches the study of political institutions or events with certain presuppositions about the nature of politics and the wider social world (even if our knowledge is quite limited). The assumptions we make (e.g. 'it is important that we have strong political leaders') affect the way we then interpret politics (e.g. 'John Major was a poor prime minister'). Similarly the values that we hold (e.g. 'violence is always wrong') affect the way we interpret political events (e.g. 'Britain was wrong to go to war with Iraq'). Theory offers a way through which the assumptions and/or values of the scholar can be laid out. Where theoretical positions are made clear this helps students understand 'where people are coming from'. For example, if someone declares sympathy with Marxist theory, then this gives an indication about the assumptions underlying their interpretation of events. One drawback of much literature on British politics is that theoretical assumptions are not made explicit. This book seeks to address the neglect of theory in two ways:

(1) The first two chapters are devoted to outlining the most influential theories and models of British politics. Key perspectives are revealed and compared, drawing attention to their respective strengths and weaknesses.
(2) Later chapters apply particular concepts and models in an analysis of contemporary British politics. Key theories are used to understand and explain patterns of change and continuity.

The traditional dynamics of British politics

Many accounts of British politics are chronological in structure. Discussion will often be focused on a particular period, e.g. the Major period (1990–7), or a wider segment of history, e.g. the immediate postwar period (1945–70). Analyses of particular governments are, usually, preceded by discussion of the policies and approach of the previous administration. One difficulty with this approach is that, while attention is paid to detailing successive events and crises, the 'bigger picture' of British political history fades from view. There is a strong preference for accounts of British government that stress the role of contingent factors and the privileged role of key actors in explaining political events (Bevir 2001). This can have two negative consequences:

(1) Political change may be emphasized at the expense of highlighting patterns of continuity.
(2) Empirical detail may be emphasized at the expense of highlighting the broader dynamics of British politics, including the key ideas and institutional relationships that endure, but alter, over time.

In contrast, this book seeks to initiate discussion of contemporary developments in British politics by drawing attention to the traditional dynamics of British politics (Chapters 3 & 4). Rather than being focused on chronology, the aim is to lay out the key ideas and institutional relationships that have profoundly shaped the development of British politics. Attention will be given to how these have changed over time, but it will be argued that many key characteristics of British politics have endured despite numerous economic, political and technological upheavals. These characteristics help explain important continuities in the practice of British government. Discussion centres in turn on key ideas followed by key institutional relationships.

Key ideas

Ideas play a multifaceted role in British politics. Ideas shape people's understanding of the political world, orienting them to act in particular ways. At the same time ideas can be used as tools either to garner support for politicians or to legitimize decisions they make. Furthermore the ideas inherited from past generations play an important role in shaping contemporary politics. Despite the importance of ideas, their treatment in the literature of British politics is patchy. Historically, many books pay limited attention to ideas in their own right, focusing more on the conflicts between different interest groups and personalities. Many of the textbooks that do examine the role of ideas limit discussion to outlining the key ideologies relevant to British politics, namely liberalism, conservatism and socialism. While these are of crucial importance, less attention is given to outlining the dominant, often cross-cutting (in ideological and party-political terms) ideas which have featured strongly in the governing discourses of British governments. As well as outlining key ideologies this book examines:

- Ideas and themes which have recurred in the discourses of most modern British governments (e.g. notions of British identity and British nationalism).
- How such themes have endured, resisted rival ideas and adapted to changing circumstances (e.g. the idea of strong, responsible government).

The impact of such ideas is illustrated with reference to trends in public policy and governing styles. It will be demonstrated that particular sets of ideas have helped sustain significant long-term patterns of continuity in British politics.

Key institutional relationships

One of the strongest features of the literature on British politics is the attention devoted to examining key institutions such as parliament, the civil service, local government and the political parties. There is a great deal of specialist literature on each of these topics. If there is a weakness in textbook treatment of institutions, it may be a tendency to treat institutions in an isolated fashion, out of broader context. In this book the focus is not so much on examining individual institutions but rather the key relationships *between* particular institutions that constitute traditional dynamics of British politics. This account will seek to demonstrate two key aspects of these relationships:

- Institutional relationships are broadly structured to ensure the dominance of the core executive (central government).
- Institutional relationships are structured in a way which favours the interests of particular elite groups.

Attention will be devoted to examining how institutional relationships have been re-formed, created and subject to increasing complexity in the postwar period. At the same time, it will be illustrated that the fundamental characteristics of many of these relationships have survived despite adaptations. Again, these constitute traditional dynamics which help explain patterns of continuity.

Contemporary developments in British politics

As highlighted above, many argue British politics is currently at a critical juncture. In recent years a set of important changes has impacted on governing style, policy-processes and the structure of government itself. For the first time, a Labour government has served two full terms in office. The Blair government has pushed through important changes in public policy and indeed to the process of government itself. Furthermore it has enacted a series of far-reaching constitutional reforms. The final section of the book surveys these changes and considers to what extent these constitute a break with the past.

The new Labour government elected in 1997 has been subject to a great deal of academic study. The literature is now voluminous. Despite the attention devoted to examining the policies, ideas and governing style of new Labour, there is surprisingly little consensus as to the significance of their period in office. Three generic interpretations are popular which respectively argue how new Labour should be considered:

- A continuation of the ideas and policies of Thatcherism.
- A renewed form of social democracy, or 'third way'.
- Continuous with the politics of 'old Labour'.

Each of these theories of new Labour is reviewed and compared in Chapter 5. It is argued there are limitations to comparing new Labour to particular ideological strands of political thought. In Chapter 5 the key policies, ideas and style of new Labour are reviewed, not just against the practices and ideas of preceding governments but against the broader traditional dynamics of British politics. Chapters 6 and 7 look in detail at new Labour's reform of the processes and institutions of government itself. These reforms are assessed through the application of the theoretical perspectives favoured in earlier chapters. The overall aim of the final section of the book is to review contemporary developments in British politics with the purpose of explaining complex patterns of continuity and change.

CHAPTER STRUCTURE AND GENERAL ARGUMENT

Chapter 1 reviews traditional models of British politics. It accounts for the historically dominant 'Westminster model'; its core assumptions and variations on the perspective. The importance of this model is explained, as are the reasons for its decline in recent decades. Perspectives using notions of the 'British political tradition' and elitist government are also offered. The chapter also accounts for the rise of pluralist theory, drawing attention to its core beliefs and arguable weaknesses. Lastly, the radical challenge to conventional theory posed by Marxist theory is assessed. Each of the models is compared and contrasted. It is argued that while most of the traditional models have struggled to account for changing political circumstances, the idea of the British political tradition remains a particularly useful tool for understanding British politics.

Chapter 2 reviews more contemporary models of British politics. These are models that have developed in response to the political crises and upheavals experienced in British politics in the 1970s and 1980s. First, the currently most influential academic model of British politics is examined, namely the 'differentiated-polity' model, associated with Rod Rhodes. The strengths of this model in breaking with the assumptions of the Westminster model are highlighted. Furthermore, the benefits of the model's core concepts, such as the 'hollowed-out' state, to understanding recent trends in British public policy are outlined. However, it is argued that the pluralist and postmodernist assumptions of the model undermine it as a convincing organizing perspective on British politics. The alternative 'asymmetric power model' forwarded by Marsh, Richards and Smith is reviewed as another important rival to the Westminster model. The merits of this model in accounting for both change and continuity are highlighted. It is argued that the model's emphasis on the importance of structured inequality and the enduring importance of the British political tradition stand out as particular strengths. The chapter also reviews two important normative perspectives, namely the 'new right' and 'third way' models. The new right critique of the British state is highlighted, as is the prognosis it offered, which proved so influential on the direction of the Thatcher governments. The 'third way' reply to this perspective is also outlined as are its proposals for change. It is argued that despite the radicalism of such perspectives they are less of a challenge to the traditions of British politics than is often assumed.

Chapter 3 examines the key ideas in British politics in more detail. The three most influential ideologies, namely conservatism, liberalism and socialism, are reviewed. It is argued that liberalism and conservatism have proved the most influential traditions of thought, while socialism's impact has been more limited and ambiguous. The chapter then looks at cross-cutting themes and ideas which have featured heavily in the governing discourses of British government. It is argued that notions of strong government, a liberal economy, pragmatism and British nationalism have proved dominant themes in the history of British politics. The idea of 'British exceptionalism' is discussed, as are its implications for both the domestic and international politics of both political parties whilst in government. It is proposed that the idea (and fear) of British decline has persisted as an on-going concern in the mindset of governments over recent decades. Lastly the chapter examines other sets of ideas which have (thus far largely unsuccessfully) challenged the dominant ideas and practices of the British political tradition.

Chapter 4 examines the key institutional relationships in British politics. It places these in context by outlining the fundamentals of the British constitution and charting the growth of the state in the twentieth century. It is argued that, while the scope and size of the state has been transformed, much of the elitist character of state management has been maintained. The chapter then considers key intergovernmental relationships, focusing on relations between central government and local government, and central government and the EU. It argues that centre-local relations in Britain have generally been subject to a range of tensions, while generally being conducted on terms favourable to the centre. Furthermore, central government has made increasing use of its privileged constitutional powers to diminish the power and authority of local councils. At the same time, the ways in which British central government has ceded powers to the EU is charted, highlighting the significant impact which EU institutions, laws and regulations now have on domestic politics. However, it is argued that notions of 'Europeanization' are exaggerated and that British government is still the main determinant of public policy in most areas. Finally, the chapter examines key democratic relations in Britain, notably the relations between government and interest groups as well as political parties and the electorate. It is argued that government generally structures relations with interest groups in a way that maximizes achievement of its goals and efficient policy implementation. The idea that 'union power' became dominant in the 1960s and 1970s is challenged, before examining the way in which the Thatcher and Major governments marginalized many key interest groups from decision-making. The relationship between political parties and the general population is reviewed, examining how far the parties have been catalysts for representation, participation and accountability within the political system. It is argued that traditionally both main parties have been dominated by elitist styles of leadership aimed at limiting participation in policy-making. Furthermore, it is suggested the development of the mass media has in many ways contributed to the further entrenchment of centralized, elitist forms of party leadership and government.

Chapter 5 conducts an analysis of the impact of the new Labour government on British politics. The main academic perspectives on new Labour are reviewed and compared. Subsequently the extent of political change under the Blair government is assessed by examining new Labour's economic policy, welfare policy, governing style and governing discourse. It is argued that new Labour's governing strategy is strongly influenced by neo-liberalism, but that other ideas including communitarianism and the third way have also impacted on public policy. It is further suggested that new Labour's clearest break with the strategy of the Conservatives is in the governing discourse they have employed. However, it is proposed that this discourse also reproduces many of the traditionally dominant themes of governing discourse as highlighted in Chapter 3. More generally, it is argued that, despite the significant policy and institutional reforms introduced by new Labour, many of the traditional dynamics of British politics remain intact.

The impact of new Labour is further investigated in Chapter 6. This chapter examines the 'modernizing government' agenda, a set of reforms introduced with the aim of improving both the function of government and the delivery of public services. Measures associated with 'integrated' government, performance innovation and providing 'citizen-centred' services are reviewed. The analysis reveals tensions within the reform strategy and problems arising from growing institutional complexity. The chapter then assesses how well the key academic models of British politics outlined in Chapter 2 can accommodate the changes associated with the 'modernizing government' reforms. It is argued that the changes offer more support to the 'asymmetric power' perspective, but that this model should be revised to take account of the emergence of new centralized forms of regulation. Furthermore, it is proposed that despite the novelty of elements of the agenda there is little within it which practically challenges the top-down view of democracy within the British political tradition.

Chapter 8 analyses the vast package of constitutional reforms introduced since 1997. The factors which have precipitated this agenda are analysed, drawing attention to the variety of movements and issues involved. The chapter sets out the main elements of constitutional reform introduced by the new Labour government, including devolution, the Freedom of Information Act, the Human Rights Act and electoral reform. The significance of each of these steps is evaluated, assessing just how far these measures reform or break with the traditions of government in Britain. It is argued that Scottish devolution and the Human Rights Act represent radical changes that pose big challenges to notions of parliamentary sovereignty. More generally, it is proposed that much of the agenda for constitutional reform has been deradicalized since 1997, with new Labour demonstrating a tendency to fall back on the assumptions associated with the British political tradition. However, it is suggested that the reforms to date may release forces and pressures for yet more radical change.

The book concludes with consideration of the overall impact of new Labour and the extent to which contemporary British politics is conditioned by traditional ideas and institutional relationships. The final chapter reflects on the use of key theoretical models in understanding and explaining British politics.

CHAPTER 1

Traditional Models of British Politics

INTRODUCTION

A number of general theoretical perspectives have been important in shaping the way British politics has been studied. This chapter outlines and evaluates such perspectives. Preference is given to analysing models which have persisted over a considerable period of time rather than those which tended to rise and subsequently fade away as particular short-term issues or controversies rose and then faded away. The chapter draws some sharp contrasts between the models. However, it is important to remember that there are often many areas of overlap between rival perspectives and there is much diversity within the broad schools of thought discussed. Each of the perspectives is subject to criticism and scrutiny, highlighting the arguable strengths and weaknesses of each. Important comparisons are drawn, although, as we will see, this is sometimes difficult because the focus of the models is often on different aspects of British politics (Tivey 1988: 3). It will also be argued that different *normative* assumptions or values underpin different perspectives. Four key perspectives are discussed:

- Westminster model.
- British political tradition.
- Pluralism.
- Marxism.

These perspectives are reviewed with a number of key questions in mind:

- What are the most important features of British politics?
- Which institutions, individuals or groups hold *power* within the British political system?
- To what extent and in what ways is British politics *democratic* in nature?
- What are the limitations and/or constraints upon participation and influence within the British political system?

BOX 1.1: *TRADITIONAL MODELS OF BRITISH POLITICS*

	Westminster model	*British political tradition*	*Pluralism*	*Marxism*
Focus of analysis	Parliament, formal institutions	Concepts of democracy	Public policy, interest groups	Class relations, the role of the state
View of power	Concentrated in hands of key individuals, e.g. ministers or prime minister	Executive dominates parliament and broader political system	Diffuse, dispersed among different groups – no one interest can dominate	Concentrated in hands of ruling class, reinforced by organization of the state
Key concepts	Parliamentary sovereignty	Parliamentary sovereignty	Policy communities, policy networks	Class conflict – capital *v* labour, employers *v* employees
Role of elections	Ensure democratic accountability	Legitimize elitist form of government (Tant version)	Only affect public policy outcomes to limited extent	Of limited importance – do not challenge ruling class power
Normative stance	Liberal democratic, supportive of status quo	Liberal variants (e.g. Birch) and radical variants (e.g. Tant)	Liberal democratic, combined with belief in group representation	Radical and/or revolutionary – committed to transforming British politics
Weaknesses	Too narrowly focused on parliament, neglects broader political processes	Over-emphasizes role of ideas, neglects importance of material interests	Over-emphasizes influence of interest groups, neglects power and resources of state	Too dismissive of democratic features of system

KEY PERSPECTIVES

Westminster model

Core features

Probably the most pervasive and influential perspective on British politics is that known as the 'Westminster model' (Judge 1993; Weller 1985; Verney 1991). Though there are many variations of the model, it has dominated textbook versions of British politics, forming (until recently at least) the most widespread, conventional and mainstream account of the key characteristics of British politics (McIntosh 1974).

BOX 1.2: *WESTMINSTER MODEL – KEY CHARACTERISTICS*

- Parliamentary sovereignty.
- Majority party control of the executive.
- Strong cabinet government.
- Accountability through elections.
- Institutionalized opposition.

Parliamentary sovereignty

Conventionally, Britain has been understood as a *unitary state*, meaning power resides exclusively in a single national authority. In this respect British government is more straightforward than some other political systems in which there is a formal division of power between different institutions (e.g. the United States). The guiding principle, which underpins the British political system, is that of *parliamentary sovereignty*. Within the Westminster model perspective, there is no higher authority than Parliament (other than, theoretically, the monarch, who holds the power to dissolve Parliament) and no other national body can question the legitimacy of its decisions. Parliament passes laws which are then implemented by other bodies, including the civil service and the courts. In theory, there is nothing to stop Parliament passing any bill it wishes, irrespective of public opinion. Furthermore, it may discard any previously made law – parliaments have no scope to bind their successors to existing legislation. The judiciary has powers to question legislation on legal grounds but ultimately cannot block or overturn it. Members of Parliament are not (constitutionally) constrained to vote in particular ways by their constituents or any organized interests.

Majority party control of the executive

Parliament is elected using the *First-Past-the-Post* electoral system. As such the system will, usually, enable one political party to obtain a majority in the House of Commons. Britain has traditionally had a two-party political system, meaning that two main parties compete to gain majority control of Parliament. The winning party is invited by the monarch to form a government. The leader of the winning party is responsible for forming a cabinet of ministers to run the executive, i.e. the decision-making machinery of government. Ministers will almost always be selected from the MPs of the majority party. Accordingly, in general, the winning party will support the actions and proposed legislation of cabinet and ministers. In effect, this means that, unlike in many political systems, the *executive* and *legislature* are effectively combined. Cabinet ministers form the executive, yet they are (usually) simultaneously members of the legislature. This fusion is further supported by traditions of strong *party discipline*. Each of the main parties seeks to ensure that back-bench MPs support their leadership (whether in government or opposition), operating a 'whip' system whereby MPs can be subject to varieties of punishment if they do not back the party line. It is thus unusual for (majority-party) back-bench MPs in the *House of Commons* to rebel against the government view on key issues. It is more common for the *House of Lords* to oppose government legislation; however, by convention the Lords can only delay legislation, not finally veto it. Hence strong cabinet government is the norm.

Strong cabinet government

This means that the executive is in a powerful position to lead government and pass the legislation it wishes. British government is usually *strong government*. Wright (2003: 48) argues that strong government is 'the big truth' about British politics, the key to understanding its character. The prime minister appoints ministers to manage the different departments of government (e.g. health or education), with the authority to issue directives and organize the administration of these policy areas. Three organizational features are important:

- Ministers are *accountable to Parliament* for the decisions they take and for what occurs within their own departments or areas of responsibility (Judge 1993).
- The work of ministers is coordinated through *cabinet* meetings chaired by the prime minister. The cabinet takes *collective* responsibility for all decisions taken by government.
- Ministers are supported by a *politically neutral* civil service responsible for implementing the desired policies of the government of the day.

Accountability through elections

The Westminster model is founded on the principle of parliamentary sovereignty rather than popular sovereignty. The only exception to this occurs during general elections, every four or five years. It is at this point that the population holds the government accountable and may choose to re-elect it or remove it from office. Similarly, individual MPs are accountable at this point to their local constituents. General elections enable each voter to make their voice heard and hence endow Parliament with democratic legitimacy.

Institutionalized opposition

In the Westminster model *opposition* is given an institutional form. The monarch invites the leader of the main losing party to form a *shadow* cabinet responsible for opposing the government. This ensures that the government of the day is held to account in Parliament.

A further defining feature of many accounts of the Westminster model is a normative belief in the virtues of the system. In other words, traditionally British political scientists tended to believe that the Westminster model provided democratic and effective government. Many subscribed to a Whig-oriented view of the British political system. They believed that the Westminster model was well suited to gradual and evolutionary change, capable of adapting where appropriate but conserving traditions and conventions that had proven themselves to be effective over a long period. They sympathized with the Westminster model's ability to provide strong, effective leadership, possessing the means to effect gradual change and cope with emerging crisis. Thus authors tended to take a benign rather than a critical view of the political system. This attitude was reinforced as the model was 'exported' to former colonies that adopted similar parliamentary procedures to those found at Westminster.

Variants of the Westminster model

Despite the self-congratulatory tone of much writing on the Westminster model, there have been significant debates between authors concerning how the model worked in practice. In particular, much attention is focused on who holds most power within the model. Disputes emerged as to whether it was the prime minister or the cabinet who were at the centre of power.

BOX 1.3: *VARIANTS OF THE WESTMINSTER MODEL – WHO HOLDS POWER?*

- *Prime ministerial model* – the prime minister dominates government and policy-making through using extensive powers of appointment, patronage and agenda-setting.
- *Cabinet model* – power lies in the collective decision-making body of cabinet; the prime minister is heavily dependent on his or her ministers.
- *Baronial model* – individual ministers have enormous power over their own departments, which they manage with relative independence from other ministers, including the prime minister.

Prime ministerial model

In the early postwar period authors such as McIntosh (1962, 1974, 1977) and Crossman (1963, 1972, 1977) (a former minister) argued that the prime minister was the dominant player within government circles. This school of thought draws attention to the extensive powers prime ministers have at their disposal, including:

- Appointing or removing ministers.
- Setting cabinet agenda.
- Appointing senior civil servants.

In addition, prime ministers have many personal staff available to do their bidding and they personally command much media attention. Lacking any specific policy responsibility, they are in a strong position to shape the overall direction of policy while ministers remain preoccupied with their designated areas.

Cabinet model

This perspective was challenged by authors such as Jones (1969), who argued that cabinet ministers were at the centre of power. They argued that prime ministers depend on the support of their colleagues for survival, therefore they cannot 'lord it over' ministers in quite the way people such as Crossman suggested. In practical terms it is difficult for prime ministers to have the knowledge or expertise of departments and policy areas that would enable them to dominate government. Also, many prime ministers seek to run a collegiate government and will seek consensual decision-making within cabinet.

Baronial model

Norton (1984, 2000) argues that ministers are somewhat akin to medieval barons, each with their own territory that they tend to guard jealously. Like barons, they have relative autonomy in the way they run their own area. Ministers take executive decisions in their departments on a day-to-day level and thus play a large role in determining policy. They are supported by senior civil servants with expertise in the relevant areas. Norton argues there are limits to collegiality between ministers – most will resent interference by other ministers within their areas of concern.

Evaluating the Westminster model

The Westminster model has, historically, been the most influential perspective within studies of British politics. However, in recent decades it has received much criticism. Alleged weaknesses of the model include:

- Narrow focus on formal institutions.
- Unrealistic view of political power.
- Increasingly antiquated and inaccurate system.
- Democratic aspects of British politics overstated.

Narrow focus on formal institutions

Much of what is included in the Westminster model is relatively uncontroversial, drawing attention to undisputed features of the British political system such as regular elections and the workings of Parliament. However, the model has been attacked for focusing almost exclusively on *formal* institutions of British politics. Critics argue that the model neglects the many informal, yet crucial, aspects of the political process. For example, little attention is given to the impact which interest groups such as business can have on the decisions a government makes. A range of organized interest groups deploy resources and efforts to influence government outside the corridors of Parliament. Also, the model cannot account for wider political struggles within society, for example the conflicts that may arise in industry between employers and employees. Furthermore, the focus on Westminster institutions means that various regional, local and sub-national institutions that wield power tend to be ignored or downplayed in terms of their importance.

Unrealistic view of political power

Many critics argue that the Westminster model offers overly simplistic views on how power operates. Smith (1999) argues that the 'who holds power?' debates within the Westminster model literature have tended to be unhelpful. This is because such perspectives tend to assume that power is concentrated in the hands of particular individuals such as the prime minister and/or ministers. In contrast, Smith argues that power is not the property of particular individuals, but rather is dispersed within and between institutions responsible for forming and implementing government policy. Even senior ministers must rely on the cooperation of others such as colleagues and civil servants in order to be successful. Individuals find themselves in exchange relationships in which they depend on the resources and goodwill of others. Thus power is more dispersed than the Westminster model suggests.

Increasingly antiquated and inaccurate system

Critics argue that even if the Westminster model has proved useful in the past, over recent decades it has been an increasingly outdated and inaccurate system of British politics. A number of factors have served to make the model less relevant in the postwar period:

- *Growth in interest groups* – there are now many more organized interest groups seeking to influence government and the policy process.
- *Entry into EC/EU* – Britain's entry to the EC in 1973 meant the UK Parliament was no longer the sole decision-making body concerning British law. Indeed, where British and European law conflicted, the latter would now take precedence.
- *'Globalization'* – many argue that nation-state governments are increasingly irrelevant as the world becomes more economically and politically integrated.

Democratic aspects of British politics overstated

As highlighted above, many advocates of the Westminster model take a benign view of the British political system, believing it to be a beacon of democracy in action. However, critics argue that the perspective overstates the extent to which Britain is democratic. For many, the holding of elections to Parliament every four or five years is a highly limited type of democracy, offering very few opportunities for people to influence government directly. The model tends to assume that groups can make their voices heard through political parties, and that institutionalized opposition ensures the government is held accountable for its actions. However, this overlooks the fact that many groups in society have little access to knowledge or resources through which they can make their voice heard to government.

The above weaknesses help explain why numerous scholars of British politics have become sceptical about the Westminster model. However, the relative paucity of alternatives, along with a general theoretical inertia, means it has survived as a key organizing perspective. In many ways it remains the key 'image' which many people have of the British political system, however inaccurate or misleading it may now be in describing the practical operation of British politics.

British political tradition

While the Westminster model seeks to map out the key institutional features of British politics, other influential authors have focused attention more on the *ideas* which underpin political practice. The aim of such perspectives is to examine how particular ideas about democracy have led to patterns of change and continuity in British politics. In so doing, a number of authors refer to the idea of the *British political tradition*, emphasizing the links between the past and the present. Greenleaf, Birch and Tant all offer different understandings of the British political tradition; however, there are many shared themes between these authors.

BOX 1.4: *BRITISH POLITICAL TRADITION – KEY AUTHORS AND IDEAS*

Greenleaf

British politics is shaped by the clash of two sets of ideas:

- *Libertarianism* – belief in individual rights and a limited role for government.
- *Collectivism* – belief in the collective good and a strong role for government.

Birch

British politics is shaped by particular ideas about democracy, including notions of:

- *Representation* – Members of Parliament have historically been elected to vote according to their own best judgement, not to (necessarily) reflect the views of their constituents.
- *Responsibility* – historically the stress has been on providing *strong and efficient* government rather than government that is responsive to the views of the public.

Tant

Democracy and popular participation in British politics are limited by:

- Elitist, 'top-down' style of government.
- Emphasis on *secrecy*.
- Ideas and practices resistant to radical challenge.

Key authors and ideas

W. H. Greenleaf argues that British politics has been shaped by the clash of two contrasting sets of political ideas, namely *libertarianism* and *collectivism*.

Libertarianism and collectivism

Whereas libertarianism prioritizes individual rights and freedom from intrusion by government, collectivism stresses the collective good and the benefits which strong and organized government can bring people. Greenleaf (1983: 13) argues that these 'opposing tendencies' make up the British political tradition and help explain the development of British politics over recent centuries. He argues that over time collectivism became the stronger theme as government became ever bigger and took on more control over economic and social issues during the twentieth century. Government gained new powers to deal with the effects of industrialization, urbanization and in order to effectively lead Britain in two world wars (Greenleaf 1983: 78). However, ideas individual rights remained a strong theme, reflecting the strength of classically liberal ideas in Britain (see Chapter 3). General political debate remained centred on the tensions between demands for individual liberty as against the need for strong government.

These themes are also present in a different, yet in many senses comparible, analysis by Anthony Birch (1964), who focuses on how different conceptions of democracy have shaped the British political tradition. In particular, Birch considers how notions of *representation* and *responsibility* have shaped the ideas and institutions that have dominated British politics.

Representation

Birch argues that historical debates concerning the British political system focused on the issue of representation. This concerned questions of whether, to what extent and how the general population should be represented in government. Historically (and despite their differences) the Tories and Whigs argued that mass participation in the political system would put order and stability at risk. Such views were challenged by the Liberals, who fought successfully to ensure that Parliament be elected by the population as a whole. However, the type of representation that MPs provide for their constituency is, arguably, a limited one. In the current system, election of an MP does not mandate him or her to vote in accordance with the majority view of their constituents on a given issue.

Responsibility

Birch notes that during the twentieth century there was strong debate as to what constituted responsible government. Liberals argued that responsible government was ensured through ministers being accountable to Parliament through their actions. Conservatives were less concerned about accountability to Parliament, stressing the need for a strong executive that could make the tough, sometimes unpopular, decisions needed to run the country in a responsible manner. Socialists often argued that responsible government should be ensured through parties offering policy platforms to be voted on by the public, which they would implement if elected. However, taken as a whole the stress has been on the need for strong and efficient government rather than responsive or participatory government (see Chapter 3). The dominant view has been that it is more important that the system works well than that a large number of people should be involved in decisions. Birch argues that the British political tradition consists of a hierarchy of:

> First, consistency, prudence and leadership, second, accountability to Parliament and the electorate and third, responsiveness to public opinions and demands ... It is this tradition ... that explains the system of disciplined party government that the country now enjoys. (Birch 1964: 245)

Drawing on Birch, Marsh (1980) argues that the British political tradition consists of a liberal notion of representation and a conservative notion of responsibility. This explains the enduring commitment to the idea of strong government in Britain, sustained in the postwar period by majority party control of Westminster. The basic belief is that a strong executive needs to have the power to take decisions to ensure that government operates efficiently. Co-joined with this is the view that *too* much accountability to Parliament, or the people, will prevent government taking the difficult decisions so as to act responsibly. Again, like many advocates of the Westminster model, Birch appears broadly to identify and sympathize with this general view. However, other authors have drawn on such ideas to construct a more critical model of British politics.

Tant (1993) brings together many of the ideas discussed by Birch, Greenleaf and others into a distinctive understanding of the British political tradition (see also Marsh and Tant 1991). Tant is concerned to emphasize the elitist nature of the British political tradition and the negative consequences which this tradition has had for democracy in Britain.

Elitist 'top-down' style of government

Tant argues that because of the narrow notion of representation described above, Britain has an elitist and 'top-down' system of government. It is elitist as government consists of a limited number of individuals who will primarily take decisions based upon their own best judgement as to the 'nation's' best interest. Due to the majority party system, government will usually be in a position to force through whatever Parliament policies it wishes, with the electorate only able to have an indirect say every four or five years in an election. MPs are under no constitutional obligation to take any notice of the opinion of their constituents and political parties are not beholden to implement the manifesto pledges they may have made in an election. The implicit view is that efficient government can be achieved only by entrusting an elite to take decisions. Tant (1993: 6) argues 'government and only government was the arbiter of the "national interest" sustained through the tradition of strong, centralised, independent and initiatory government.' In summation, the British political tradition believes government 'knows best'.

Emphasis on secrecy

In the British political system sovereignty is deemed to reside in Parliament – government is viewed as the sole authority which no other interest can legitimately challenge. Tant argues that a negative consequence of this structure is that Britain has one of the most *secretive* governments in Western society. The release of information to the public occurs only at the government's discretion and historically even the courts have not had the power to compel government to release its documents. As civil servants are deemed non-political it is argued their anonymity must be protected by not releasing records of decision-making within Whitehall. Furthermore civil servants and others are constrained from speaking out about publicly by the various *Official Secrets Acts*. Indeed, the orthodox view has been that secrecy is necessary for effective and responsible government. Such a perspective argues:

> the people's representatives [require] to have a large measure of discretion and autonomy in descision making 'on behalf' of the people and in their ultimate interests. . . . In this view government is a specialized vocation; government must therefore be unfettered, free and independent, in order to make sometimes difficult decisions in the national interest. (Tant 1993: 44)

Ideas and practices resistant to radical challenge

Tant is keen to highlight the implications of the top-down elitist form of government. He argues that over the last two centuries a variety of political movements aiming to make British politics more democratic and participatory have been thwarted through the ideas and practices of the British political tradition. For example, on occasions in the past the Labour party has sought to pursue a participatory approach to government. Members would participate in policy debates and would agree a party programme of policies which would then (in theory) be implemented by a future Labour government. However, in practice this did not occur. Labour governments (and the wider parliamentary Labour party) frequently implemented policies at odds with the wishes of the Labour party membership. In power, Labour governments believed they had to be 'independent' and 'responsible', making their own personal judgements as to the best course of action, very much in line with the British political tradition (Tant 1993: 191). Tant argues that despite the Labour party initially being a threat to the traditional system of government in Britain they became 'one of its major guarantors' (ibid.). Similarly, popular movements for change have also been resisted. For example, the Campaign for Freedom of Information argued that government should be more 'open' and that information leading to important government decisions should be released to the public. The Labour government of the late 1970s failed to implement a manifesto pledge to create a Freedom of Information Bill. Furthermore, the Conservative governments of 1979–97 were implacably opposed to such a bill, arguing that ministers were constitutionally accountable to Parliament for the release of information and thus the campaign was 'inappropriate and unnecessary' (Tant 1993: 201) (see Chapter 7 for recent developments on this issue). Thus the British political tradition was able successfully to resist radical challenges, keeping the existing system intact.

Assessing theories of the British political tradition

The main strength of the work of Greenleaf and Birch is the attention they give to examining key ideas in British politics. These ideas help us to make sense of the institutions and practices by drawing attention to the conceptions of democracy and government which underpin them. They move the study of British politics away from the descriptive study of institutions to a more interpretative approach. Through drawing attention to how ideas have survived and adapted, this work helps us to understand patterns of change and continuity. Tant is particularly effective in demonstrating how the ideas of the British political tradition have helped perpetuate elite rule and resisted the challenges of radical political movements. The key ideas that have dominated British politics are explored at greater length in Chapter 3.

Work on the British political tradition is sometimes criticized for being *idealist*, i.e. it gives too much importance to the role of core ideas above other factors which are important in politics. For example, Greenleaf is criticized for conceptualizing British politics as a constant tension between libertarian and collectivist ideas. Rhodes and Bevir (2003) argue it is misguided to see British politics in terms of a clash of unchanging core ideas, rather ideas and traditions themselves change over time. An alternative school of thought in British politics argues that ideas are less important than such authors believe. A range of authors, sometimes dubbed 'sceptics', argue that ideas tend to be used as instruments or tools that politicians use to manipulate opinion and to gain or maintain power (e.g. Middlemass 1979; Bulpitt 1983). For example, Bulpitt argues that British governments have tended to be principally concerned with *winning elections* and projecting an image of *governing competence*. Particular ideas (e.g. 'Keynesianism' or 'monetarism') serve as devices which politicians draw on pragmatically or opportunistically. For authors such as Bulpitt, British politics is not so much about the pursuit of lofty ideals but more about the raw business of elites holding on to power. It is perhaps Tant's analysis of the British political tradition that can best accommodate the challenge of the sceptics. In outlining how particular ideas have helped *perpetuate* an elitist style of government, he gives due attention to both the ideas themselves and to how different groups lose or benefit from them. The theoretical perspective favoured in the remainder of this book draws on this notion of the British political tradition.

Pluralism

In the immediate postwar period, traditional views of British politics stressing strong party government continued to dominate. However, in the 1950s an alternative model began to emerge. A number of British scholars began to be influenced by work done by American political scientists. Such research focused on identifying the important role played by pressure groups or interest groups in the US policy process (e.g. Truman 1951). Subsequently, attention was paid to the groups involved in policy-making in the British context including business and trade unions. Studies revealed that many different groups played a role in forming policy and thus that such groups should be recognized as crucial elements in the British political system. Such work gave birth to the British variant of the perspective known as *pluralism*. A wide variety of variants of pluralism has emerged, but most share the following assumptions.

BOX 1.5: *PLURALISM – KEY CHARACTERISTICS*

- Power is *diffuse*, many different *interest groups* (e.g. business or trade unions) influence the political process. It is not the preserve of politicians or bureaucrats.
- Interest groups are the *key* actors in the political process, reflecting the concerns of different groups in society.
- The government plays a relatively passive role in policy-making and is independent of particular interest groups. It generally seeks to find a balance between different viewpoints.
- It is unlikely that any single group can dominate the policy process.
- Conflict and negotiation between many interest groups is beneficial, increasing participation in politics and hence enhancing democracy.

Key characteristics of pluralism

Power is diffuse

A core assumption of pluralism is that power is *diffuse*, not concentrated. This contrasts with the Westminster model which views power as being concentrated in the hands of individuals, such as the prime minister or cabinet members. In contrast, pluralists argue that, in practice, power is not the preserve of particular individuals or institutions but rather is dispersed among different groups. Crucially, the focus for pluralists is not on Parliament or political parties but rather on the whole range of groups involved in the policy process. They argue that attention should focus on the way such groups compete, lobby and negotiate to influence policy. Elections are less significant in determining policies than many assume since:

- General elections only take place every four or five years, limiting the influence that the electorate can have on the policies implemented.
- Parties tend to be elected on broad manifestos rather than detailed policy proposals. The main work of practical policy formation is conducted later.

Thus pluralists argue that people as isolated individual voters have relatively limited effect on the policies that subsequently emerge. Instead, people exert influence on the policy process through organized *interest groups*. Pluralists argue that interest groups develop spontaneously to represent and/or promote the views and interests of particular groups in society. So, for example, trade unions emerged in education to represent the professional interests and opinions of teachers.

Interest groups are key

In general, pluralists argue that interest groups are the key actors in influencing policy. On any particular issue there will tend to be a range of groups involved in seeking to influence government policy, often with contrasting views. In general, interest groups will have access to relevant government departments and be involved in discussions on forming policy. For example, both employers' interest groups (e.g. Confederation of British Industry) and employee interest groups (e.g. trade unions) are likely to have access to the Department of Trade and Industry when new health and safety legislation is being considered. Interest groups are crucial for a number of reasons:

- They have legitimacy in representing members of the public to government.
- They bring expertise of particular policy areas and/or may be involved in the implementation of new policies.
- They have a mix of resources, skill and knowledge at their disposal which they deploy to influence government and others.

Government's limited role

For pluralists, government itself is less important in shaping policy than other models of British politics assume (e.g. Westminster model). The political process is conceived mainly as one of conflict between a large number of interest groups. In classical versions of pluralism government is viewed mainly as a neutral arbiter, acting as a 'referee' to ensure that conflict and negotiation between various interest groups is conducted fairly. In this view government will not have strong biases in favour or against particular groups. In general, it will seek to find a balance between the different interests to achieve a policy outcome that can be respected as reasonably equitable. Many pluralist models emphasize that the government itself is segmented, meaning that particular policy decisions tend to depend on the relationships between sections of government and key interest groups in that area. For example, historically agricultural policy has been determined largely through close working ties between the Department of Agriculture and the main interest group in this area, the National Farmers' Union. Later versions of pluralism accept that the government is not always passive or neutral in the policy process; nonetheless they stress that interest groups play a vital role in shaping policy (Richardson and Jordan 1979).

Difficult for any single interest group to dominate

Pluralists also take issue with perspectives that argue certain interest groups (e.g. businesses) may dominate policy-making and that some groups may end up without having their voice heard (see discussion of Marxism below). Pluralists say this is unlikely for a number of reasons:

- There are many policy areas and most interest groups are interested only in a limited range of these (e.g. teachers' unions are likely to have little interest in what is happening in agricultural policy).
- Even if a particular interest group is powerful it is unlikely to dominate a policy area for an extended period. This is because 'counterveiling' interest groups are likely to emerge to challenge their influence. Thus, for example, employer interest groups are unlikely totally to dominate a policy area as trade unions may be likely to lobby in opposition to their demands.
- Even if particular groups have many more resources than others (e.g. businesses may have more finance available for lobbying activities) this does not mean they will dominate a policy area. Most pluralists argue that considerable influence can be exercised through the activity and skills of interest groups – they need not have extensive resources to make their voice heard effectively to government.

Pluralism enhances democracy

For many authors, pluralism is not only an accurate account of the British political system, it is also a welcome state of affairs. Pluralists view the emergence and interaction of a vast range of different interest groups as beneficial to society in general. Interest groups offer individuals the opportunity to participate in politics in a way that is more direct and influential than simply voting in elections. In this way liberalism departs from classical liberal theories about representation based on individual preferences and votes. Interest groups offer a way for groups to organize a collective voice and articulate particular demands to government. Processes of conflict and bargaining help ensure that policy outcomes have legitimacy, and wide participation makes for a healthy democracy.

Assessing pluralism

Pluralist perspectives provide a powerful corrective to some of the claims of the Westminster model, in particular, the idea that Parliament and/or party government is the key to all decision-making is challenged. Pluralism draws attention to the wide variety of groups which often influence government as well as the networks and policy communities that exist between interest groups and parts of government. It emphasizes the complexity of policy-making and that power is not the exclusive property of government or cabinet.

However, a drawback of pluralist analysis is that it may overstate the potential for groups to interact with and influence government. Studies of policy networks indicate that in general it is only a select group of interests which have regular interactions with government and that many other viewpoints have no direct access or input to the policy process (Marsh (ed.) 1992). The fact that there is a *plurality* of groups does not mean there is pluralism (Marsh 2002). Central government possesses many more resources than most interest groups and can alter arrangements to favour certain interest groups over others. Thus while many different groups may exercise power there are asymmetries which mean government is in a strong position to get its way much of the time. Related criticisms of pluralism include:

- *Equate consultation with influence* – too often pluralists infer that because an interest group has been consulted on policy it must have influenced the policy subsequently adopted. However, because a government listens to a viewpoint does not mean it will be influenced by it in its final decisions.
- *Overestimate ease of access and representation* – pluralists tend to view the political system as relatively open and accessible. However, there are sectors of society, e.g. lone mothers or the unemployed, that may have little opportunity to organize collectively to make their voice heard to government.
- *Neglect ideological context* – pluralists tend not to consider the dominant ideas in society which shape the context in which policies are formed. The ideas (e.g. belief in a market economy) shape beliefs of what is 'realistic' policy.

Thus, pluralists often take a 'rose-tinted' and uncritical view of the political process. Such perspectives are too ready to take claims as to the democratic nature of British politics at face value. However, most pluralists accept that there are inequalities in British politics and that outcomes can often favour some interests more than others. In addition pluralism is a theory which has undergone a variety of mutations to take account of changes in British politics since the 1960s. Over time, a number of scholars became less optimistic concerning the reality and/or desirability of pluralism in British politics. Indeed, some authors opted to embrace other theories as political and economic conflicts intensified in the 1970s. During this decade an alternative perspective emerged named *corporatism*, which argued that only particular groups were in a position to influence government. 'Insider groups', such as employers, held sway, whilst 'outsider' groups, such as environmental lobbyists, were excluded. Corporatism emerged as a theory to take account of the attempts by successive Conservative and Labour governments in the late 1960s and 1970s to implement incomes and prices policies. These governments experimented with 'tripartite' arrangements in which unions, employers and government would try to reach agreement on general economic policy. In return for their influence on government, employers and unions were expected to keep their members in line in support of the agreed economic policies. However, 'tripartism' proved a failure when agreements collapsed during periods of rising inflation and unemployment. A number of scholars questioned whether unions and employers had the influence claimed, arguing that 'tripartism' was mostly an attempt by the government to exert control over other key groups. In any case, the theory quickly became obsolete when the Conservative governments in the 1980s abandoned any attempts at tripartism and dismantled the institutions associated with it. This period also provoked further criticism of conventional pluralist theories. Thatcher's marginalization of the trade unions, and privatization of key industries, dispelled any lingering notion that government itself was somehow a neutral or passive player in policy-making. Pluralist theory did survive such changes, mainly by adopting a more qualified version of the perspective than was found in the 1960s. However, a number of its erstwhile supporters abandoned the theory to embrace a new right perspective (see Chapter 2) while the perspective also came in for vociferous criticism from a Marxist viewpoint.

Marxist models

Marxist models draw inspiration from the work of the political economist Karl Marx and the numerous authors influenced by him. There are various strands of Marxist thought, but most share several core features.

BOX 1.6: *MARXIST MODELS – KEY FEATURES*

- Only *limited* parts of British government are 'democratic'.
- Economic interests profoundly influence political processes.
- Dominant ideologies help perpetuate social and economic inequalities.
- Government is concerned primarily to promote the interests of the ruling class.
- The state seeks to suppress class conflict.

Key features

Limited nature of 'democracy'

In contrast to many of the models discussed above, Marxists adopt a much more critical stance toward the role of government and the state. To begin with, Marxists insist that the British political system is much less democratic than many people assume. Indeed, they argue that in many ways the democratic features of the system such as elections and the Houses of Parliament act as convenient window-dressing for a more sinister reality. Marxists draw attention to the fact that these democratic features only constitute a *part* of the organization of the state. While Members of Parliament are elected through regular election, vast other sectors of the state are not subject to any direct popular control. These include the civil service, public corporations, the Bank of England, the judiciary, the military and the security services. Such institutions constitute what Dearlove and Saunders (1991) have termed the 'secret state', organizations which administer society but which are not directly controlled or influenced by the general public. This means that 'democracy' in Britain is highly restricted. Marxists such as Ralph Miliband (1982: 27) argued that, while the British political system holds out the *promise* of popular participation and influence in politics, this promise is not realized in practice. Theories such as pluralism (above) are regarded as part of an *ideology* of democracy which permeates society (see section below). For Marxists the state is in fact a barrier to genuine democracy, acting to quell dissent and limit popular influence on political processes.

Influence of economic interests

For Marxists, the key to understanding British politics rests in exposing the profound role which *economic* relations and interests have over the political process. Miliband argued that Britain should be thought of as a 'capitalist democracy' in which society is fundamentally shaped by the relations between capital and labour. It is argued that Britain, like other capitalist societies, is characterized by vast inequalities of power and wealth. Those who own the 'the means of production' (e.g. factories, businesses) exercise control and accumulate wealth, while the remainder of society must sell their labour to survive. Marxists such as Miliband argue that the wealthiest groups constitute a 'ruling class' whose influence over what the government does is profound. Apart from the direct influence the ruling class has on government (see discussion below) they can also exercise powerful influences on other groups in society (Miliband 1982: 7). Most insidously, through their ownership of much of the mass media they are in a position to influence the thinking of the population through promoting certain attitudes and values in newspaper columns. Thus many Marxists focus on the way *ideology* (see Chapter 3) which favours ruling-class interest is perpetuated within society.

Dominant ideologies help perpetuate social and economic inequalities

Karl Marx argued that in capitalist society the dominant ideas would be those of the ruling class. In his materialist understanding of history the ideas which emerge in a given era are conditioned by particular economic arrangements and people's relationship to them. As the ruling class own the means of production they have substantial control over the ideas propagated within society as a whole. Thus the main ideas expressed about politics, economics, morality and science are likely to be constructed to explain, justify and support the prevailing social and economic order. The existing structure of society and its values will be presented as natural or desirable. Ideologies will thus misrepresent or mask the reality of inherently exploitative class relations. The working class will be encouraged to identify with such ideologies, to endorse ideas which actually serve to preserve ruling-class power. So, for example, tabloid newspapers will encourage striking workers to abandon industrial action with the argument that the 'British national economic interest' will suffer because of the strikes. In this instance workers are being invited to identify with a fictitious idea, i.e. that there is a collective 'British' national economic interest. Nationalist ideas are being deployed to create the idea that workers and bosses are bound together by shared identities and economic concerns. However, this nationalist ideology serves to obscure the underlying truth that workers and bosses have contradictory interests (i.e. workers seek a decent livelihood, bosses seek profit maximization). Thus the influence of ideology may cause workers to abandon a strike which is objectively in their own best interests. More generally, the ruling classes perpetuate their dominant position in society through manufacturing the consent of the working-class majority through ideologies.

Government promotes interests of the ruling class

It is argued that, generally speaking, government acts to promote the interests of the ruling class rather than the majority of the population. This occurs for a number of reasons, including:

- *The power of business* – possessing large amounts of wealth and resources, large businesses are well placed to influence the political agenda, e.g. they may donate to political parties, run advertising campaigns on issues or threaten to withdraw investments if they do not favour particular government policies (Dearlove and Saunders 1991). Business interests own and control large sections of the media such as newspapers which help shape popular opinion.
- *The personnel of the state* – the key positions in the organization of the state are mostly occupied by people from a wealthy, well-educated background (e.g. the majority of senior civil servants went to public school and Oxbridge). As such they are linked with, or have the same values as, those who run British business. Thus, though state officials are not practising capitalists, they tend to be tied to the capitalist

ruling class either through family, or school background and wealth (Miliband 1967).

Other Marxists, such as Poulantzas (1973), emphasize the constraints placed on government by operating in a capitalist economy. Structurally, government is dependent for success on the prosperity of British business and is thus constrained to forward the interests of the ruling class. Despite Marxists' stress on the influence of the ruling class, they argue that government retains a *degree* of autonomy in how it acts. Thus what it does may be influenced to an extent by other pressure groups in society such as trade unions or popular movements. On occasions popular pressure may be so strong that government implements change which does not find favour with business. However, they are keen to stress that even where other groups achieve some success (e.g. lobbying for higher spending on public services) concessions and reforms are generally made with a view to securing the long-term stability of the capitalist framework.

State seeks to suppress class conflict

The power of the ruling class over the state has a couple of important implications – in general the state will:

- *Seek to suppress class conflict* – for Marxists there is constant conflict between the interests of the ruling class and the working class. For example, the drive for profit may lead business to lay off workers or cut wages, thus generating conflicts between employers and employees. In general the state will act to protect business interests by acting to minimize the threat of industrial action such as strikes. For example, the Thatcher governments introduced legislation making many types of industrial action unlawful. In the 1960s and 1970s both Conservative and Labour governments made (ultimately unsuccessful) attempts to involve trade unions in national economic decision-making in return for showing restraint in their pay claims. More generally, Marxists argue that the apparatus of the state, including police, courts and security services are used to suppress challenges to the interest of the ruling class. During the miners' strike in 1984–5 police used paramilitary tactics to break up pickets and the leadership of the National Union of Mineworkers was infiltrated by MI5 spies.
- *Seek to contain pressures for change* – many Marxists argue that one of the most insidious roles of the state is in containing and even absorbing pressure for changes in the political system. Miliband uses the example of the Labour party. Historically, on many occasions Labour presented itself as a party of the workers, devoted to introducing large-scale redistribution of wealth and extending public ownership. In so doing it represented the demands and wishes of many millions of voters while constituting a direct threat to the interests of business and the ruling class. However, despite Labour victories in particular elections, such changes did not materialize. Miliband (1970) argues that on each occasion the hopes of the labour

movement were betrayed by the Labour party leadership who reneged on their radical commitments after winning power. The Labour leaders themselves came from relatively privileged class backgrounds and more generally the parliamentary Labour party became 'cut off' from the influence of grassroots Labour support. Thus in power Labour never took the steps needed to transform a state geared to promoting the interests of the ruling class. Coates (2001) argues that even when Labour governments have made moderate positive changes (e.g. boosting spending on public services) they have usually had to reverse these policies soon after in the wake of economic crisis.

Like theories of the Westminster model, Marxist models emphasize strong patterns of continuity in British politics. However, Marxists view this continuity in mainly negative terms. Anderson (1964) and Nairn (1976) argue that the domination of the ruling class in Britain has left the country with an antiquated set of political institutions ill-suited to the contemporary political world. They argue that Britain's long-term economic decline can be explained by the complacent failure of the ruling class to modernize British industry and promote long-term investment. More generally the state has served to reproduce patterns of vast inequalities in wealth and opportunity in society.

Assessing Marxist models

The particular strength of Marxist approaches is the way in which they draw attention to the links between political processes and other aspects of the social world, particularly economic relations. They challenge the comfortable assumptions of perspectives such as the Westminster model and/or pluralism, both of which tend to assume that British politics is essentially democratic. Marxist perspectives explain unequal outcomes in politics with reference to social class and the way in which structured inequalities in society are reproduced. Furthermore, they can help explain why particular sets of political ideas, such as socialism, have often struggled to make an impact on the current parliamentary system.

Nonetheless, in recent years the Marxist viewpoint has been less influential than in previous decades. This may owe something to the popular perception that Marxist ideas had become irrelevant following the downfall of Communist governments in Eastern Europe after 1989. However, of more significance may be difficulties within the theories of authors such as Miliband. Miliband grants that both civil servants and politicians have *some* degree of autonomy in what they do and that not all decisions are simply determined by the views and interests of the dominant capitalist class. However, it is unclear just how much autonomy these actors have. This links to a broader criticism of some Marxist literature that it places too much emphasis on economic relations in explaining politics, to the neglect of other factors that may be important, for example, gender, race and culture. Tivey (1988: 105) argues that, while mainstream literature neglects consideration of non-democratic elements of politics, Marxist perspectives may be too dismissive of the remaining democratic elements. In other words, Marxists may be a little quick to write off the genuine impact and difference that political groups can make through participating in albeit constrained and limited democratic processes.

However, Marxism's influence on the study of British politics has been significant and a number of contemporary authors may be described as 'post-Marxist' (e.g. Gamble 1994; Hay 1999.) Such work takes ideas from Marxist critiques of the state and capitalism but combines these with theoretical concepts and ideas from other schools of thought.

CONCLUSION

Historically, the Westminster model has proved the most influential perspective on British politics. It remains a key 'image' referred to by politicians and civil servants to justify and explain the functioning of government. Nonetheless, few would now argue that it accurately reflects the day-to-day work of government. The domination of the perspective owes much to the relatively uncritical stance taken by past generations of political scientists towards the British political system. Indeed, much earlier literature on British politics adopts a celebratory tone, with the Westminster system regarded as a beacon of best democratic practice for the world. Though a more sober attitude emerged, the Westminster model remained unrivalled for many British political scientists, even though they criticized some of its assumptions. Pluralist perspectives emerged to challenge the narrow institutional focus of the traditional model. This work did much to change perceptions about the key relationships in British politics, highlighting that power was more dispersed than conventional analysis had allowed for. Although pluralism originally overestimated the access and influence that interest groups had on government, the perspective survived in revised forms. It remains an important influence today through its contribution to contemporary models of British politics such as the 'differentiated polity' (see Chapter 2). However, both the Westminster model and pluralism have been criticized for exaggerating the extent to which British politics is representative and democratic. For critics, such perspectives are at best partial in their analysis, at worst they are theories which provide powerful elites with a mask to hide their dominant position in the political system.

However, others authors assert elite dominance as one of the overriding features of the political system. Some writers on the British political tradition consider the domination of the executive, and the top-down system of government, as a necessary means of ensuring efficient government. Alternatively, Marxist perspectives argue that such a system operates to reinforce systematically the power of wealthy groups in society and perpetuate inequality. Such strongly critical perspectives tended to be resisted by mainstream political scientists. However, they played a significant part in academic debates, helping to precipitate various revisions and adaptations of traditional models. Criticism of the system was blunted by the dominance of liberal democratic assumptions among scholars of British politics, combined with a general antipathy towards grand theorizing. Consequently, theories of British politics remained a neglected area of enquiry, leaving ever more outdated perspectives such as the Westminster model to hold influence beyond their shelf-life.

The traditionally dominant models of British politics only began to be widely questioned in the 1970s as successive governments faced economic and political crises. This period, followed by the changes wrought by Thatcherism and international economic trends in the 1980s, led to re-evaluation of core assumptions regarding the nature of British politics. Though scholars increasingly pointed to the inadequacy of the traditional models in the face of such change, relatively few alternative models emerged. It was only in the 1990s that traditional perspectives began to be displaced. Nonetheless, each continues to exert a significant influence on analyses of British politics.

CHAPTER 2

Contemporary Perspectives on British Politics

INTRODUCTION

Having considered the most influential traditional models of British politics, we now turn to consider more contemporary perspectives. As we will see, traditional perspectives remain crucial points of reference for students of British politics. However, changes within the political system itself, as well as in prevailing normative interpretations concerning British politics, have led to the formation of a range of new perspectives. We focus on two types. First, we examine general models of how British politics functions, which offer an alternative to the Westminster model. Second, we review contemporary normative perspectives on British politics that have been influential on politicians and policy-makers in recent decades. The former perspectives, the 'differentiated-polity' model and the 'asymmetric-power' model, aim to provide useful organizing perspectives with which to understand British politics. The latter perspectives, those of the 'new right' and 'third way', aim to offer a critique of how British politics functions and offer views on how it *ought* to operate.

In this review we draw attention to the key features of each perspective. We compare and contrast models before offering a view of which models and features are most useful in understanding British politics. We emphasize the continuing importance of the ideas associated with the British political tradition (see Chapter 1) and assess how far contemporary models break (or seek to break) with this view of the nature of British democracy.

KEY MODELS

Differentiated-polity model

As Chapter 1 argues, the Westminster model has received sustained criticism. Despite this, over many years there were few developed alternatives to the model. Rod Rhodes sought to fill the vacuum with his 'differentiated-polity' model. In recent years the 'differentiated-polity' model and its associated concepts have become highly influential on contemporary studies of British politics and public policy. Indeed, Holliday (2000) argues the perspective is 'fast becoming accepted academic orthodoxy'.

Rhodes (1997: 3) argues the 'differentiated polity' is characterized by 'functional and institutional specialization and the fragmentation of policies and politics'. He argues there are a number of key features (see Box 2.1).

BOX 2.1: *DIFFERENTIATED-POLITY MODEL*

- *Intergovernmental relations* – the state should not be thought of as unitary. There are a range of networked relationships between public sector organizations and between central and local government.
- *A segmented executive* – in practice the prime minister can have only limited power over individual government departments. As a result decision-making is segmented rather than integrated.
- *Power dependence* – policy actors are dependent on one another for mutual success. There is a limit to the extent to which any group can dominate the agenda as they are reliant on the compliance and cooperation of other groups.
- *Policy networks* – policy networks are now the dominant mode of governance as opposed to markets or hierarchies.
- *Governance (rather than government)* – actors outside the core executive, such as interest groups, have a vital role in making and implementing policy. In addition the government itself is divided on policy issues and decision-making involves exchange between actors at both central and local levels.
- *A hollowed-out state* – the state has lost powers 'upwards' to international organizations through globalization and European integration. Simultaneously it has lost powers 'downwards' and 'sideways' to the private sector and agencies.

Intergovernmental relations

For Rhodes, academic descriptions of the relations between different branches of government had long been too simplistic. He argues that even in the 1970s the commonly used phrase 'centre-local' relations was inadequate. In the 1980s such terms became much more problematic as the Conservative governments sought to bypass local authorities by creating many special-purpose bodies. He uses the term 'intergovernmental relations' to denote that government is now a matter of complex interactions between various actors and groups including the European Union, Parliament, Whitehall, local government, special purpose bodies, regional institutions and regulatory organizations.

Rhodes is keen to debunk the idea that Britain is a 'unitary state' with a single centre of power. Rather the state is 'differentiated' into a maze of functions and policy networks. Rhodes draws on Luhmann's (1982) notion of a 'centreless society' which invokes the idea that society is now too complex to be considered 'unified' in any clear way, rather it consists of a multiplicity of autonomous subsystems. He argues '... there is not one but many centres linking many levels of government – local, regional, national and supranational' (Rhodes 1997: 3). Crucially, these different centres are interdependent and their interaction is fundamental to the operation of government. Government officials at different levels regularly interact, sharing attitudes and opinions and cooperating on policy issues. However, interactions now also extend beyond circles of government officials to encompass other groups such as the private sector. New patterns of interaction include self- and co-regulation; public- private partnerships; cooperative management; and joint-entrepreneurial ventures (Rhodes 1997: 51).

There are two important aspects to the type of intergovernmental relations Rhodes articulates. The interdependence between different levels makes coordinating government a difficult task – 'interdependence confounds centralisation' (Rhodes 1997: 3). This means central government, or the core executive, is unable to exercise the kind of coordinated top-down control of government which models such as the Westminster model would imply are possible. Second, the British state has been subject to a process of 'imbrication' (Cerny 1990) in which the public, private and voluntary sectors of society have become interlocked and intertwined (Richards and Smith 2002: 21). As such it is difficult for government to separate clearly its own interests from those of other groups.

A segmented executive

Rhodes argues that it has long been taken for granted that the UK has a strong executive. Perceptively he noted that such assumptions underpin long-standing debates in British politics such as whether Britain has 'prime-ministerial' or 'cabinet' government. For Rhodes, such debates obscure the reality that 'the executive in Britain can be characterized as much by fragmentation and interdependence as by strength' (Rhodes 1997: 13). Ministers in fact have a large degree of control over their 'own turf', i.e. their individual departments. They are subject to no higher legal authority and on a day-to-day level are unlikely to face immediate challenge.

One consequence of this structure of government is that policy areas tend to be contained within particular 'funnels' of government. Policy tends to be formed in a vertical manner – typically departments will adopt policy with limited or no consideration of how it may adversely affect or impact on the policies being pursued by other key departments. This is exacerbated by tendencies to 'departmentalism' which Richards and Smith (2002: 22) describe as 'a pathology that prompts ministers to think of the micro-political interests of their own department at the expense of the macro-political goals of their own government'. Departmentalism makes for a number of consequences. First, ministers will often be locked in battle with colleagues, seeking to secure more resources and power for their own 'patch'. Second, there is a reluctance to engage in cross-cutting work with other departments on issues which might be of importance to both. Finally, tendencies to self-interest lead to departments engaging in what Rhodes calls 'bargaining games' with other key actors in the policy process.

Such is the fragmentation of policy-making that a complex series of coordinating mechanisms and networks are crucial to policy formation. These include, for example, interdepartmental committees and informal personal relations between officials. Furthermore, the growth in size of the core executive over recent decades has exacerbated the difficulties of achieving effective central coordination. Thus Rhodes cautions against any conception of the core executive as a simple unified whole.

Power dependence

Rhodes argues that traditionally there have been two models of 'centre-local' relations in Britain:

- The *agent* model in which central government is dominant – local authorities merely implement nationally determined policies.
- *Partnership* models in which central and local government are co-equals (with local authorities holding much power) – each depends on the other.

However, Rhodes argues that in reality different branches of government are neither fully dependent nor fully independent of one another. In fact they are *interdependent* (Rhodes 1997: 8). Each needs resources from the other in order to achieve their objectives. Therefore, they enter exchange relations. Governing organizations will deploy resources and use bargaining tactics to try and maximize outcomes favourable to them. At the same time, they will try to avoid becoming dependent on other 'players' in the governing game.

Rhodes argues that actors and organizations enter exchange relations at all levels of government. What is distinctive about this 'power-dependence' model of exchange relations is that the exercise of power is rarely a zero-sum game. In other words it is infrequently the case that one actor or organization 'wins' while others 'lose'. It is wrong to think of the prime minister dominating ministers, ministers dominating civil servants, or central government dominating local government. Each needs resources from one another to achieve their goals. For example, ministers need civil servants to implement policies and civil servants need ministers to win resources for their department (Richards and Smith 2002: 24). Also, Marsh *et al* (2001: 239) argue 'a minister is unlikely consistently to push for a line which her/his civil servants oppose because s/he knows that will cause problems in terms of the smooth running of the department'. Generally, then, power is a positive-sum game in which groups and actors exchange resources to achieve objectives.

Policy networks

Different interests exert influence on the British policy process. Decision-making on a day-to-day level involves processes of aggregation of and intermediation between different interests. For Rhodes (and many other writers) 'policy networks' are a convenient way of analysing these processes. It is argued that policy areas tend to have a range of actors involved in influencing decisions such as ministers, civil servants, pressure groups and special advisers. To understand a policy area, it is necessary to identify the range of actors involved, to establish who is in the 'network'. Different policy areas will have different networks – for example, the network around health policy will consist of different government officials and pressure groups than the network around environmental policy.

For Rhodes, the concept of 'policy networks' is crucial to understanding the British political system – 'policy networks of resource-dependent organisations typify the British policy process and are a basic building block to understanding the shift to governance' (Rhodes 1997: 13).

Networks are viewed as crucial for a number of reasons since they:

- Limit participation in policy-making.
- Define the role of actors in the policy process.
- Decide what issues will be included and excluded from the policy agenda.
- Shape the behaviour of actors through rules of the game.
- Favour certain interests over others.
- Substitute private government for public accountability.

This conception of networks challenges traditional perspectives of British politics such as the Westminster model in at least two ways (see Marsh and Rhodes 1992; Marsh and Smith 2000). First, it challenges any notion that there are clear boundaries in the operation of government. Policy-making is not conducted through formal institutions but through informal networks. Power is not concentrated in institutions such as government departments, but is diffused between different actors within networks. Second, and relatedly, power may be distributed in a horizontal, rather than vertical, way between different institutions. The exercise of power cannot be understood through traditional notions of hierarchical government.

For Rhodes, such networks are self-organizing (see below). Central government cannot determine the way they function and operate. As such, networks challenge the power of central government and throw into question the notion that sovereignty lies in Whitehall or Westminster (Richards and Smith 2002: 27).

Governance (rather than government)

The term 'governance' has become widely used in academic circles in recent years. Despite this (or because of it) the term has no single commonly accepted meaning. However, most definitions would accept that governance is 'a change in the meaning of government, referring to a *new* process of government' (Rhodes 1997: 15). Rhodes's version of governance has become one of the most widely used as it combines and builds upon a range of other perspectives (see Rhodes 1997: 48–51). For Rhodes (1997: 53) there are four characteristics of governance:

(1) Interdependence between organizations. Governance is broader than government including non-state actors. Changing the boundaries of the state means the boundaries between public, private and voluntary sectors become shifting and opaque.
(2) Continuing interactions between network members, caused by the need to exchange resources and negotiate shared purposes.
(3) Game-like interactions between network members, rooted in trust and regulated by rules of the game negotiated and agreed by network participants.
(4) Networks are not accountable to the state: they are self-organizing. Although the state does not occupy a sovereign position, it can indirectly and imperfectly steer networks.

At the core of governance are *self-organizing*, interorganizational networks with significant autonomy from the state. State control of networks is limited for a number of reasons including lack of legitimacy, the sheer complexity of the policy process and the complexity of institutions involved (Kickert 1993). Central government lacks the power to control the networks and hence they become responsible for organizing themselves.

In such circumstances, government's role is significantly more limited than in the past. Because of the importance of networks, and the onset of institutional fragmentation, government must seek to 'steer' rather than 'row'. As it no longer has direct control of public services, the British state should use its considerable resources to try to 'steer' these networks in the direction it feels is appropriate. However, because networks have a great deal of autonomy, the 'steering' from central government can only be imperfect.

However, Rhodes argues that British governments have been slow to recognize the reality of governance. For example, he explains policy failures under Conservative governments (1979–97) largely as a consequence of applying 'an inappropriate elite, command operating code' to policy-making. The Conservatives attempted to impose change without the consent of the self-organizing networks which ultimately determine whether policy will be implemented successfully. As Marsh and Rhodes (1992) argue, public policy under successive Thatcher governments were featured by significant 'gaps' between the original goals of policies and the policies actually implemented in practice. In short, the Conservatives had failed to appreciate the central importance of networks in delivering public policy. The transfer of power away from central government towards self-organizing networks is a key feature of what Rhodes terms the 'hollowing-out' of the British state.

A hollowed-out state

Perhaps the best-known feature of the differentiated-polity model is that of the 'hollowed-out' state. Rhodes's notion that the British state has become 'hollowed-out' over recent decades has become one of the most referred to concepts within political science, public administration and other commentaries on the changing role of government. 'Hollowing-out' refers to the idea that central government has lost much of its power and authority in the policy process as a result of a series of changes. Power has been ceded (Rhodes 1997: 53):

- *Upwards* to bodies such as the European Union and global financial institutions such as the IMF.
- *Downwards*, by losing functions to agencies and special-purpose bodies.
- *Outwards*, through privatizing, market-testing public services and the formation of self-organizing policy networks.

A number of processes have driven this hollowing-out:

Privatization and marketization

In the postwar period, government owned and was responsible for running all key public utilities such as gas and electricity as well as important British industries such as steel. Over 18 years in power Conservative governments (1979–97) sold almost all public companies to the private sector. Consequently, the British government's involvement in economic affairs was substantially reduced. In addition, the Conservatives sought to inject market-type mechanisms into the public sector – for example, through encouraging schools to compete for pupils. As a consequence, central government ceded direct control of a range of public services 'outwards' to private sector and other public sector bodies.

New managerialism

Relatedly, the Conservatives introduced what became known as New Public Management (NPM). NPM aimed at improving the efficiency and effectiveness of the public sector by restricting costs and improving service delivery. It was argued that traditional hierarchical methods of organizing public services were often inappropriate. NPM sought to apply private sector management techniques in the delivery of public services through introducing targets and performance indicators and empowering public sector managers with more freedom to make decisions. Allied to this, government functions were decentralized and delayered with the creation of agencies 'hived-off' from central government.

Europeanization

Many have argued that the British state has increasingly ceded power upwards to the European Union. British politics has been 'Europeanized' through a range of treaties such as the Single European Act (1986) and the Maastricht Treaty (1993). In particular, these treaties instituted qualified majority voting – a mechanism which means individual governments such as the UK no longer have control over a range of policy areas and may have to implement policy to which it is opposed. The European Commission can initiate and draft European legislation and there are now transnational policy networks spanning all levels of government. British central government 'is one player, albeit a powerful one, in these networks' (Rhodes 1997: 23).

Globalization

Arguably, changes in the international system, both economically and politically, are placing new pressures on national governments. 'Globalization' usually refers to processes that are increasing integration and interconnectedness between different nation states and regions. Features of change include financial integration, facilitated by advances in information technology, as well as the growth in multinational corporations, which operate across state borders. In addition, there has been a marked increase in recent years of international governmental organizations. Globalization helps account for the external hollowing-out of the state – the British state now has less autonomy in decision-making for at least two reasons. First, government is under pressure to set tax rates and flexible work practices that are apparently necessary to attract investment from multinational corporations. Second, the growth in international governmental organizations means power has been ceded 'upwards' to such bodies.

Internal hollowing-out has also been facilitated by the growth of policy networks (outlined above) which limit the influence of central government in decision-making. In combination, these 'hollowing' factors are fundamental to understanding the shift from a unitary state to a differentiated polity (Rhodes 1997: 19).

Evaluating the differentiated-polity model

The differentiated-polity model clearly represents an advance on the Westminster model. The emphasis on resource-dependency and the 'differentiated' nature of the political system offers a much more realistic view of how British government works in practice. Furthermore, the differentiated-polity model can account for many of the changes in the British state over recent decades, offering insight into the impact of external and internal change.

The differentiated-polity model is now the most utilized organizing perspective on contemporary British politics and use of the terms 'governance' and 'hollowing-out' have become commonplace. In addition, there is now a vast literature devoted to analysing 'policy networks' and a general acceptance that networks are now an important part of the British political system.

Despite the influence of the differentiated-polity model in mainstream political science (and beyond), the perspective has received some criticism. The model has been criticized on both theoretical grounds and also on the basis of empirically grounded studies of British politics and public policy.

Theoretical criticisms focus on the philosophical assumptions which inform the differentiated-polity model. Assumptions include:

- *A belief in pluralism* – Rhodes's position argues that power is dispersed and that many interests can have effective input into the policy process.
- *A belief in 'postmodernity'* – the differentiated-polity model is influenced by perspectives which argue Western societies are moving from a modern era involving top-down hierarchical government to a postmodern era where decision-making is more horizontally organized, involving a range of actors and groups.

Criticisms from empirically based papers variously argue that the differentiated-polity model:

- *Misrepresents* the changing British state – rather than being 'hollowed-out' the state is becoming more *congested* with the proliferation of government agencies, taskforces, units and area-based initiatives (Taylor 2000).
- *Fails* to account for ongoing processes of *centralisation*, rather than fragmentation. It is argued that successive governments have actually enhanced the scope and range of central government power over the policy process. For example, Davies (2001) reveals the ways in which central government has extended its influence over urban regeneration. In the face of such purposeful centralization he argues that the notion of 'governing without government' displays a 'fatal conceit'.

In summation, it is argued that Rhodes's belief in a pluralist dispersal of power leads him to overlook the continuing critical importance, if not dominance, of the core executive in the policy-making process. A number of authors stress that central government continues to hold significant power to set the agenda and to form and re-form networks. It is argued that government usually has far more resources in terms of personnel, finance and communications than other policy 'players'. Insofar as partnership working and networks have become the main form of governance, the state remains the dominant partner within these networks (Clarence and Painter 1998).

Thus, for some authors the differentiated-polity model goes too far in accepting pluralist assumptions about dispersal of power and the accessibility of the policy process. Indeed, there is a real danger that the continuing power of the core executive becomes obscured behind exaggerated notions of 'governance' and the belief that government is merely 'one player amongst many'.

Furthermore, to the extent that the differentiated-polity model has been influenced by postmodern perspectives it appears that the model has inherited the latter's ambiguity concerning (some would say indifference towards) notions of structural inequality. For there is limited mention within the differentiated-polity model of the material imbalances between different groups in the policy process, and scant account is offered for the fact that many groups and interests are not represented within governing networks. Relatedly, no explicit recognition is given of the fact that processes of governance occur within a civil society characterized by massive inequalities in terms of wealth, social class, education, gender and race. For these reasons some authors have sought to generate an alternative organizing perspective.

Asymmetric-power model

If the differentiated-polity model was an overdue response to the Westminster model then the asymmetric-power model may be a timely response to the Rhodes perspective. The asymmetric-power model was proposed by Marsh *et al* (2001) in the context of research into changing patterns of governance in Whitehall (see Box 2.2). The model was further promoted as an alternative to the differentiated-polity model by Richards and Smith (2002) and by Marsh et al (2003). This account of the asymmetric-power model draws on these pieces as well as some supporting contextual literature.

BOX 2.2: *ASYMMETRIC-POWER MODEL*

- *Structural inequality* – British politics does not take place on a level playing field. Socio-economic conditions create structural inequalities which both facilitate and constrain the actions and likely success of individuals and interest groups in the British polity.
- *British political tradition* – a belief that Whitehall, the core executive, knows best. This is underpinned by a view of democracy with a preference for strong and decisive rather than responsive government.
- *Asymmetries of power* – the relationship between government and other participants is asymmetrical. Government has a unique set of resources: force, legitimacy, state bureaucracy and legislation which are unavailable to other actors.
- *A strong, segmented executive* – the core executive is not unified but power remains concentrated at this level. Departments are key actors, though the centre has taken steps to reassert forms of greater control over policy and organization. The continued strength of the executive and its control of significant resources means that, while the government sometimes fails to get its way, it still continues to 'win' much, even most, of the time.
- *A limited pattern of external constraint* – the British state still has considerable autonomy and powers despite external changes and significant constraints.

Structural inequality

Marsh *et al* (2001: 247) argue that students of politics too often neglect the broader socio-economic structural context in which British politics takes place. Though this context does not determine what happens in the political process, it does play a crucial role in both constraining and enabling action. As Richards and Smith (2001: 282) argue, actors continue to have unequal access to political processes and political power; for example, the poor, ethnic minorities and women are systematically discriminated against. Members of the core executive are overwhelmingly white, middle-class and male (Marsh *et al* 2003: 309). It is argued that there is too much emphasis on agency (the power of actors) in models such as that of the differentiated polity. Marsh *et al* insist it be recognized that British politics is not a level playing field and that there are 'enduring slopes and gullies' which favour some interests over others but many groups are still excluded from the policy process.

British political tradition

Marsh *et al* argue that a weakness shared by the Westminster model and the differentiated-polity model is a lack of attention to the dominant *ideas* held by politicians and civil servants. In rectifying this they draw directly on notions of the British political tradition (see Chapter 1 for fuller discussion).

British politics continues to be underpinned by a top-down view of democracy which stresses:

- *A limited, liberal notion of representation* – the emphasis is upon the holding of periodic, relatively free and fair elections. There is little emphasis on Members of Parliament forwarding the views of his or her constituents. Referendums (i.e giving the people a direct say) are used rarely and only where the government finds it politically expedient to do so (Marsh *et al* 2003: 311).
- *A conservative notion of responsibility* – the emphasis is on the need for strong and decisive, rather than responsive, government. (Richards and Smith 2002: 283). The convention of ministerial responsibility ensures executive government by placing responsibility for decision-making in the hands of ministers. Thus a leadership-focused rather than participatory view of democracy is forwarded (Marsh *et al* 2003: 312).

Marsh *et al* argue:

> the Westminster model present(s) a false picture of how the British political system works. The key features – parliamentary sovereignty, ministerial responsibility and collective responsibility – do not function as the model suggests. However, unsurprisingly, it is the view of democracy shared by the actors in the core executive, it legitimises their authority and power. As such it affects how the system works. It has shaped the process of constitutional and organisational reform and continues to maintain elite rule. The code that underpins the British political system is still one that emphasises that Whitehall, that is the core executive, 'knows best' (Marsh *et al* 2001: 247).

Thus the British political tradition contains a limited conception of democracy, advocating strong, centralized executive power. Therefore politics within the core executive remain closed and elitist despite waves of managerial reform (Marsh *et al* 2003: 313).

Asymmetries of power

Marsh *et al* argue that there are asymmetries of power in the British political system. They accept that the process of governing has become more complex in recent years and that resources have shifted to some extent towards actors other than government. Networks between government and private and voluntary sector bodies are important to the delivery of public services. However, while government does often depend on other groups for resources, these groups 'continue to depend on the government which has a unique set of resources – force, legitimacy, state bureaucracy, tax-raising powers and legislation – which are unavailable to other actors' (Richards and Smith 2002, 283). Thus the relationship with most interest groups remains *asymmetrical.* For instance, government has the power to:

- *Sanction the membership of networks* – for example, the trade unions became excluded from important policy networks under the Conservative governments (1979–97).
- *Reassert central control where necessary* – for example, government may introduce legislation to increase its power over a policy area.

Overall, government has greater capacity than many other groups to respond to the changed environment of governance (Richards and Smith 2002: 272). It is argued that only interests which themselves possess crucial resources such as knowledge, expertise, finance and access to the media have consistent privileged access to and influence over government (ibid: 283). Marsh *et al* argue that these interest groups are invariably either:

- *Economic,* such as the City of London, the Confederation of British Industry or the Institute of Directors, or
- *Professional*, such as the National Farmers' Union or the British Medical Association.

However, even where government may be quite dependent on such groups it still retains resource advantages. For example, the Home Office has strong resource-exchange relationships with the Association of Chief Police Officers (ACPO). The government listens to the ACPO as they have a great deal of influence over how government policy is implemented at a practical level (Marsh *et al* 2001: 184). Despite the importance of the ACPO in policy-making in the law and order field they can still be overridden by central government. For instance, in the mid-1990s the government pushed through the Police and Magistrates Court Act in the face of opposition from the ACPO. The Act sought to establish more central government control over law and order by allowing ministers to set annual objectives for police forces (ibid: 197).

A strong, segmented executive

Marsh *et al* and Rhodes are in agreement about the segmented nature of the executive in Britain. The core executive is not unified and the majority of important decisions are made within individual government departments. This belief stands in contrast to accounts of British politics which stress the unifying role of individual actors, such as the prime minister. For example, many commentators stressed the idea that Mrs Thatcher dominated decision-making within government in the 1980s (e.g. Kavanagh 1987; King 1985). Through her strength of personality and leadership qualities Thatcher was viewed as having effective control over government. However, commentators such as Marsh and Rhodes (eds) (1992) argue that in many policy areas Mrs Thatcher herself did not intervene and even her intervention in some high-profile areas like social security was limited. Marsh *et al* argue that it is individual ministers and officials who tend to dominate decision-making within individual departments. While the prime minister retains great power to intervene in the affairs of departments, in practice the volume, scale and complexity of policy decisions that must be made within central government set limits as to how far the prime minister can get involved in departmental decisions. Consequently, departments are the 'key actors and institutions at the centre of the policy-making process' (Marsh *et al* 2001: 249)

However, while Rhodes draws attention to the limits of the power of the core executive, stressing its dependence on other actors, Marsh *et al* stress the continuing *strength* of the core executive within the policy process. The majority of resources remain concentrated within Whitehall departments and thus they remain key players in policy areas. Indeed, the core executive can, and has, taken steps to further assert control over the diverse institutions of governance. For example, Conservative governments removed certain powers from local government and invested them in special-purpose bodies appointed by central government. Also, over the last 25 years there have been various attempts to bring greater coherence to central government – for example, the Treasury has become increasingly involved with policy initiatives in different departments (Marsh *et al* 2001: 238).

Marsh *et al* accept that power is not usually a zero-sum game. On occasions, there are zero-sum games – for example, when fox-hunting was recently banned the anti-hunting lobby 'won' and the pro-hunting lobby 'lost'. However, because most relations within government and between government and interest groups are based on exchange relations, zero-sum games are very rare. For instance, senior civil servants and ministers are usually dependent on one another to achieve their goals. Marsh *et al* cite the example of welfare reform under the Conservatives. They argue that the Secretary of State for the Department of Social Security, Peter Lilley, had success in pushing through welfare changes by gradually coaxing civil servants to accept that it was in their interests (as well as the government's) to bring about change. This was in contrast to the previous Secretary of State, John Moore, who had floundered after trying to impose change without the goodwill of his officials (Marsh *et al* 2001: 172–4).

Thus Marsh *et al* agree with commentators such as Rhodes that British politics is based on exchange relations. However, they insist that such relationships are usually asymmetrical. Two features are particularly important:

- The most crucial actors in the policy process remain those located within departments, i.e. *ministers* and *civil servants* – 'these two sets of actors continue to act as the guardians of the policy process which, in turn, continues to be predominantly top-down, closed, secretive and elitist' (Marsh *et al* 2001: 180).
- There are asymmetries in the resources available to actors and groups – in general the prime minister has more resources than ministers, ministers have more resources than civil servants and departments more resources than interest groups (Marsh *et al* 2001: 239).

Because some actors have more resources than others does not mean they will always be more influential on policy. A lot depends on how well actors use the resources available to them. However, the strength of resources available to central government means that it continues to dominate the policy process much, even most, of the time (Marsh *et al* 2001: 248).

A limited pattern of external constraint

Marsh *et al*'s criticism of the differentiated-polity model is strongest in relation to Rhodes's notion of a 'hollowed-out' state. They concede that the pattern of external constraints on government is changing and that British government can have little if any impact on international financial markets. However, they take issue with the hollowing-out thesis, particularly notions of the British state being hollowed 'outwards' and 'upwards'.

Marsh *et al* argue that Rhodes overstates hollowing 'outwards' to interest groups and policy networks. They argue:

- In most networks it is departments who are the most important actors due to their possession of the most resources.
- Relatedly, it is departments who decide who is consulted and who is excluded from networks. In particular, groups with limited resources are vulnerable to changing views of departments.

Thus for Marsh *et al* the crucial role of individual departments in policy networks needs to be taken more seriously than the general literature on policy networks (and that on the differentiated-polity model) suggests (Marsh *et al* 2001: 236). Also, they contend that networks are of more limited use in studying relationships *within* and *between* departments as:

- Networks in the core executive are too fluid to analyse.
- It is the wider culture of Whitehall which provides the rules of interaction rather than the specific networks (Marsh *et al* 2001: 237).

Similarly, Marsh *et al* argue that Rhodes overstates the extent of hollowing 'upwards' via processes such as Europeanization and globalization. They contend it is unhelpful to conceive of globalization as 'hollowing-out' the British state because:

- British governments have long been constrained by international conditions. For example, in the 1960s and 1970s (supposedly a pre-globalization period) British governments found their economic policies undermined by the instability of sterling (Richards and Smith 2002: 140).
- It is unclear that global trade is in fact becoming 'globalized'. Hirst and Thompson (1996) argue that trade is no greater now than in the pre–1914 era and that the majority of trade is regional rather than global.
- Globalization is, at least to some extent, a discursive construction – it is an idea which influences the thinking of government rather than an inexorable process. Hay (1999) suggests globalization has been used by British governments as a rhetorical device to justify neo-liberal policies, such as low taxation and economic deregulation. The aim is to make it appear that there is 'no alternative' to such policies. However, in reality the government retains a significant amount of autonomy in economic affairs.
- Relatedly, British government retains an important strategic role in guiding the British economy. Markets cannot fulfil this strategic role, hence they are dependent on government (Marsh *et al* 2001: 249).

Furthermore, Marsh *et al* argue that it is a mistake to view international institutions such as the IMF, UN or EU as simply constraints on British governments. They argue that, just like power (see above) state-global relations cannot be conceived of as zero-sum games (Marsh *et al* 2001: 250). For one thing, processes such as European integration may be viewed as *enabling* the British state to have a greater say in international and domestic affairs. By pooling elements of sovereignty in some ways the British state gains more influence over Europe and within the international community. Also, the European Union offers ways for the British state to increase its domestic affairs. Government may invoke EU directives and regulations to implement policies they favour with the benefit that if such measures are unpopular the finger of blame is likely to be pointed at Brussels rather than Westminster. Buller (2000) argues that the Conservatives used their support for the Single European Act as a means to entrench their 'free-market' policy stance within Britain. At other points, Buller suggests the Conservatives postured opposition to EU integrationist measures to project an image of governing competence and the belief that they would 'stand up for Britain' against the Brussels bureaucracy. Richards and Smith (2002: 155) argue that the EU has had a surprisingly limited impact on the formal structure, organization and rules of Whitehall. Marsh *et al* emphasize that the impact of the EU on any given department is strongly affected and mediated by the institutional interests of that department. In some cases, departments are happy to increase EU coordination of policy, e.g. the Home Office supported cooperation in tackling drugs. However, in other areas departments will resist integration in areas where each wishes to protect its autonomy, e.g. the Home Office has strongly opposed attempts to centralize immigration policy (Marsh *et al* 2001: 241). Thus one cannot simply view the EU as a blanket constraint on the British state – in reality the EU both constrains and/or *facilitates* British government in a range of complex ways.

Richards and Smith argue that the state has not been so much 'hollowed out' as *reconstituted*. While the boundaries of the state have changed through processes such as privatization, this has not necessarily reduced the role or power of the state. The core executive has retained many of its powers and its dominant role in the policy process.

Evaluating the asymmetric-power model

It can be argued that the asymmetric-power model offers a more convincing organizing perspective that of the differentiated polity. The differentiated-polity model is particularly effective in highlighting the trends associated with the transition to governance. However, the pluralist and postmodernist assumptions informing the model mean that the extent of decentralization and increased participation in the policy process are exaggerated. The strength of the asymmetric-power model is that it combines an account of the transition to governance with recognition of the enduring power of the core executive and the continuing influence of the British political tradition on the mind-set and practices of elite participants in British government. Importantly, the asymmetric-power model gives acknowledgement of the enduring structured inequalities, both in the organization of government and in society more generally.

Both the differentiated-polity model and asymmetric-power model draw attention to the need to be sensitive to, and to account for theoretically, ongoing processes of change in the British state. Models of British politics need to be able to help explain contemporary practices in the British polity and, if they cannot, must be discarded or appropriately amended. Due to its emphasis on the continuing power of the core executive and structural inequalities, this book favours the asymmetric-power model as an organizing perspective. However, the changes covered above refer mainly to those prior to the election of new Labour in 1997. A key question is how effectively the asymmetric-power model can accommodate changes occurring in British government in recent years. As we will see in Chapter 7, recent changes may suggest adaptation of this model.

KEY NORMATIVE PERSPECTIVES

In the last chapter we saw that normative assumptions play an important role in shaping models of British politics. Theories such as Marxism or pluralism offer not just a clear view of how British politics works but with a value-laden vision of how it *ought* to work. We now turn to consider contemporary normative perspectives on British politics, both of which (it can be argued) have had a crucial role in shaping the kinds of changes introduced by successive governments over the past 25 years. These are respectively 'new right' and 'third way' perspectives. Below, the intellectual roots of each position are reviewed, outlining its analysis of the problems facing British politics, before sketching its proposals for change. Subsequently, a comparative evaluation of both perspectives is offered.

New right

From the margins to the mainstream

The roots of the new right perspective are in the work of academic authors such as Friedrich von Hayek (1944), Milton Friedman (1963) and Robert Nozick (1974). In von Hayek's *The Road to Serfdom* he railed against the trend in Europe towards planned economies with high levels of state intervention in the economy and society. In the 1970s the views of such authors became increasingly influential on sections of the political right in Britain. New right think-tanks, such as the Institute for Economic Affairs, the Adam Smith Institute and the Centre for Policy Studies began to 'sprout like mushrooms' (Gamble 1994) and had strong ties with Conservative politicians such as Keith Joseph and Margaret Thatcher. Though diverse in views, the new right generally combined a belief in traditional Conservative attitudes such as family values and law and order (neo-conservatism) with a more radical commitment to a free market economy in which the government should have limited involvement (neo-liberalism) – see Box 2.3. Though formerly on the margins of political debate, in the 1970s the new right began to build intellectual and political credibility through its response to the various problems and crises experienced by successive British governments. These included:

Recognition of British economic decline

In the 1960s academics and politicians became increasingly conscious of the fact that, following the decline of the British Empire, the UK economy was experiencing relative economic decline (Weiner 1981; Barnett 1986). In the postwar period the British economy was experiencing much lower growth than its main competitors.

Relations with the Trade Unions

In the late 1960s and 1970s both Labour and Conservative governments had serious problems in relations with trade unions. Various attempts to agree income policies broke down and a range of protracted industrial disputes occurred, notably the miners' strike of 1974 which brought down the Conservative government of Ted Heath and the 'winter of discontent' which felled the subsequent Labour government in 1979.

Perceived failings of Keynesian economics

In the 1970s Britain experienced constant problems of spiralling inflation and rising unemployment. This led people to question Keynesian economics, particularly when in 1976 the Labour government felt compelled to appeal to the International Monetary Fund for funds to finance the budget.

The new right perspective gained ground as it offered a relatively coherent and radical diagnosis of these problems, along with ideas for rectifying them.

BOX 2.3: *CORE ASSUMPTIONS OF NEO-CONSERVATISM AND NEO-LIBERALISM*

Neo-Conservative assumptions

- The state should exercise moral authority and enforce traditional family values and the need for discipline and self-restraint.
- The state must crack down on crime and punish offenders.
- The welfare state should be dismantled and the 'dependency culture' associated with it.
- A traditional sense of British identity and patriotism must be preserved.

Neo-liberal assumptions

- The market is the most effective, innovative and moral means of organizing the economy.
- Individual liberty is secured by minimal state intervention in the economy and society.
- The state is likely to act in favour of interest groups rather than to the benefit of the general public.
- The state is likely to be inefficient and self-interested.

The new right analysis

The new right argued that such problems arose for a number of reasons:

- The British state had become 'overloaded' – in the postwar period government had become involved in too many areas. For example, ever greater national resources were being spent on welfare, raising unrealistic expectations of what government can provide people with. Relatedly, government found itself under increasing pressure from organized pressure groups each seeking to have their own sectional demands satisfied.
- The demands on government were leading to high taxes on business. Consequently, the private sector's profit-making and wealth-creating potential was being weakened by having to subsidize the public sector. Subsequently, the economy as a whole suffered.
- Free from the rigours of the market, the public sector tends to act in a self-interested, self-maximizing way. Public sector employees will look to expand their own control over resources and will organize services in a manner convenient to them rather than the public.
- The creation and expansion of the welfare state has had adverse

effects, including making and encouraging people to be dependent on state benefits. This has helped precipitate moral decay and the decline of traditional family values. Furthermore it undermined the entrepreneurial spirit necessary to economic success.

The new right argued that the British government needed to adopt a radically different set of assumptions including:

- Non-intervention in the economy as this distorts the operation of the market. Optimal economic conditions occur when the market is free to develop spontaneously without government interference. In effect new right theorists were calling for the reassertion of *classically liberal* economics (see Chapter 3).
- Government should limit itself to a minimal role in providing law and order, defence and essential services.
- The welfare state does not secure 'social justice', rather it results in the deserving paying for the undeserving.

From such assumptions the new right generated a range of ideas which they argued could be used to overturn the damage caused by Keynesian state-interventionism and the welfare state.

The new right prognosis

Central to the new right economic policy was a belief in *monetarism*. Drawing from the work of Friedman, the new right argued that the principal problem facing the economy was not unemployment, but inflation. Rather than use Keynesian interventionist strategies to secure full employment (which just generated more inflation), government should seek to regulate the money supply. By restricting the flow of money in the economy 'sound money' would result, thus eradicating inflation. In the longer term sound money would enable markets to flourish, creating new jobs in the economy. Furthermore, the harmful effects of state intervention should be reversed in a series of other ways including:

- The 'rolling back of the state' from intervention in the economy – where possible, public services should be turned over to the more efficient private sector. More generally the goal of government should be to ensure that the market is allowed to develop in as unencumbered a way as possible. Thus regulations, red tape and taxes on both businesses and individuals should be reduced.
- Government must distance itself from the distorting influences of interest groups. Legal restrictions must be placed on groups such as the trade unions whose actions can threaten the development of the free market.
- Spending on the welfare state and the public sector must be reduced. This will facilitate lower taxes and free up more money for investment in the wealth-creating private sector. The structures of the welfare state must be dismantled to eradicate the 'dependency culture' it has created. Government should promote traditional family values and a

sense of national pride to foster the kind of moral and self-reliant attitudes necessary for a successful society and economy (in this sense they were promoting a return to 'traditional conservatism' – see Chapter 3).

New right ideas were influential on the thought and actions of Conservative governments (1979–97). Such ideas were essential to what became known as 'Thatcherism' and informed a range of key policy changes and reforms of government (see earlier discussion of differentiated-polity model and introductory sections in Chapters 5, 6 and 7). Certainly, not everything the Conservative governments did can be explained with reference to new right ideology (see Marsh *et al*). As with all governments, changes were often *ad hoc*, ill thought through and by short-term political expediency. Much of the structure of the welfare state remained intact despite the onslaught of Thatcherism. Nonetheless, major restructurings of the state such as privatization and public service reform owe much to the new right. Indeed, some argue that new Labour and Tony Blair also embrace elements of the new right perspective and that they have continued with many reforms introduced by the Conservatives. However, new Labour has become strongly associated with an alternative perspective, that of the 'third way'.

Third way

Over many years the political left in Britain, particularly the Labour party, struggled with the issue of how to respond intellectually to the new right and Thatcherism. The left criticized policies such as privatization and public spending restrictions but was divided on what type of alternative policies should be followed. Indeed, as time went on many thinkers and politicians on the left became more sympathetic to certain Thatcherite ideas. It was often argued that the left needed a 'big idea' to organize its policy and values around (and to differentiate itself from the new right). For many, Anthony Giddens's notion of the 'third way' has become new Labour's big idea.

For Giddens the third way involves:

- A rejection of two other ways, namely neo-liberalism and state-interventionism.
- A renewal of social democracy, for a modern context.
- A combined commitment to a dynamic economy *and* a socially just society – a 'third way' approach.

Beyond neo-liberalism and state interventionism

As is covered below, the third way has a strong belief in the benefits of a dynamic market economy. However, it is also critical of the new right and neo-liberalism on a number of grounds.

Neo-liberalism presupposes government has no responsibility needs to be taken for the social consequences of market-based decisions (Giddens 1998: 33). Yet, a dynamic economy will necessarily produce negative consequences for some individuals and communities, however beneficial changes are for the economy in general. For example, efficient business decisions may result in factories closing, leading to high unemployment in particular areas. The Conservative governments (1979–97) were criticized for failing to take any responsibility for those who fell out of work, particularly in the early 1980s and early 1990s. Many argue that the Conservatives were following the new right view that it is not up to government to 'correct' the market and that individuals themselves must take all the responsibility for gaining employment in the marketplace. Indeed, Giddens argues that there is a contradiction between the free-market goals of the new right and their commitment to family values. Unemployment pressures families and can help precipitate relationship breakdown. Furthermore, Giddens argues that neither 'trickle-down' economics nor the 'minimal state' can provide the public services people want and deserve. Indeed, the Conservatives' perceived neglect of public services was a contributory factor in Labour's election victory in 1997.

Despite the limitations of the new right perspective, Giddens is also critical of traditional left-wing perspectives. He argues that, as an alternative economic model to capitalism, socialism proved a failure. It produced tyrannous regimes in Eastern Europe and failed to generate the levels of economic growth and prosperity achieved in the West. He also criticizes the more moderate politics pursued by left-wing governments in the West during the postwar period, which are usually referred to as 'social democracy'. Traditional social democracy believes in a strong role for the state in economic and social life through Keynesian economics, state ownership of key industries and a comprehensive welfare state. However, though such policies had many positive aspects, including the pursuit of egalitarianism, for Giddens they sometimes led to perverse consequences. Like the new right, Giddens (1998: 16) points to heavy-handed state intervention as having produced a legacy of decaying, crime-ridden housing estates and a welfare state that creates as many problems as it solves. Moreover, he argues state-interventionism has become increasingly unsuited to the contemporary world.

A renewal of social democracy

However, despite the third way's explicit rejection of traditional social democracy and certain left-wing ideas, it is still presented as a 'renewal of social democracy'. It locates itself on the centre-left of politics. However, it is argued that social democracy can survive only by adapting and modernizing its ideas to deal with the dilemmas of the contemporary world. These dilemmas include:

- *Globalization* – Britain, like other nations, cannot avoid the process of globalization which 'pulls away' powers which the state formerly held

towards international capital and multinational corporations. In particular, this makes Keynesian economic strategies unworkable.
- *Individualism* – globalization has also brought about a retreat of tradition and custom. British society has become more pluralistic with an increasing diversity of lifestyles. This 'new individualism' challenges the 'collectivist' assumptions of much traditional left thinking.

Thus Giddens argues that the political left must pursue its values in this changed context. This means embracing globalization and accepting that in the absence of any alternative to a market economy it is sensible to make that economy as dynamic and efficient as possible. Rather than being hostile to (or sceptical about) markets, Giddens (1998: 35) argues the left should 'get comfortable' with them. However, the pursuit of a dynamic economy should be combined with a continuing social democratic commitment to social justice.

Marrying economic efficiency and social justice

Traditionally, the goals of market efficiency and securing left-wing goals such as social equality have been viewed as being incompatible. However, Giddens argues they can and should be combined. This 'third way' vision includes a number of elements:

'What matters is what works'

Rather than relying on outdated right- or left-wing ideology, public policy should be organized pragmatically. It should not be assumed that either markets or the state can best provide services, rather, public services should be run in whichever way works best in practice. Relatedly, public, private and voluntary groups should be encouraged to work in *partnership* with one another to secure the best possible services for citizens.

Democratic renewal

Relatedly, there is a need to move beyond the polarized between those who say 'government is the enemy' and those who say 'government is the answer'. Rather, there is a need to renew democratic processes for the modern world. This entails working positively within international bodies such as the European Union as well as decentralizing and devolving power within Britain through constitutional reform. Political institutions must reconnect with the desires and needs of citizens in order to secure legitimacy.

Promoting equality through 'social inclusion'

While the new right condones inequality, much of the traditional left has sought to ensure equality of wealth. However, Giddens argues that equality should be thought of as *inclusion* within the mainstream of society. Those groups that suffer problems such as poverty, unemployment, lack of education and training are often effectively excluded from the opportunities enjoyed by society in general. Government, in combination with businesses and local people, should introduce initiatives aimed at rebuilding local communities and offering groups access to work, education and other opportunities.

Promoting 'positive welfare'

The new right is hostile to the welfare state while the traditional left is attached to it. Giddens argues that the welfare state should be retained but modernized under the theme 'no rights without responsibilities'. For example, the state should provide benefits to the unemployed but they must also take some responsibility for finding work. Government should provide opportunities for education and training but individuals must be responsible for taking up these opportunities.

As we will see in Chapter 5, the third way concept has been embraced by new Labour and Tony Blair. Furthermore, third way ideas have played an arguably important part in influencing the reforms introduced by new Labour since 1997.

COMPARING NEW RIGHT AND THIRD WAY PERSPECTIVES

Giddens seeks to differentiate third way politics clearly from that of the new right. Certainly, the concepts and language used to justify the perspectives differ (Fairclough 1999). However, some commentators have questioned whether the perspectives ultimately offer very distinct positions. Apparent similarities include:

- A commitment to the free market, deregulation and low taxation regimes for business.
- A belief that unchecked public service providers tend to be self-interested and risk averse.
- A commitment to the retrenchment of the welfare state.

Commentators such as Callinicos (2001) and Anderson (2000) argue the third way is actually about the capitulation of the British centre left to Thatcherite and new right ideas. Anderson (2000: 5) argues 'the hard-core of [neo-liberal] government policies remain ... but are now carefully surrounded with subsidiary concessions and softer rhetoric'. Callinicos argues that, unlike socialism, one of the two 'ways' Giddens opposes is very much alive, namely neo-liberalism, an economic doctrine which all Western governments, including new Labour, still appear to be beholden to.

Driver and Martell (2002: 86) argue the third way *is* different from the new right but not quite in the manner Giddens suggests. The third way does not transcend left and right but rather mixes values and ideas from each. The consequent difficulty is that in the end ideas and policy prescriptions are actually contradictory. For example, the commitment to providing opportunities for education may conflict with the success of the market economy. However, the 'mix' of the third way does contain *both* neo-liberal and social democratic ideas.

In Chapter 5 we seek to evaluate in what ways 'third way' thinking has been influential on new Labour and whether and to what extent it has broken with Thatcherite and new right politics.

The new right, third way and the British political tradition

Whatever differences may exist between new right and third way perspectives, it is fair to say that both make quite bold claims as to their uniqueness and radicalism. After all, the new right emerged in response to what it saw as the hegemony of state-centred politics in the postwar period. Thus its commitment to a minimal state and the free market was presented as a far-reaching radical alternative. As outlined above, the third way is constructed as a transcendence of the ideologies and policies which dominated twentieth-century politics. It was argued earlier that British politics has been fundamentally shaped by belief in centralized, elitist and representative government. In concluding an evaluation of new right and third way perspectives it is important to consider just how far (in principle) such critiques offer a break with the ideas contained within the British political tradition (see Chapter 1). There are a number of areas of comparison.

A liberal economy

Gamble (1994) summarizes 'Thatcherism' as the commitment to the 'free economy and the strong state' – combining new right themes of minimal state intervention in the economy but strong leadership on matters such as law and order and defence. While this may be an appropriate label for 'Thatcherism' it could also serve well as a summation of the British political tradition (Marsh and Trent 1991). It can be argued that British economic policy has been characterized by a lack of intervention in the economy. No British government of the left or right has created the kind of 'developmental' interventionist state which authors such as Marquand (1988) argue emerged in countries such as Germany. In this light the new right commitment to 'roll back the state' was misleading – the British state has not been *highly* interventionist, even in the postwar period. The third way's emphasis on 'globalization' and the constraints it places on domestic economic policy may be regarded as similarly overblown – Britain's economic policy has been profoundly affected and influenced by international economic pressures at a number of points during the postwar period (see Chapter 4).

Strong leadership

At the same time, the British state has always long been 'strong' on matters such as defence – notably with the commitment of all postwar governments to an independent nuclear deterrent. The lack of a codified constitution and a parliamentary majority system has generally ensured 'strong government'. The new right perspective offers no challenge to the power of government in this sense. Indeed, it reinforces the British political tradition's emphasis on the idea that government should be able to take strong decisive action (e.g. on crime or terrorism) even when this may breach civil rights. The stress is on responsible rather than responsive government. In this area the third way appears potentially much more radical – the commitment to decentralized and devolved systems of government has the aim of 'reconnecting' with the people, to establish more responsive forms of government.

Accountability and responsibility

The new right perspective seeks to decrease state ownership and extend private control of the economy. This is radical inasmuch as, in principle, government cedes responsibility for providing particular public services. However, the new right view does not challenge the principle of parliamentary sovereignty – that government is accountable to voters through elections every few years. Again, the third way is potentially more radical in that the emphasis on partnership and involving communities and voluntary groups in decision-making appears to spread accountability and responsibility for public services to other groups. In principle, then, it may challenge the 'government knows best' philosophy of the British political tradition.

Consequently, while the new right perspective is broadly compatible with the British political tradition, the third way perspective appears to challenge its assumptions in some significant ways. Yet, as we will see in Chapters 5, 6 and 7, despite the influence of the third way and related ideas on new Labour's reform agenda, the British political tradition has exercised a crucial influence over its use of state power.

CONCLUSION

Alternative models of British politics are underpinned by different assumptions and values. The study of British politics is never fully objective or theoretically innocent. Authors always bring a set of political and ethical values to their study of the subject. This is most clear in the normative perspectives of the new right and third way. In different ways these perspectives seek to overcome problems and dilemmas which have arisen in postwar British politics. From such perspectives we can see clearly how a particular analysis of British politics can generate particular conclusions about whether and how British politics should be changed. Each continues to influence contemporary politicians in their exercise and contestation of power. Therefore, debating perspectives on British politics is not merely an abstract academic issue – it is also a question of how British politics is 'lived' and which groups and interests benefit or lose out within its current structure.

More generally, it is a notable feature of the study of British politics that so little energy has been devoted to theorizing on the topic. This has both fostered confusions and resulted in relatively antiquated understandings of British politics having persisted due to the lack of alternative models. Fortunately, in recent years perspectives such as the differentiated-polity model and asymmetric-power model have emerged to stimulate much-needed debate on this topic.

One reason that such models are debated and are useful for students of British politics is that the subject matter is always undergoing change. In the face of globalization, governance and a changing civil society, it is important that we have models and theories with which to make sense of change. Of particular concern is the question: in what ways do such changes alter the structures of British politics and in what ways does the state retain its traditional features?

The development of models such as the differentiated-polity model and the asymmetric-power model exposes the weaknesses of the Westminster model which had so long dominated studies of British politics. Not only was the Westminster model an inappropriate account of the practical functioning of British politics, it became ever less useful following the extensive changes in the British state during the 1980s and 1990s. The differentiated-polity model highlights the onset of 'governance' and growing importance of 'networks' in understanding the operations of the British polity. The asymmetric-power model draws attention to the continuing patterns of structural inequality in Britain which make the dominant pluralist accounts (and also the differentiated-polity model) of British politics problematic. The asymmetric-power model stresses the continuing power of the executive and how changes in state structure have generated opportunities for the central government to extend its powers, not merely cede them.

The analysis offered in the remainder of this book is sympathetic to both theories of the British political tradition and the asymmetric-power model. These will provide useful gauges and assumptions against which to assess contemporary developments in British politics in Chapters 5, 6 and 7. However, to contextualize such analysis properly it is necessary to look more closely at the traditional ideas and practices that have dominated British politics.

CHAPTER 3

Traditional Dynamics of British Politics I: Key Ideas

INTRODUCTION

This chapter examines the key ideas in British politics. The aim is to lay out the different kinds of philosophical and moral belief, which have shaped the institutions, policies and practices of British politics. As we will see, particular sets of ideas have played a powerful and dominant role.

Examining ideas – why bother?

It is difficult to overstate the importance of ideas in British politics. Sometimes people dismiss the notion that abstract ideas play much of a role in the practical 'nitty-gritty' of real world politics. It is argued that politics is about action rather than abstraction, practicalities rather than philosophy. Often people (including many politicians) will declare themselves to favour a 'common-sense' approach rather than an ideologically influenced stance. However, any perspective or opinion on politics is shaped by a received set of ideas. Any notion we have on topics such as democracy, government or individual rights is a result of the ideas we have acquired from others, whether through education, family or the mass media. There is no neutral position from which we can understand politics. Any political action we take (irrespective of whether this is understood as 'ideological' or 'common-sense') is shaped by webs of beliefs we have inherited from the world around us. Thus to understand British politics it is crucial to review the sets of ideas which have influenced politicians and the policies they have pursued.

Ideas are also important in other ways. Ideas not only influence individuals but also may be used as a tool with which individuals can influence others. So, for example, politicians may promote particular ideas, e.g. 'lower taxes', not necessarily through strong personal belief, but in the hope that the idea will bolster support for his or her political movement. Particular sets of ideas are often strongly associated with particular *interests*. Societal groups will often seek to benefit themselves through arguing for particular ideas which, if followed, will tend to result in better outcomes for themselves. Ideas can therefore be weapons with which different interests battle for outcomes which favour them. In summary, ideas are important as they:

- Influence *all* kinds of political opinion and action.
- Construct a view of the world, including our sense of moral right and wrong, e.g. ideas such as 'freedom', 'equality', 'justice'.
- Are used to promote particular interests, i.e. desired outcomes for particular groups.
- Are a means through which individuals or groups can manipulate or influence others.

Ideas and their varying influence

The first section deals with the main political *ideologies* which have dominated British politics. The key principles of conservatism, socialism and liberalism are outlined and contrasted. In each case, attention is given to both the interests associated with such ideas and, in particular, the *policies* which such ideas have influenced. Furthermore, attention is drawn to key *conflicts* between ideas, which have shaped the path of British politics in the postwar period. The second section looks at crosscutting themes that have been influential on British government, particularly themes with a long historical pedigree such as strong government, pragmatism and British nationalism. These ideas are used to help explain significant patterns of continuity in British government. The final section examines 'counter-discourses', sets of ideas which have not proved dominant in British politics (over the long term) but have played a role in challenging mainstream opinions and informing political conflicts.

DOMINANT IDEOLOGIES

The term *ideology* was first used in the nineteenth century by the French philosopher Destutt de Tracy to refer to the 'science of human ideas'. Ideology has been defined in innumerable ways over the last two centuries; however it is generally used to refer to sets of ideas or assumptions that shape people's understanding of the world. Leys (1983: 14) argues that ideology is 'any set of social ideas that becomes part of the operative assumptions of the political practice of a particular social group'. Ideologies are usually understood to be coherent in that the ideas within an ideology will tend to be consistent with one another. However, such is the diversity within different broad ideological schools that one often comes across ideas that stand in tension with one another. For this reason Bevir (2001) prefers to speak of broad *traditions* of ideas, webs of belief that are linked with one another but are not necessarily consistent. This section reviews the three dominant traditions of ideological thought, i.e. sets of ideas that have dominated British politics over the past two centuries.

BOX 3.1: *IDEOLOGIES*

	Conservatism	*Classical liberalism*	*Progressive liberalism*	*Socialism (social democratic version)*
View of human nature	Imperfect, tendencies to selfishness and folly	Individuals capable of rational pursuit of self-interest	Cautiously optimistic, individualism can combine with social concern for others	Optimistic, disposed to be cooperative and creative where free from constraint
Core values	Tradition, custom, reverence for family and nation	Individualism, freedom from external constraint	Equality of opportunity	Equality, community
Role of government	Elite rule, tough on law and order	Minimal state, protection of property rights	Active state, ensuring welfare	Active state, ensuring welfare and redistribution
Economy	Laissez-faire (modern strands)	Laissez-faire	Mixed economy	Mixed economy
Inter-national affairs	Narrow protection of British national interest	Promotion of free trade, economic deregulation	Promotion of free trade and human rights	Promotion of international collaboration and human rights

Liberalism

Context

The most significant and dominant set of political ideas in Britain has been, and remains, *liberalism*. In many ways liberal ideas are the founding blocks of modern British politics – liberal assumptions have become so ingrained that they have almost become second nature. Arguably even 'rival' perspectives such as conservatism and socialism share many core beliefs with liberalism. However, it is important to remember that when liberalism emerged it represented a highly revolutionary set of ideas, fundamentally challenging many long-standing traditions and social hierarchies. A number of seismic political, religious, economic and intellectual changes have been important in the ascendancy of liberal ideas to their dominant position, not just in Britain, but in the wider Western world.

Liberalism emerged from the political upheavals of the seventeenth, eighteenth and nineteenth centuries – in the eighteenth century America won its independence from Britain and established a constitution guaranteeing individual rights for citizens and limiting the powers of government. In 1789 the French aristocracy was overthrown in a revolution seeking to establish new sets of individual rights. Liberal ideas underpinned both these revolutions. Though Britain did not undergo quite such dramatic political change, many key liberal theorists were British (e.g. John Locke 1690; John Stuart Mill 1859) and their ideas played a key role in the limitations placed on the power of the monarch and the rise of modern representative government.

Core Liberal ideas

There are five general principles of liberal thought:

- *Individualism* – individual people are seen as the basic unit of society. In this way liberalism contrasts with other philosophies which view society as consisting of collectives such as nation, social class or ethnic group. As such, the rights of people as *individuals* should take priority over collectivist notions. Individuals possess inalienable *rights* of expression and thought, which no other authority may legitimately constrain. In addition, individuals should have the right to keep (or freely exchange) any property they possess.
- *Freedom* – people have the right to individual liberty. Government must not infringe on the individual's ability to make their own decisions, follow their conscience and express their opinions.
- *Toleration* – respecting individual rights means that people must tolerate the views of others, even in circumstances where they may strongly disagree. For example, people should show tolerance to those with different religious or political beliefs.
- *Equality* – as individuals are the basic unit of society, all must be attributed equal worth. All people should be equal before the law and have the right to political representation. Thus liberalism is *anti-hierarchical*, and no individual is regarded as intrinsically of greater value than another.
- *Rationality* – liberalism is cautiously optimistic about human nature. Individuals are viewed as the best judge of their own self-interest. Where people are free to make their own decisions, using their own reflexive powers, outcomes will tend to be positive. It is not appropriate for politicians, religious leaders or anyone else to make decisions for people in their daily lives.

These ideas have been profoundly important in the development of British politics, to the extent that most are now taken-for-granted core assumptions in contemporary society. However, liberalism is a very broad school of thought with many influential and contrasting strands. In order to look more closely at its political impact it is necessary to focus on two broad traditions of liberal thought, namely classical liberalism and progressive liberalism.

Classical liberalism and its impact

Classical liberal ideas derive from the work of earlier key liberal thinkers such as John Locke and John Stuart Mill. Four general features are identifiable:

Negative freedom – individual freedom is assured by the absence of restriction by government or any other external force. Classical liberal writers believed that government will often tend to infringe freedom in arbitrary ways, such as through arrest or unjustified taxation. Thus freedom requires non-action by government, leaving individuals to do as they wish. Importantly, *all* individuals are *equally* subject to the constraints of the law.

Minimal government – government should have a role only insofar as it protects individual rights and freedoms. State action must therefore be limited to protecting civil liberties, such as individuals' right to keep property they have bought or inherited. Individuals must be free to exercise individual rights, except where they may be acting in ways that infringe the rights of others. Therefore the exercise of freedom must take place within the boundaries of the law. Beyond this protective role, government has no business interfering in society. In order to prevent government overstepping this minimal role, the classical liberal argues that there should be a separation of powers in government. By dividing up government into branches, e.g. separating the executive and the legislature, it was hoped no one group would be in a position to abuse governmental power. Separating powers would create 'checks and balances' on government action, thus mitigating against arbitrary misuse of authority.

Laissez-faire economics – political economists such as Adam Smith (1776) believed that a limited role for government was also crucial to generating economic prosperity. Individuals should be free to enter economic exchanges based on their own rational judgement as to what will benefit them best. The competition between producers will ensure that goods people want will be available at a price and quality consumers find acceptable. Though people enter market exchanges for selfish reasons (e.g. pursuit of profit) the outcome of such interaction will be for the general good of society. What Smith called the 'invisible hand' of the market will ensure social 'goods' such as employment and wealth. Government intervention risks distorting the market, stifling individual initiative and thus reducing wealth and productivity. Classical liberals were conscious that laissez-faire economics would produce inequalities that would leave some in poverty. However, it was often argued that the threat of poverty and destitution is needed to motivate people to adopt values of hard work and thrift.

Representative government – a key way to prevent the misuse of government power is to give people a say in the formation of government. Thus classical liberalism argues for the extension of the franchise to allow all adults to vote. The belief was that individuals were the best judge of their own interest and that participation in the political process would foster responsibility and moral character.

Impact of classical liberalism

Classical liberal ideas gained ascendancy in the late eighteenth and early nineteenth century (the term 'liberal' only becoming popularized in the nineteenth century). The ideas played a crucial part in shaping modern politics. Classical liberalism contributed to:

- *The emergence of parliamentary democracy and the party system of government* – liberal ideas were deployed to secure successive extensions of the franchise eventually to include all adults in Britain. In so doing they overcame Conservative arguments that allowing the general population to vote would lead to 'mob rule'. The birth of representative government led to the development of the party system, as we currently know it – with two main parties competing to become the government.
- *Development of British capitalism* – classical liberalism became the ideology used to justify the effectively revolutionary transition of Britain from its feudal past into the first developed capitalist country, via the industrial revolution in the eighteenth and nineteenth centuries. Government's role in the economy was limited with an emphasis on securing 'sound money', i.e. ensuring that government spending did not exceed its income. Of central importance was the promotion of the idea of *free trade* across national boundaries, enabling Britain to become the dominant global economic power.
- *Power of new entrepreneurial class* – extension of the franchise and changing economic relations created a shift in power away from the old aristocracy (the Tory landlords) towards the newly prosperous class who owned British industry.
- *Changing political debate* – though classical liberalism directly promoted the interests of the new capitalist class, the ideas associated with it such as equality and individual rights had a resonance far beyond this group. Such ideas altered the terms of political debate in Britain, breeding developments in thought which the classical liberals could not have predicted.

Classical liberal ideas stressing a minimal state and the free market were given new life and practical application in the 1980s through their influence on the policies of Margaret Thatcher and the new right (see Chapter 2).

Progressive liberalism and its impact

Along with the economic growth generated by economic liberalism came large inequalities in wealth. Writers in the liberal tradition became concerned about the large numbers of people in poverty and dire social circumstances. Theorists such as T.H. Green (1901) concluded that many people were denied the kind of opportunities which classical liberalism assumed people to have. It was argued that some groups lacked either the education or means with which they could effectively compete in the marketplace. Problems were exacerbated at times of economic downturn where many may experience unemployment. From these perceptions a new type of liberal thought emerged known as progressive liberalism (sometimes referred to as 'new' liberalism). Four general features of progressive liberalism are:

- *Positive freedom* – progressive liberals believe that negative freedom (see above), i.e. freedom from government interference, is insufficient to secure freedom for all individuals. Without help, many individuals would suffer from poverty, ignorance and unemployment which can be an unfortunate by-product of the market. Progressive liberals believe that the state has to take on responsibilities to assist individuals in overcoming such disadvantages. Thus government can play a *positive* role in releasing people from the circumstances holding them back, thus promoting the 'common good' (Green 1901). Importantly though, Green argued that there was a strong moral onus on individuals themselves to make the best of the opportunities afforded to them.
- *State provision of welfare* – theorists such as L.T. Hobhouse (1922) argued that the state should take a paternalistic attitude to individuals in society. Those in need of help, the poorest, should receive financial support from government to ensure they do not live in squalor. The state should guarantee a minimum standard of living below which no one should fall. Furthermore, the state should provide access to opportunities, such as education, through which people may develop the skills and knowledge needed to participate in the marketplace. Government provision of welfare should be funded through taxes raised on wage earners, thereby redistributing wealth from the richest to the less well off.
- *Mixed economy* – progressive liberals questioned the classical liberal assumption that the market would always allocate resources in the most effective way. Though holding on to the belief that the market was essential for wealth production, they argued that the state should also play a role in organizing the economy. Progressive liberals argued that where monopoly ownership restricted competition, the state might have an obligation to intervene to correct the effects of the market. His arguments were a precursor to the later thoughts of people such as John Maynard Keynes who questioned classical liberal belief in a continuous equilibrium between supply and demand in the economy. In particular, Keynes argued that during times of economic downturn the government should take active measures to stimulate demand in the economy. Where appropriate, government should borrow and invest to secure high employment and boost economic activity. Thus the economy should have a mix of private enterprise and public management.
- *Liberal imperialism* – progressive liberals argued that international economic prosperity was undermined by struggles between different world powers for markets. These struggles undermined free trade, created instability and made wars probable. It was argued that powerful nations should seek to establish agreed international

frameworks and rules of behaviour in order to promote free trade of goods and minimize conflict. Liberal imperialist ideas proposed that Britain could not only promote its own interests internationally but also measures of benefit to other nations.

Impact of progressive liberalism

Progressive liberalism made a huge impact on twentieth-century British politics, helping to expand the size of government and increasing its involvement in social and economic life. Three sets of developments were of particular significance:

'Social reformism'

The Liberal government (1906–14) enacted reforms that established a new role for government in securing welfare. Measures included introducing old-age pensions, establishing health and employment insurance and other welfare measures.

Creation of the welfare state

Building on measures enacted by the wartime coalition government during the Second World War, the Labour government (1945–51) established what is now referred to as the welfare state. Most of the reforms were laid out in a report produced in 1942 by the liberal William Beveridge who called on government to tackle the five 'giants' of Want, Disease, Squalor, Ignorance and Idleness. The report was groundbreaking in acknowledging that problems such as unemployment and poverty were not a result of individual failure but were social problems with roots in the economic system. The postwar Labour government enacted Beveridge's recommendations including the creation of:

- Benefits for the unemployed, sick and disabled.
- Old-age pensions for all.
- A National Health Service, free for all at the point of use.

These benefits were to be paid for through National Insurance contributions and general taxation. The Labour government also implemented:

- The 1944 Education Act making secondary schooling compulsory and free for all children up to age 15.
- A massive house-building scheme to make public housing accessible and affordable.

In total such reforms aimed to offer people access to comprehensive public services 'from the cradle to the grave'.

Keynesian economics

Following the emergence of mass unemployment in the 1930s, the Beveridge report had also recommended that government take steps to ensure full employment. The postwar Labour government broke with traditional economic orthodoxy to embrace economic ideas associated with the progressive liberal economist John Maynard Keynes. Keynes argued that government had to take responsibility for economic planning, being prepared to borrow to invest in the economy in times of economic downturn. Such investment would boost employment and thus boost demand for goods. Keynes argued that government should also intervene at points where there was too much demand, taking the heat out of the economy by increasing taxes. Through these types of intervention government could help the smooth operation of the market, helping it avoid falling into the slumps that a hands-off laissez-faire approach tended to precipitate. Moreover, the economic strategies employed by both Labour and Conservative governments between 1945 and the 1970s were often justified using Keynesian arguments (though the extent to which they were actually Keynesian as opposed to classical liberal is debatable).

Conservatism

Conservatism has consistently remained a powerful strain in British political thought. Its success has in many ways been paradoxical. As a perspective, or disposition, conservatism tends to be hostile or sceptical towards change. At the same time the historical success of conservatism owes much to its ability to adapt to change and adjust to new circumstances.

Context

In many ways conservatism emerged as an identifiable school of thought in reaction to political and economic upheavals in the eighteenth and nineteenth centuries. A seminal text is Edmund Burke's *Reflections on the Revolution in France* (1789). The French revolution and ensuing violence created shock waves among the British aristocracy. Burke's book amounted to a wholesale attack on the rationalist liberal ideas which influenced French revolutionaries. Moreover, he argued that traditional customs and institutions should be *preserved* in order to ensure stability and harmony in society. Conservative thought grew further in the nineteenth century as life in Britain became transformed through industrialization and urbanization. In the face of such change many were nostalgic for the more stable feudal economic relations and forms of rural life, which were fast disappearing.

Core assumptions of conservatism include:

- *Human imperfection* – Conservatives are pessimistic regarding human nature. People will often act selfishly and are susceptible to corruption. Behaviour owes much to underlying emotions and passions, rather than detached reason. Thus Conservatives are sceptical about liberalism's stress on rationalism, believing it is folly to organize society based on the assumption that individuals will act rationally. Rather, people must be subject to frameworks of discipline that will discourage them from acting in selfish and irresponsible ways.
- *Strong government* – government must take a strong lead in maintaining peace and stability in society. Individuals must be subject to the rule of law that is enforced by government agencies. Transgressions of the law must be stiffly punished to maintain order and make an example of wrongdoers.
- *Hierarchy and elite rule* – people are born with different abilities and talents. Inevitably some will have more abilities than others, meaning that social hierarchies are inevitable. Inequalities are thus natural and not something that can or should be eliminated. Consequently political leadership should be the preserve of those with the skills and abilities to lead effectively. Such skills can be nurtured through elite schools and universities.
- *Traditionalism* – Conservatives take a sceptical attitude towards proposals for change. Change is often motivated by short-sighted self-interest. However, even where the motivations for change are virtuous, the outcomes can be harmful. Conservatives cite the disruption and violence usually associated with political revolutions as examples of how pursuit of high-minded ideals can lead to tragic consequences. Conservatives prefer to rely on experience and accumulated knowledge rather than abstract planning. Thus Conservatives argue there must be respect for:
- *Established institutions* – long-standing institutions have worth by the fact of their very longevity. Their survival indicates their importance to the social fabric, being sustained through the accumulated wisdom of successive generations. They should not be abolished or substantially reformed without strong reasons for change – similarly, traditional customs and practices have value through their survival, indicating their importance to stability and harmony in society.
- *Nation and family* – in contrast to liberal emphasis on people as individuals, conservatism stresses how people's identity derives from their ties to family, community and nation. The traditional family is viewed as the bedrock of society, to be valued and protected. Conservatives also believe that people gain shared values and a sense of pride from their national identity. *Patriotism* is thus a feature of conservatism – celebration of symbols of national importance, e.g. Union Jack, monarchy and military, help foster harmony and unity. The key duty of government in international affairs is to protect the nation's interest and to secure the best outcome for Britain in an anarchic world.

- *Pragmatism* – love of tradition and scepticism about human rationality mean that Conservatives take a cautious attitude towards change. Conservatives do not always oppose change but argue that it should be pursued in a gradual manner. Change should be justified based on experience or practical grounds rather than through abstract reasoning or logic. The approach should be pragmatic, adapting institutions or practices to meet pressures for change, yet resisting wholesale alteration.

Strands of conservatism and their impact

Conservative ideas have played a huge role in the development of British politics. They were deployed to considerable effect in the nineteenth century against the newly ascendant classical liberal ideas. Although many changes were enacted which Conservatives opposed, they also had considerable success in resisting further changes and keeping most of the traditional features of British politics intact. Successes included maintaining a strong powerful role for the aristocracy (and the survival of the monarchy), despite the rise of the new entrepreneurial class and the extension of the franchise. For example, the House of Lords continued to be made up of the landed gentry who gained their place through accident of birth. More generally, the British constitution was subject only to gradual change, with key traditions and conventions of parliamentary behaviour being preserved. There are a number of strains of Conservative thought, each of which have impacted on British politics in important ways. Three main strands are:

Traditional conservatism

Traditional conservatism takes a hard-line stance in defence of traditional institutions and customs of behaviour. These ideas have contributed much to the development of the English legal system. This strand of thought has also manifested itself in opposition to progressive reforms in recent decades such as women's rights to abortion, homosexual rights and uncontrolled immigration. Traditional Conservatives view such changes as undermining the traditional family model and British way of life. These attitudes have done much to fuel arguments against the immigration of (particularly) non-white people to Britain since the 1950s. In the 1960s the Conservative politician Enoch Powell argued that immigration was 'literally mad' and would provoke large-scale violence. Powell argued that those descending from people born in the former colonies could never legitimately be called 'British'. Such attitudes were echoed in later decades with ongoing resistance to immigration and asylum-seekers. Opponents accuse traditional Conservatives of overtly or covertly perpetuating prejudicial views towards minority groups.

Paternalist conservatism

While maintaining the Conservative view that inequalities are inevitable, paternalist Conservatives argue that the wealthy and powerful must take responsibility for helping the less fortunate. In this view all social classes are part of an organic whole and depend on one another. In the mid-nineteenth century the Conservative prime minister Benjamin Disraeli advocated a 'one-nation' politics, introducing reforms to tackle some of the worst social consequences of the industrial revolution. The 'one-nation' view also called on the wealthy to assist the poorest through support for voluntary associations and charity. Paternalist conservatism had its strongest influence in the postwar period as the Conservative governments between 1951 and 1964 maintained and expanded the welfare state established by the preceding Labour government. Leaders such as Harold Macmillan argued that welfare provision was a necessary safety net and that government had a duty to manage economic affairs and public services. For many, acceptance of new institutions such as the National Health Service was a pragmatic step that would increase social harmony and help pacify a strong Labour movement. However, paternalist conservatism has also promoted continuity in key institutions such as the monarchy who, it is argued, will look after the interests of its subjects. Furthermore this school of thought defended the hereditary principle in the House of Lords, arguing that the landed gentry will benignly cater for the interests of the lower orders as well as their own.

Liberal conservatism

Liberal Conservatives share classical liberalism's desire for minimal intervention in the economy. Individuals should be free to participate in the market and generate wealth, free from government constraint. However, liberal Conservatives believe that individuals cannot be trusted to act responsibly in other spheres of life. A strong state is needed to ensure law and order and social institutions are needed to foster a sense of duty and responsibility to the nation. Liberal conservatism became influential in the nineteenth century as the Conservative party sought to broaden its support beyond its aristocratic base. The adoption of liberal economic principles enabled the party to attract support from business. The Conservatives became known as the defenders of business and property rights, bringing together the aristocracy and the newly wealthy under a common political umbrella. The blend of liberal economics with commitment to a strong state proved a winning political formula for the Conservatives for much of the twentieth century. Though the party embraced more interventionist, Keynesian-orientated policies at points in the postwar period, they subsequently 'returned' to liberal Conservative ideas under the leadership of Margaret Thatcher. Liberal Conservative ideas were used to embrace monetarist economics, the 'rolling back' of the state through privatization of public utilities and a 'tough' stance on law and order.

Socialism

In the broad sweep of British political history, liberalism and conservatism have been the most influential ideologies. However, socialist thought has played a significant role and has inspired many important political struggles in the twentieth century. There have been many fierce debates over both what 'socialism' means and, relatedly, how far such ideas have impacted on the British political system.

Context

Like liberalism, socialist thought developed in the context of the industrial revolution. However, while liberalism celebrated emerging capitalist relations, socialist thought took a much more critical view. Socialists pointed to the terrible conditions in which many people lived, working very long hours for minimal pay and enduring squalid, unhygienic housing. Meanwhile, the owners of industry grew rich from the profits generated by other people's work. Socialist thinkers argued that such inequalities were a product of the inherently exploitative nature of capitalism. Thus socialism developed as a challenge to the new social order, questioning the Liberal and Conservative ideas that were being used to justify it.

Core assumptions of socialism include:

- *Collectivism* – socialism is more optimistic regarding human nature than either liberalism or conservatism. People are viewed as basically good, generally being disposed to cooperate with one another for common benefit. Individual thought and action is viewed as a product of people's environment. So, if someone acts selfishly or harms others this tends to result from the circumstances surrounding them. Wrongdoing does not emerge from innate 'evil' but from social conditions, e.g. poor living conditions may make someone more likely to commit crime. Given decent living conditions and access to opportunities (such as education) people are likely to be creative and work in harmony with others.
- *Equality* – socialism promotes the idea that people should have equal chances to prosper in society. This goes further than liberalism's commitment to equality of opportunity. For socialists it is also necessary to challenge the vast inequalities of wealth which emerge from market relations. Without tackling these, 'equality' means little as the poorest will lack the resources to participate effectively.
- *Class differences* – socialists argue that under capitalism society is divided into distinct economic classes. The working class, the majority, sell their labour in the marketplace and survive through the wages they earn. The ruling class, the minority, own industry and business, and make money from the profits generated by these. This wealth gives the ruling class great power as well as privileged access to

education and services. Historically socialism is committed to improving conditions for the working class.
- *Strong government* – many strands of socialism argue that the state should be used as a powerful mechanism to transform society. Socialists should make use of government to redistribute wealth and opportunity and to tackle inequality. Furthermore, government should take an active role in planning the national economy.

Strands of socialism and their impact

Socialism became a substantive political force in Britain in the twentieth century. In 1908 trade union groups who aimed to gain representation in Parliament formed the Labour party. A range of affiliated groups advanced (varying kinds of) socialist ideas within the party and in 1918 Labour adopted 'clause 4', which advocated the 'common ownership' of industry. However, to assess the impact of socialist ideas it is necessary to differentiate between different strands. These include:

Marxism

In its traditional guise Marxist socialism calls for a political and economic revolution to overthrow capitalism to end class-based society (Marx and Engels 1848). In comparison to a number of European societies Marxist ideas made a relatively limited impact in Britain. Marxism consistently remained a minority viewpoint in the Labour party and in the British trade union movement. Many socialists sympathized with large elements of the class-analysis of Marxism, yet there was little appetite for the revolutionary change advocated. Marxist ideas gained more of a hearing at the point of high industrial militancy such as in the 1970s. In 1984–5 the National Union of Mineworkers was led by a committed Marxist, Arthur Scargill, who viewed the miners' strike of that year very much as a class war. More generally overtly Marxist ideas tended to be confined to smaller far-left groups such as *Militant* and the *Socialist Workers' Party*. However, interestingly, writers in the social democratic and revisionist traditions of socialism still regarded Marxism as 'the' socialist position to reassess and move beyond.

Social Democracy

Social democracy (sometimes referred to as 'reformist' or 'corporate' socialism) believes that the market produces inequalities and damaging social consequences. At the same time it believes the market can play a positive role in wealth creation. Therefore the state must assume a key role in planning the economy, with markets being subject to regulation and control. A balance of public and private ownership is desirable, with the state taking active measures to provide welfare and enact redistributive measures. Social democratic ideas developed as the Labour party committed itself to competing for parliamentary power against the Conservatives. The belief emerged that Labour could transform society by peacefully gaining power through elections and making use of the powers of the state. An important source of such thinking was the *Fabian Society*, an affiliated group which argued that socialism could be achieved through gradual, step-by-step reforms enforced through a strong central state. Such change would require government taking more of the economy into public ownership and extending welfare provision. Social democratic thinking was influential on the postwar Labour government's programme: nationalizing 20 per cent of British industry, creating the welfare state and adopting Keynesian economics (see above discussion of liberalism). To this extent social democratic thinking overlapped strongly with progressive Liberal ideas. This is perhaps not surprising as key founders of the Labour party such as Keir Hardie and Ramsay MacDonald had originally been members of the Liberal party. Many in the Labour party wanted the reforms of the Attlee government (1945–51) to be built upon by taking much more of British industry into public ownership. However, these calls were resisted by the party leadership and future Labour governments in the 1960s and 1970s did little to extend nationalization.

Revisionism

In the 1950s a number of significant figures in the Labour party began to reflect on the party's achievements and the direction which socialist thought should take in the future. Anthony Crosland's book *The Future of Socialism* (1956) argued that the ownership of industry was now less important to social justice than many had assumed. Indeed the experience of state ownership in Communist countries indicated that too much state control of economic affairs could lead to inefficiencies and abuse of individual liberty. According to Crosland it was unnecessary for socialists to pursue their goals through traditional class struggle and the idea of socialism competing to replace the capitalist system. The goals of greater equality and reduction of class privilege could be achieved by adapting the existing system. A mixed economy, run along Keynesian lines, could sustain full employment and produce the economic growth that could be used to improve conditions for the less well-off. For Crosland a key strategy for socialists was to redistribute wealth through taxing high earners and using these funds to improve welfare and education. Revisionist ideas were influential on Labour party leaders over the next two decades. Keynesian economics ideas remained important and the Labour government of 1964–70 moved to end selection of pupils in state schools, introducing a new comprehensive system in which pupils would no longer be chosen for particular schools based on ability or social background. Labour governments in the 1960s and 1970s boosted spending on public services, though were forced to backtrack when economic problems emerged. Many members of the Labour party opposed the policies of the Labour governments in these decades, believing them a 'betrayal' of socialist ideas. Bitter battles were fought at party conferences between the revisionist-orientated leaders of the party and members who advocated a stronger socialist programme including policies such as more nationalization, higher levels of taxation and welfare spending, and nuclear disarmament. Following Labour's defeat in 1979, for a brief period such ideas gained the ascendancy within the Labour party and in 1983 the party stood on a radically left-wing manifesto. During this spell a number of high-profile revisionists left the party to form the *Social Democratic Party* (which later merged with the Liberal party to become the Liberal Democrats). However, following Labour's landslide defeat in 1983 the moderates in the party began reclaiming control.

In the 1980s a new type of revisionist analysis emerged as the political left in Britain struggled to respond to the triumph of 'Thatcherism'. Leading figures in the Labour party argued that changes in British society and the international economy meant that socialists had once again to reconsider their policies and ideas. During the 'modernization' of the Labour party under Neil Kinnock (1983–92) and John Smith (1992–4) the party gradually abandoned Keynesian economics and their oppositions to the Conservative's privatization of key public services. The 'efficiency and realism' of markets was accepted and redistributive polices were moderated. These reforms paved the way for the emergence of 'third way' ideas under Tony Blair's leadership (see Chapter 2).

Some critics argued that revisionist perspectives abandoned too much of traditional socialist thinking to properly be considered 'socialist'. Certainly, many of the ideas of revisionism are similar to ideas within the liberal tradition, particularly as revisionism departs from socialism's historical opposition to capitalism. Of the three ideologies discussed socialism has, in the British context, proved the most defensive and least self-assured set of ideas to have significantly impacted on British politics. In many ways it is the poor relation of Liberal and Conservative traditions. This weakness arises in part from the limited number of years Labour was in government pre-1997. Between 1951 and 1997 Labour was in power for only 11 years. However, more generally socialism's relatively limited success may be explained by the fact that it posed the most far-reaching changes to the status quo, in turn provoking opposition from some of the most powerful groups in society.

GOVERNING DISCOURSES: DOMINANT IDEAS AND COMMON THEMES

This section focuses less on the conflicts between different ideologies and more on examining the ideas which have tended to dominate British politics. Attention is drawn to ideas that have often cut across party political debates and to themes which have been common to the discourses of British governments, particularly in the postwar period. Such ideas help explain large areas of continuity in British politics. Stress is placed on themes of strong government, a liberal economy, pragmatism and empiricism, and notions of 'Britishness'.

Strong government and a liberal economy

As the above discussion indicates, there is no easy equation between particular political parties and political ideologies. Liberalism has been the dominant ideology, yet for most of the twentieth century the Liberal party was a minor party. Much of what successive Labour and Conservative governments can be easily equated with classical and/or progressive liberalism. However, the different ideologies influencing British politics have of course fuelled political conflict within and between political parties. The conflict between Keynesian interventionist strategies as against more classical liberal (or monetarist) economic policies has arisen at different points within both main political parties. The Labour and Conservative parties have adopted sharply contrasting ideological stances on issues such as the extent of welfare, redistributive policies and how far 'equality' is a desirable goal. However, despite the continual conflicts within British politics, and the competing traditions of thought, it is possible to argue that a couple of broad ideas have been generally dominant. The dominance of Liberal and Conservative ideas has contributed to an emphasis on:

- *Strong government* – as we have seen, conservatism has had a strong impact on the attitude of government to the constitution. There has been much pride in the traditions of British government, which place sovereignty in Parliament and, relatedly, power in the hands of the executive. Broadly, the British political system is viewed as having proved its worth by its survival and adaptability over the centuries. The Conservative party historically has been suspicious of mass participation in politics and maintained the need for a strong centre capable of taking difficult and necessary decisions despite the unpopularity. In this area the Conservative emphasis on the need for strong leadership has dominated over Liberal warnings against overpowerful government. The general belief in strong government has been given support by much British socialist thought. For example, the Fabian school of British socialism argued that a strong state was needed to take the reforming measures needed to transform British society.
- *Liberal economy* – classical Liberal ideas dominated as British capitalism developed and they have remained crucially important up to the present day. As argued above, historically much Conservative thought came to incorporate *economically* Liberal ideas with the emphasis on minimal intervention in the economy. British governments have generally sought to maintain 'sound money' through keeping a tight rein on public spending and balancing the budget. There was a move away from laissez-faire economics under the postwar Labour government towards more interventionism and planning. However, it should be remembered that this change owed more to the liberal ideas of Keynes and Beveridge than to socialist doctrine. Although Keynesianism involved more government management of the economy it still largely left the market to manage its

own activity (indeed, some economists argue Keynesianism was just a revised version of classical Liberal economics, rather than a departure from it). Furthermore, many scholars have questioned just how 'Keynesian' postwar economic policies were, stressing the continued influence of classical Liberal ideas regarding keeping a balanced budget. Kerr (2001) argues there was a recurrent struggle between Keynesian and classical Liberal ideas within the key economic institutions, leading to numerous turns in economic policy between the 1950s and 1970s. Certainly, Keynesian ideas came in for sustained criticism in the 1970s and were completely abandoned by the Thatcher governments in favour of a return to many classical Liberal assumptions.

Pragmatism and empiricism

The above sections indicate the huge impact that ideologies such as conservatism and liberalism have had on British politics. Indeed, there have been occasions when politicians have argued their case using strongly ideological language (e.g. Mrs Thatcher). However, there is a long-standing tendency for British politicians to couch their arguments in less zealous terms. Frequently, politicians will present policy choices as *pragmatic* rather than ideological decisions.

Above it was argued that a key element of Conservative thought is the advocacy of pragmatism. However, belief in a pragmatic approach has much wider resonance within British politics. The emphasis on pragmatism has deep cultural roots. Norton (1984: 35) suggests this relates to the fact that Britain has never been subject to the kinds of external constraint which have resulted in a more rationalist approach to politics in other countries. For example, Britain has never had to justify its political system from 'first principles' like the American founding fathers (ibid.), or to rebuild its constitutional framework following defeat in war as Germany had to do following the Second World War. Rather the British political system has evolved in a generally piecemeal way. Consequently Kavanagh (1990: 66) argues:

> British politicians are noted for their pragmatism ... politicians have not been sympathetic to abstract argument either of a Marxist or right wing kind, but are hard put to be 'worked up to the dogmatic level', to quote Bagehot.

Thus they generally present policy as 'common sense', the most beneficial decision based on the circumstances. Indeed, politicians will often cite the absence of ideology as a virtue, presenting themselves as 'down-to-earth' realists rather than starry-eyed ideologists. For example, the former Labour Prime Minister Harold Wilson (1964–70, 74–6) made pragmatism one of his key themes, making his ignorance and disinterest in theorists such as Karl Marx well known. The emphasis on pragmatism helps explain why British politicians have generally been considered 'moderates' and why many rules and procedures have survived over decades without serious challenge.

Arguably, resistance to abstract ideas and planning has been a feature of broader British political culture. For example, the Labour movement has eschewed both revolutionary ideas and any strong attachment to other brands of socialist thought. Trade unions have tended to remain narrowly focused on improving material conditions for employees in particular sectors through 'free collective bargaining' with employers. In the 1960s and 1970s both Labour and Conservative governments tried to involve trade unions in national economic planning in exchange for their exercise of wage restraint. These experiments in 'corporatist' practices (see Chapter 1) failed with grass-roots trade unionists unwilling to accept these arrangements.

The tendency towards a pragmatic stance can be linked to general belief in *empirical* approaches to problem-solving. Empiricism has been a strong school of thought in British philosophy, following the work of David Hume (1748). Empiricism argues that it is best to base decisions on experience rather than on abstract ideas. Indeed, Britain has generally been hostile to continental philosophy championing abstract theorizing and rationalist approaches. Empiricist philosophy has permeated approaches to public policy-making where the emphasis has been on trial and error and incremental change, rather than wholesale reorganization based on grand plans. Norton (1991: 35) argues that empiricism is ingrained, being both a descriptive and prescriptive term: 'To the Englishman it is both what is and what he believes has always been.' Again, the cautious approach which empiricism encourages helps explain continuities in British politics.

Whether pragmatism and empiricism have proved the virtuous approaches many British politicians claim them to be is questionable. As Britain's economic and political decline became apparent in the 1960s (see below) a range of authors came to question the values and practices of the governing elite. Diverse writers such as Barnett (1986), Anderson (1964) and Nairn (1976) argued that an antiquated, amateurish approach to government had prevailed, resulting in Britain failing to develop the kind of modern state institutions that could lead to success in the international economy. Failures to plan adequately and make decisive interventions were seen to have precipitated decline.

British nationalism

In Chapter 1 it was emphasized that in the past many writers on British politics have heaped praise on the British political system. Kingdom (1991: 54) argues: 'Many texts dwell with pride on the idea of Britain's unique insularity (physical and metaphorical) and the conviction implicitly or explicitly, that its political system is superior.' The idea of Britain as an exceptional nation has played a crucial role in the discourse of British politics. More generally notions of 'Britishness' and changing conceptions of Britain's role as a world leader are fundamental to understanding the course of twentieth-century politics. There is a good deal of literature which examines British foreign policy and Britain's changing role within international politics. However, perhaps curiously, few textbooks on British politics focus on the way in which ideas of British identity have been constructed and how these affect *domestic* politics as well as international affairs. Notions of 'Britishness' tend to be taken for granted often implicitly endorsing assumptions about British exceptionalism. In this subsection, key ideas about British identity and Britain's role in the world are examined with a view to understanding both changes and continuities in such ideas. The importance of such ideas to the governing discourse of successive British governments will be illustrated.

British and English nationalism

Within textbooks on British politics the term 'nationalism' is usually only introduced to discuss nationalist politics within *areas* of Britain such as Scotland or Wales. However it is necessary to understand the idea of 'Britain' as the product of particular nationalist ideas and projects. Nationalism as a concept refers to the idea that the world is naturally divided into particular units which each has the rights to govern themselves. It was not until the Union of the Crowns in 1603 that new emblems of a distinctively 'British' identity were created. The centralization of power at Westminster in London from 1707 helped consolidate the notion of 'Britain'. According to Gamble (2003: 26): 'Great Britain was a continuation of England and a vehicle for England ... it is very hard to disentangle the two and say what England is apart from Britain.' Fundamental to constructing notions of British nationalism was the pursuit of Empire. Using its naval powers Britain conquered large areas of the globe, including substantial parts of Africa and Asia. British military and appointee politicians took charge of governing these colonies while British business plundered the national resources of the country and exploited the labour of native peoples. Meantime Britain 'led the world' in other ways with the development of parliamentary democracy, the first industrial revolution and the establishment of London as the centre of world commerce and finance. Such events were used to create particular beliefs or myths regarding British identity, including:

- *British exceptionalism* – the belief that Britain had a unique, privileged role in the world. Some saw Britain, along with Israel, to be God's chosen people (Gamble 2003).
- *National superiority* – Britain's role as world leader in military, political, economic and technological terms was taken as evidence of Britain's racial superiority over other nations.

Beliefs regarding British superiority led to the celebration of traditional symbols and customs of Britain such as monarchy and the Union Jack. They also led to the survival of particular traditions of political culture into the twentieth century. As well as belief in national superiority, R.W. Johnson (1985) argues there was a culture of:

- Deference to authority (knowing 'one's place' in society).
- Secrecy and high politics (key decisions should be left to leaders).
- Anti-egalitarianism and status hierarchy (there is a natural order in society).

The stress on tradition, social divisions and patriotism is of course a key part of the *Conservative* ideological tradition discussed above. The fact that the British state had avoided both foreign invasion and internal revolution helped sustain a Conservative outlook. Indeed, Johnson argues that in large part British national culture has been a *Tory* culture. However, it was due to the power of this culture that nationalist ideas became absorbed into other political ideologies in Britain. For example, drawing on socialist ideas the Labour party initially opposed the idea of working-class people fighting for 'the nation' in an imperial war. Yet, by the beginning of the First World War it had (like the Liberal party) come in line to support the British public going to fight against Germany 'for King and Country'. In fact, Labour's later creation of the welfare state after 1945 gave the idea of 'British exceptionalism' a new dimension and renewed vigour as British government pioneered new ideas through the creation of universal benefits and public services. This was one of the first welfare state of its kind and was used to reinforce Britain's understanding of itself as a world leader. Though ideas about British identity underwent changes in the course of the postwar period, notions of British exceptionalism and nationalism continued to play a powerful role.

Britain as an imperial power, a 'world player'

As the German and US economies developed, Britain gradually lost its role as leading economic power. This decline became particularly evident after the Second World War when Britain was saddled with debt to the USA. A combination of economic pressures as well as political demands for independence forced Britain to begin dismantling the Empire. However, the determination to remain an imperial power remained. As the Empire declined British governments sought to hold on to influence through construction of the Commonwealth which would keep close trading ties between Britain and the former colonies.

While Britain sought to reconstruct a leading international role through the Commonwealth it began to contemplate seeking influence through the newly developing European Economic Community. In the 1960s the idea of European integration emerged as one of the biggest controversies in British politics, a status it retains to the present day. For some, British participation was tantamount to giving up on Britain's unique role as world leader, becoming merely one nation among others in the European project. Others argued that European integration offered a new means to play a leading role while Britain's other spheres of influence were in decline. What has been common to both anti-

European and pro-European political discourses over the last 40 years has been the claim to be prioritizing the British national interest and preserving Britain's role as an important world player.

UK/US 'special relationship'

One way Britain has sought to maintain a globally important role is through the 'special relationship' with the United States. As the cold war between the United States and the Soviet Union developed after the Second World War, Britain perceived the need to ally itself with the military power of the US against the threat of a Soviet invasion of Europe. Successive British governments adopted a pro-Atlanticist stance in which they would seek to work closely with the USA and generally support American actions and international policies. It was hoped that by supporting the US publicly Britain could weld private influence over them, working together with shared attitudes. Both the Conservative and Labour parties had members concerned about an Atlanticist position, yet the respective leaders maintained this stance. Doubts from some regarding Atlanticism were understandable since it was the USA who had effectively taken over Britain's role as world leader. America's own often lukewarm stance towards the 'special relationship', notably expressed in their failure to support British action in the Suez crisis of 1957, makes the British government's continued support for it even more mysterious. However, Gamble argues two factors were important in explaining Britain's belief in Atlanticism:

- The special relationship was a crucial idea through which Britain could reconcile itself from relegation from the front of world politics. In British eyes it gave the UK a key purpose in acting as a broker between the United States and Europe (Gamble 2003: 98).
- The special relationship was particularly palatable to Britain because of the core ideas which both America and Britain held dear. These included the 'idea of global economy governed by free trade, sound finance and respect for property rights ... principles of democracy, human rights and rule of law' (Gamble 2003: 102). Underpinning such ideas were belief in an 'Anglo-Saxon' model of capitalism in which the emphasis is on individualism and minimal state intervention. This contrasted with more interventionist and collectivist traditions in many European countries.

The special relationship persisted in the postwar period, receiving renewed vigour in the 1980s with the close relations that developed between President Reagan and Mrs Thatcher due to their shared free market views and policies.

Decline

Over the last three decades British governments have been haunted by the idea of *decline* (see Barnett 1986; Anderson (1964); Nairn (1976); Hutton 1995; Hay 1996). Alongside the loss of Empire, Britain has also experienced long-term economic decline, a trend that worsened in the postwar period as British economic productivity fell relative to other key European countries. Concern came to a peak in the 1970s as high inflation and rising unemployment bedevilled postwar economic expansion. Faced with what some have called 'post-hegemonic' trauma British politicians have searched either for scapegoats or for means by which Britain's traditional status can be revived. Right-wing politicians argued that trade union power and the welfare state had undermined market activity. Decline also became part of left-wing political discourses that tended to blame long-term failure to invest in British industry. The Conservative government elected in 1979 pledged to 'reverse decline'. The recapture of the Falkland Islands after Argentina's invasion in 1982 led to an outpouring of British nationalism and jingoism, with the Conservatives keen to promote the idea that Britain's international power was reaffirmed (Labour also supported the war). However, the mood was short-lived and Britain found itself pulled into greater European integration. Relative economic decline persisted under successive Conservative governments and, in the mid-1990s, Labour sought to portray itself as prospective agents of national renewal with the slogan 'new Labour new Britain'. In so doing, Labour began connecting itself with traditional symbols of British identity such as the Union Jack and the British bulldog. Once again the idea being pushed was that Britain needed to regain former status and national pride.

COUNTER DISCOURSES: CHALLENGING DOMINANT IDEAS

The above section highlights the ideas that have traditionally dominated British politics and governing discourses. However, it would be a grave mistake to believe that many of these ideas have not been subject to significant challenge. Indeed there have been numerous sets of ideas which have posed a challenge to beliefs in strong central government, constitutional conservatism and traditional British nationalism.

Radical liberalism

As outlined above, liberal ideas were crucial in the development of representative democracy in Britain. However, some argued for a more extensive overhaul of traditional practices in government, namely the *radicals*. The radicals had a considerable political presence in the nineteenth century, constituting a minority of the Liberal party. Radicalism argued for a more far-reaching notion of popular sovereignty in which political power would be exercised in a more 'bottom-up' manner. It was proposed that elections be more frequent and that candidates should stand on platforms advocating particular policies. Members of Parliament should be *delegates* of popular will, responsible for implementing the will of the majority. This challenged the dominant Liberal view that perceived Members of Parliament as representatives, elected to exercise *their own* best judgement. It was argued that rather than elections being a way of legitimizing government they should actually be used to mandate government in its actions. Radicalism failed in its aims, perhaps because it called for change that would have fundamentally altered the British political system, challenging the tradition of top-down, elitist, strong government.

Despite being the 'third party' since the early twentieth century the Liberal party, and subsequently the Liberal Democrat party, has been a strong advocate of far-reaching constitutional change and moves to a more devolved, federal system of government. It has consistently argued for a change from first-past-the-post to a proportional representation system. Such a change would almost certainly result in coalition government, thus challenging single-party control of the executive. This would remove one of the traditional key components of 'strong government'. The Liberals have also consistently called for devolution of power from Westminster to the regions of Britain. Their commitment to federalism poses a challenge to the idea of the unitary state and the centralization of power in London at Westminster. The Liberal Democrats have also (along with an array of pressure groups) campaigned for constitutional reforms such as a Freedom of Information Act and rights protecting civil liberties (see Chapter 7).

Participatory Democracy

Radicalism is not the only vehicle through which calls for a more participatory and less centralized political system have been made. Notions of participatory democracy have been influential in the Labour party, though these ideas have frequently been suppressed and opposed within the party (see discussion of British political tradition, Chapter 1). A particularly radical version of this idea was popular within the party in the early 1980s as the left of the party promoted the Alternative Economic Strategy (AES). The AES called for 'bottom-up' democracy not only in the Labour party but within society and the economy more generally. This would involve extra-parliamentary political activity and workers' control over industries.

Anti-imperialism

Similarly the Labour party has included strong currents of opinion opposed to Empire and its legacy. Many equated Empire with conservatism and considered British rule in the colonies to be repressive and quite counter to the socialist goals of equality and self-determination. The Atlanticist stance adopted by Labour's leadership was opposed by many members who viewed the United States as the linchpin of capitalism and a new malign imperial force in the world. The Labour left opposed Britain's membership of NATO and called for the dismantlement of Britain's independent nuclear deterrent. This stance was bolstered by much popular opposition (both within and beyond the Labour movement) to the Vietnam War and to nuclear weapons via the *Campaign for Nuclear Disarmament.* Nuclear disarmament became Labour party policy during the 1950s and 1980s, but never became the stance of Labour in government. In the 1990s significant numbers of Labour members and MPs opposed Britain's support for and military involvement with the United States in the 1991 Gulf War. However, Labour's shadow cabinet gave support for the war.

Celtic nationalism

The enduring idea of Britain as a unitary state led from Westminster has been subject to a range of criticism from nationalist movements within Britain. These include:

- *Irish nationalism* – the nationalist and republican movements in Northern Ireland continue to campaign for an end to British rule. Whilst unionists staunchly defend British sovereignty, many are in favour of devolving power from Westminster to a Northern Irish assembly.
- *Scottish nationalism* – Scottish nationalist ideas gained ascendancy in the 1970s and the Scottish National Party has proved an active opposition in the Scottish Parliament. Scottish nationalists call for Scotland to become completely independent from England in dissolution of the Act of Union. These ideas pose a fundamental challenge to the idea of 'Britain' as a nation-state.
- *Welsh nationalism* – there are calls for the protection of the Welsh language and the distinctive cultural customs of Wales. Since the establishment of the Welsh Assembly, a degree of power has been devolved from Westminster to enable a significant degree of self-government in Wales.

Chapter 7 looks at recent developments regarding constitutional change, highlighting the significant impact that ideas such as electoral reform, nationalism, devolution and constitutional reform have begun to make in recent years.

CONCLUSION

Later chapters consider how far and in what ways the traditional dynamics of British politics have been challenged since 1997. However, in the broader history of British politics ideas such as radicalism, participatory democracy, and Celtic nationalism have all been resisted or pacified. This owes much to the resilience and periodic adaptations of the dominant ideas in British politics. Liberalism has been the dominant set of ideas in British politics over the last 150 years, leading to the development of modern representative government and sustaining a preference for limited government involvement in the market economy. Despite the clashes between liberalism and conservatism, these strands of thought have become intertwined, with a Liberal economy being combined with Conservative belief in strong government. These ideas are at the heart of the British political tradition. Historically, some strands of socialist thinking have posed challenges to this tradition while others have adapted to it. The cross-cutting tendencies for British politicians to embrace 'pragmatic' rather than grand-conceptual approaches to change have contributed to the survival of dominant ideas from the past.

Other key aspects of British political thought are notions of British nationalism and Britain's role in the world. Ideas of 'Britishness' developed in the age of Empire have continued to exercise an important role, even as illusions of grandeur have dissipated. In particular the idea that Britain remains, or should reassert itself as, a privileged player in international politics has persisted. In the postwar period a dominant strategy to this end has been to stress the shared political and cultural outlook of Britain and the United States. Britain has seen itself as uniquely placed to broker between the United States and Europe, given its shared heritage with each. However, Britain's attitude to European integration has remained ambiguous. Generally, governments have argued that integration is in the national interest and will increase Britain's international influence. Against this has been the fear that British identity and sovereignty will be lost, subsumed into a larger European entity with different values. The spectre of economic and political decline has loomed large over British government in recent decades, provoking both searches for scapegoats as well as domestic and international remedies.

However, it is important not to treat the dominant ideas of strong government, a Liberal economy, pragmatism and British nationalism as somehow an inevitable outcome of past interactions. As we have seen, such ideas have been contested and many have survived through their ability to adapt to changing circumstances and rival ideas. Furthermore, the survival of these broad ideas does nothing to diminish the fierce clashes of political opinion over the past two centuries. For example, twentieth-century politics was in many ways the story of a struggle between classical and progressive strands of liberalism. The establishment of the welfare state and Keynesian economics marked a watershed in British politics, yet classical Liberal ideas fought a rearguard action culminating in the politics of 'Thatcherism'. Notions of British national superiority have dissipated following the loss of Empire yet intense debates have developed as to how Britain can best maintain a powerful world role.

As we have seen, political struggles and the interests of particular groups influence ideas. Furthermore, the survival of particular ideas relates to the survival and development of key institutional relationships in British politics. These relationships are examined in the next chapter.

CHAPTER 4

Traditional Dynamics of British Politics II: Key Institutional Relationships

INTRODUCTION

This chapter reviews key institutional relationships in British politics. This discussion is contextualized by charting the terrain on which such relationships have been constructed. Thus the first section of the chapter charts the traditional features of the British constitution and its implications for the practice of government. Attention is then turned to the development of the British state, examining the growth of government involvement in civil society and the economy during the twentieth century. The second section looks first at key intergovernmental relations, examining the traditional relationship and tensions between central and local government. Focus is then placed on the development of relations between British central government and the European Community/European Union (EC/EU). The final section reviews key democratic relationships in British politics, looking first at relations between government and interest groups, before examining the relations between the political parties and the general population. The chapter examines how these sets of relations have evolved, particularly in the postwar period, drawing attention to important patterns of change. Overall it is argued that the relations between political institutions, and between these institutions and civil society, have been dominated by the power of central government, with the party system and changes in the media helping to sustain traditional top-down, elitist forms of decision-making.

CONTEXT: CONSTITUTION AND STATE

British constitution

Institutional relationships in British politics are underpinned by a somewhat unusual constitution. In many nations, such as the USA, there is a written constitution that lays out the structures, branches and powers of government and their relationship to citizens. In Britain no single document exists and much of what is understood as the constitution is a series of established conventions (Dicey 1885). The modern constitution owes much to rules established in the Glorious Revolution of 1688 after which practical political power was substantially transferred from the monarch to Parliament.

There are four principal 'sources' of the British constitution:

- *Statute* – Acts of Parliament become written law, binding on all citizens and enforceable through the courts.
- *Common law* – established by the judiciary, decisions made in one court of law set precedents against which similar future cases must be judged.
- *Convention* – particular practices of government such as 'collective cabinet responsibility' become established and are then followed in future, though they are not rules enforced by any external authority.
- *Royal prerogative* – special powers are exercised by the prime minister (or ministers) on behalf of the monarch. These include powers to declare war, make treaties, issue orders to armed services and to appoint the civil service.

The key historic principle of the British constitution can be summarized as 'the Crown in Parliament is Supreme'. Vested with the monarch's authority, Parliament is sovereign, acting as the source from which all other authority formally derives. Acts of Parliament are binding and in theory there is no constraint on the kinds of laws Parliament may pass. Parliament may overturn any previous legislation. Other bodies such as the courts or lower tiers of government all act on the authority of Parliament. In this way the British constitution differs from others such as the US which includes a formal separation of powers between the legislature, executive and the judiciary. Yet historically British government was praised for the 'checks and balances' in the system, notably the split in authority between the House of Commons and the House of Lords. Moreover, the fact that the constitution was not formally written and proceeded substantially through convention was seen to provide a *flexibility* that served political institutions well, giving them leeway to react to new circumstances and pressures (Johnson 1980). So, for example, in response to industrialization and liberalism government was able to extend the franchise, paving the way for modern party political competition. In reaction to demands for democratic legitimacy, acts were passed in 1911 and 1949 limiting the powers of the unelected House of Lords in relation to the elected House of Commons. Indeed the constitution was not an issue of great political controversy for most of the twentieth century. However, in the 1970s the constitution began to be examined in a more critical light. Traditional features that have been questioned include:

- The principle of parliamentary sovereignty in *effect* gives the executive overwhelming legislative power. Through the party whip system government can usually pass bills it wishes through Parliament and the judiciary lacks power to overturn legislation. Thus there are few 'checks and balances' in the system.

- Formal power is centralized in Westminster, while regional and local branches of government lack autonomy as well as independent legitimacy.
- Individuals have no formal protection against the (potentially) arbitrary power of government. For example, there is no bill of rights. Indeed, the populations of Britain are still formally *subjects* of the Crown rather than *citizens* as enshrined in a written constitution.

Chapter 7 considers the ways in which the traditional constitution has been challenged in recent years, particularly since 1997. Below, the ways in which parliamentary sovereignty has been compromised by Britain's involvement in the EU is discussed. Nonetheless, the traditional constitution has played an important role in conditioning the types of institutional relationships which have become pivotal elements of British politics. These are discussed in the later sections of this chapter.

Development of the British state: change and continuity

Birth of the modern state

It was only in the mid-nineteenth century that government in Britain began to take the form of a modern state. In the 1840s and 1850s arrangements were subject to bureaucratic rationalization, leading to the development of distinct government departments which were accountable to Parliament (via ministers) and staffed by politically neutral and anonymous civil servants (Rhodes 1994). The Northcote-Trevelyan Report in 1854 formalized such arrangements, abolishing appointment by patronage and opening up recruitment to the civil service for competition. The changes caused disquiet among the aristocratic managers of the then civil service, though they maintained the power to determine which kinds of people were finally recruited. However, though these reforms were consolidated in subsequent decades, creating a recognizable modern state structure, the scope and responsibilities of government did not change substantially in the remainder of the nineteenth century. Government's key duties were seen as protecting law and order and securing property rights, reflecting the prevalence of laissez-faire Liberal ideas (see Chapter 3). Though the state had begun to take on greater economic and social duties it was not until the twentieth century that the state grew and became embroiled in provision of welfare (Harling 2001).

Growth of the state

A range of factors conditioned the growth of the state in the twentieth century, including (adapted from Smith 1999: 43–52):

- *Industrialization and urbanization* – the development of industry and the relocation of large numbers of people into urban areas created unanticipated problems. Deprivation and poor services created pressures for new types of state activity to deal with social problems.

- *Changing class relations* – the industrial revolution created a newly prosperous middle class which challenged the power of the aristocracy. The emergence of an urban working class posed a further threat to the old social order.
- *Intellectual and technological development* – traditional Liberal ideas became challenged by more rationalist and collectivist ideas, including those of Jeremy Bentham and the Fabian Society. The emergence of such ideas was connected with scientific and technological advances that made new forms of organization and management structure possible. Technology provided the techniques of information control and surveillance necessary to develop a bureaucratic state.

Though the above factors contributed to the growth of the state (notably the creation of pensions and National Insurance in 1906), its development was accelerated exponentially during the two world wars. The war effort required that the state become involved in managing affairs in which it previously had had no involvement. Though laissez-faire ideas retained influence after the First World War, by this point a range of government departments had established competencies and expertise in areas of economic and social policy, which were not surrendered. Traditional liberal economic ideas came under increased criticism in the 1930s as mass unemployment emerged during recession. In the Second World War the state took on responsibility for an unprecedented range of functions including food, economic welfare, home security and shipping (Smith 1999: 44). Consequently many government departments developed areas of policy specialism as well as mechanisms for delivery. The development of state functions during the war altered perceptions of what government could and should be capable of achieving. As covered in Chapter 3, the postwar Labour government made good on the recommendations of the Beveridge Report to establish state management of health, education and welfare. These reforms led to the development of expertise and competence in large government departments which in practice meant they had a great deal of autonomy in deciding on policy. In 1946 public spending constituted 38 per cent of GDP compared to only 11 per cent in 1912 before the First World War. Postwar governments fostered the further development of the welfare state leading to more public spending and the expansion of key departments until the 1970s. However, in the 1960s relative economic decline led governments to begin questioning the emerging structure of the state and its ability to operate efficiently and effectively.

The survival of elitism

The expansion of the state and the development of powerful specialist departments owed much to the skill of senior civil servants to make use of external pressures to develop the competencies of government. As the size and complexity of the state grew, so more and more policy decisions were taken by civil servants rather than ministers. Ministers became even more dependent on their officials to sift through information and offer them sound advice. However, in the 1960s many came to question how effective the civil service was and whether it could carry out the extent of modernization viewed as needed to revive British prosperity. Some questioned the elite character of the senior civil service, particularly the narrow social backgrounds of permanent secretaries and the prevalence of *generalists*, i.e. people with a broad arts education rather than a specialized background in science or industry. Indeed, it is striking that despite the growth of the state and extension of its function the essential structure of the civil service in the 1960s was mainly unchanged since the Northcote-Trevelyan Report. The prime minister, Harold Wilson, sought to modernize the civil service by establishing the Fulton Committee that reported in 1968, recommending a series of steps to professionalize the service. However, efforts to implement the proposals were limited, with the civil service resisting any far-reaching reform by stealth. This resistance added to perceptions that the civil service was something of a self-serving, self-perpetuating elite which was resistant to change. Informed by a new right critique of the state the Conservative governments (1979–97) sought fundamentally to shake up the civil service. Again early attempts produced limited change; however, in the late 1980s and 1990s radical steps were implemented including:

- *The 'Next Steps' initiative* – the Ibbs Report (1998) argued that government departments were too vast in scope and size and too ready to resist change. On the report's recommendations responsibility for service delivery (i.e. implementation) was devolved to new executive agencies to be headed by a chief executive. This would leave an elite core of civil servants (about 5 per cent of the service as a whole) in central government responsible for policy decisions (Richards 1997).
- *Privatization and contracting out* – a range of government functions were sold off to the private sector or contracted out for private sector management.

These reforms were far-reaching and constitute an important restructuring of the state. Yet their impact on the traditional character of the civil service should not be overstated. Theakston (1995) notes how senior civil servants (in grades 1–3) successfully insulated themselves against the impact of privatization and marketization, retaining traditional powers of appointment. It remains the case that fast-stream recruits to the senior civil service are predominantly generalists rather than specialists, and the social background of most appointees follows a traditional pattern. In 1996, 42 per cent of civil servants had attended public school, while 46 per cent had graduated from Oxbridge. In 1994 still only 9 per cent of senior posts (grades 1–4) were women, 1 per cent were from an Asian background and 0.3 per cent were from an Afro-Caribbean background (grades 1–5) (Roberts *et al.* 2003). Consequently concerns have persisted as to how a predominantly white, male, upper-middle class and elite educated senior civil service can properly represent the interests of a diverse society. Furthermore, despite the above reforms, the basic character of relations in the executive has not altered. Key decisions are taken by ministers and officials in a top-down, closed and secretive manner. Kingdom (1999) argues: 'the 19th century model of the mandrinate (senior civil service) has survived two world wars and the Keynesian revolution ... despite bold words from reformers, it is not time to write its obituary' (Kingdom 2003).

Holding the purse-strings: the pivotal role of the Treasury

One of the most influential institutions in the development of the British state is the Treasury. As holder of the 'purse-strings' of government, it has played a crucial role in shaping economic and (less directly) social policy. Historically the Treasury has been the key source of advice to government on public spending levels and how to manage the financial markets. It has generally dominated economic decision-making in government and has acted as a constraint on the ambitions of big-spending government departments.

As Britain fought in the First World War the Treasury ceded some of its traditional economic authority as the state took on new responsibilities and spending commitments to fight the war. After the war it argued for a return to the laissez-faire economic orthodoxy, prioritizing a balanced budget and fiscal restraint. It continued to defend traditional liberal economic theory even as economic recession and high unemployment emerged in the 1930s and as others began to argue for an alternative approach based on the ideas of Keynes.

However, the experience of the Second World War changed thinking within government and the Treasury again lost its firm grip over economic policy during the war effort. It initially struggled to regain authority after the war as the welfare state developed and a range of government departments expanded to meet demand for services. However, it maintained an important negative role during postwar expansion, seeking ways to limit increased spending in its annual negotiations with departments. While successive governments were influenced by Keynesian economic strategies (see Addison 1975) the Treasury was never wholly won over to this mode of thinking and classical Liberal economic ideas remained popular among many Treasury officials. Authors often explain the Treasury's ongoing attachment to orthodox economic ideas because of its formal and informal links with:

- *The Bank of England (BoE)* – the Bank of England prints money, operates on foreign exchanges and protects the value of sterling. Despite being nationalized in 1946 it retained strong autonomy while sharing with the Treasury responsibility for setting rates of borrowing and interest rates. (Dearlove and Saunders 1991: 211)
- *The City of London* – the Bank of England is based in the centre of the financial market area of London and maintains close ongoing

discussions with key players there. The Bank of England effectively acts as lobbyist for the City to government, principally through its links with the Treasury.

Close ties between these institutions has led some to speak of the 'City-Bank-Treasury nexus' (Ingham 1984). This network is viewed as powerful as it is through the Bank of England that the view of markets on key issues is mediated to government. Stability in the markets can be important to governments concerned to prevent disinvestment in Britain or pressure on the value of the pound. Links between the institutions have sustained the Treasury's preference for classical Liberal economic strategies favouring a balanced budget and constraints on spending. This preference created a number of conflicts and problems in postwar economic policy, including:

'Stop and go'

As governments sought to stimulate demand in the domestic economy (Keynesian policy), the Treasury remained committed to defending the value of sterling internationally (classical Liberal policy). The two policies frequently came into conflict as a flood of cheap imports (cursed by the high exchange value of the £) undermined domestic expansion. The usual response of government was a 'U-turn' on its domestic policy and to pursue a classic Liberal deflationary policy to reduce demand. A 'stop and go' pattern of altering domestic economic policy emerged (see Kerr 2001).

Power struggle

The Wilson government (1964–70) was concerned that the Treasury's unwillingness to advocate more interventionist economic policy meant Britain's manufacturing base was being left to decline. In response it established the Department of Economic Affairs (DEA) to develop a National Economic Plan with policies aimed at actively reviving industry. However, a power struggle ensued with the Treasury unwilling to cooperate with the DEA whilst undermining it by maintaining deflationary policies. The Treasury prevailed and the DEA was abolished in 1970.

The power of the Treasury meant that over the postwar period the interests of the financial markets were continually privileged over the needs of British industry that required modernization. Many authors have argued that the neglect of manufacturing played an important role in Britain's ongoing economic decline (for example see Hutton 1995; Hay 1996). Relatedly, concern has persisted about the accountability of the Treasury and indeed the 'City-Bank-Treasury' nexus. The Bank of England's operational expertise means it is difficult to hold it accountable for its actions or assess how far its reading of financial market opinion is accurate. Heclo and Wildavsky (1981) carried out an investigation into the 'shadowy realm' of central government which concluded that the Treasury exercised a subtle and powerful influence over other departments through shaping their expectations about priorities and spending levels. However, over time the Treasury has established yet tighter control over the departments. In 1994 the Major government introduced the Fundamental Spending Review, a process in which departments had to explain their spending and adhere to targets set by the Treasury. As we will see in Chapter 5, the Treasury's role and influence has expanded further under new Labour.

KEY GOVERNMENTAL RELATIONSHIPS

Centre-local relations

In British politics attention tends to focus on central government and the goings-on in Westminster and Whitehall. However, approximately a quarter of public spending occurs at a local level with many key services being delivered by local councils and other special-purpose bodies. For example, local councils (whether in the form of unitary authorities, metropolitan district councils, county councils or district councils) are responsible for delivering services such as education, social services, housing, planning, refuse collection and roads and traffic. The fact that local councils carry such responsibilities, and that they are democratically elected in their own right, makes them a significant element of government in Britain. The relationship between central and local government is therefore a crucial dynamic in British politics, one which has proved particularly fractious and controversial in recent decades (see Stoker 1988; Burne 1990; Elcock 1997).

BOX 4.1: *CENTRE-LOCAL RELATIONS – AREAS OF TENSION*

- *Democratic authority and legitimacy* – local councils have their own democratic legitimacy, yet are fundamentally subordinate to central government, having no enshrined place in the constitution.
- *Finance* – local authorities are predominantly financed by central government. Disputes as to appropriate levels of local spending and taxation are commonplace.
- *Party politics* – conflicts between central and local government (including reorganization of local government) are frequently influenced by efforts to achieve party political advantage. However, whilst in power both parties (at Westminster) have tended to favour more centralization.
- *Delivering efficient services* – central government has implemented numerous reforms of local government to tackle perceived inefficiencies in local service delivery. In response, local councils have sought to resist central intervention, believing they themselves are best placed to address local needs.
- *Use of special-purpose bodies* – many local services are delivered through special bodies appointed by central government. The Thatcher governments stripped local authorities of control of some services, placing them in the hands of new special-purpose bodies. This angered many who believe such bodies to be undemocratic.

There are a number of important dimensions to centre-local relations, each of which has produced tensions. These include:

Democratic authority and legitimacy

One of the ironies of British politics is that, despite the highly centralized system that emerged in the twentieth century, many public services were historically developed in a 'bottom-up' fashion. The structure of public services in the eighteenth century was ad hoc in nature with a range of statutory, non-statutory and private bodies delivering provision across often unclear geographic areas. Just as central government took on a larger role in service provision in the nineteenth century, so it looked to ways of implementing such services at a local level. Local authorities were created to rationalize the previously ad hoc arrangements and to establish elections for councillors. Legislation in 1835, 1888 and 1894 in turn established borough, county and district councils. It is important to note that local councils have no enshrined position in the British constitution. This contrasts with other countries in which local government has a codified place within the nation's political system, protecting its powers and legal authority. However, in Britain the authority of local government comes from the centre – there is nothing in the British constitution that would prevent central government from abolishing local government altogether. However, as local government took shape in the twentieth century many viewed it as a strong addition to the British democratic process. As local councils were elected, in a sense, they had their own democratic legitimacy independent of central government and could thus act as a check and counterweight on its power. Furthermore, it created a means by which local service provision could be responsive to local needs. Nonetheless it is important to emphasize the long-standing constraints on local government:

- Local councillors are not (constitutionally speaking) legitimate *representatives* of a local population. Despite being locally elected, they fulfil a role in administering a range of services and responsibilities as defined by central government. Local areas are represented through their Member of Parliament.
- The *ultra vires* rule prevents local authorities from taking action not sanctioned by law or which exceeds their lawful authority.
- Local government has been consistently vulnerable to central government reorganization of its role, duties and powers.

Despite these constraints, as the state itself expanded in the twentieth century so the size and power of local government grew. As demands emerged for measures to tackle poverty and squalor, local councils took on new areas of responsibility, often replacing voluntary provision and buying out private owners of utilities. Between 1900 and 1938 total expenditure of local government increased fourfold (Dearlove and Saunders 1991: 474). The size and scope of local government meant that despite its constitutionally weak position it wielded a great deal of practical power. Many authors stressed local government's strength in being able to bargain and negotiate with central government, given that ultimately local authorities had to implement key public services 'on the ground' (see discussion of centre-local models in Chapter 2). In contrast, Bulpitt (1983) argues that prior to the 1960s a 'dual polity' was in operation in which central and local government fulfilled different roles. Central government preserved for itself control over 'high politics' in areas such as the economy, law and order, welfare and foreign policy. Local government played a more administrative role in areas of 'low politics' such as education and local services, in which the central had less interest. Certainly, between 1900 and the 1960s the general structure of local government remained unchanged. Yet central government did take steps to curb the power of local government, for example removing its organization of poor relief in the 1930s and of hospitals in the 1940s.

In the postwar period central government became concerned about the quality of local services and the organization of local government itself. The 1972 Local Government Act reorganized local authorities into a 'two-tier' structure of county and district councils. Larger urban areas were placed under the auspices of vast metropolitan county councils (services in London had already been coordinated with the creation of the Greater London Council in 1965). However, concerns about the efficiency of local government and the calibre of local councillors persisted. Informed by a new right critique of the British state (see Chapter 2), the Conservative government elected in 1979 implemented a range of reforms to limit and reorganize the powers of local government including:

- A vast range of financial constraints (see below under 'finance').
- Abolition of the metropolitan counties and the Greater London Council.
- Privatization of many local services and the transference of authority of many others to 'special-purpose' bodies (appointed by central government).

Over time the cumulative effect of such reforms was to radically alter the role of local government, reducing both its size and power. Many railed against the reforms as anti-democratic, reducing local democracy and increasing the power of unelected public bodies. However, constitutionally the Conservative reforms were fully legitimate. Under the doctrine of parliamentary sovereignty central government is within its rights to reorganize local government as it wishes. Indeed, the reforms were consistent with the British political tradition's emphasis on a top-down view of democracy, which gives greater weight to strong central leadership over responsiveness to public opinion.

Finance

Local government is funded by a mixture of locally raised monies, as well as funding from central government. In the early part of the twentieth century much of local government expenditure was covered by funds raised in the local area. However, in the postwar period increases in population size and the expansion of welfare services meant local government was increasingly dependent on central government grants. Nonetheless local councils retained much autonomy in the scope and quality of the local services they provided. However, as the nation hit troubled economic times in the mid-1970s the Labour government viewed local government as a target for spending cuts. The subsequent Conservative governments continued with this trajectory, citing local government as a source of much waste of public funds. Measures implemented included:

- Introduction of the block grant, in which central government would decide the appropriate levels of grant for each local authority. Overall grant levels were substantially reduced.
- Introduction of 'rate-capping' – placing limits on how much money local authorities could raise locally.

Thus the Conservatives identified finance as a key mechanism through which they could assert indirect control over local government. However, local councils often displayed much initiative in circumventing the aims of the Conservatives, variously increasing levels of local taxation and reorganizing their accounts to prevent service cuts. In the late 1990s the Conservatives abolished the rates system, introducing the 'poll tax' – a flat rate tax on local services. However, there was much public outrage at this new regressive form of taxation. The protests against the poll tax helped provoke the downfall of Mrs Thatcher and the scheme was later replaced with the 'council tax' – a system based on property. Nonetheless, the more general stringent constraints on local spending remained in place.

Party politics

Many of the tensions between central and local government have been overlain with competition for party political advantage. The rise of the Labour party in the early part of the twentieth century owed much to the party's establishment of itself within the rapidly expanding field of local government. In spite of this, up until the 1960s most local councils were controlled by independents, i.e. councillors with no formal party political allegiance. However, party political competition grew in importance. Debates on reorganizing local government following the Maude Report (1967) were strongly affected by how the proposals for reform would affect the vested interests of the political parties. In 1972 the Labour government enacted legislation to create new unitary authorities that it believed would benefit Labour because of its strong support in urban areas. However, the incoming Conservative government in 1974 scrapped the plans to keep a two-tier system in which they believed they could better exploit their support in the shires. More generally, party political tensions emerged when one party was in power and opposition parties ran local authorities. This was particularly the case in the 1980s when the Conservatives wished to pursue a strongly new right agenda, yet Labour controlled most councils. Particularly acute cases emerged when strongly left-wing councils, with an overtly anti-Thatcherite agenda, were elected in places such as London. The abolition of the Greater London Council and the metropolitan counties was overtly motivated by the Conservative government's irritation with these sites of resistance to their agenda.

However, though in the 1980s Labour argued for more power and autonomy for local government, this owed much to their weak national position at the time. Whilst in power at Westminster, both Labour and Conservative parties have sought to sustain the power of central government. They have sustained this position even when at the cost of their own parties at a local level.

Efficient service delivery

In the postwar period a key concern of successive Westminster governments has been how to ensure efficient local service delivery (Clarke and Stewart 1988). Balanced against this has been the need to make local councillors accountable to local people and responsive to the community. Arguably, it has been the former goal that has taken precedence in the various reorganizations of local government. Following the Bains Report in 1972 the old committee system of decision-making was replaced by introduction of a new corporate management structure. The reforms brought a new wave of professionals into the administration of local government. Many councillors complained that the introduction of corporate management was moving power away from democratically elected councillors towards a non-elected elite of local government officials. Yet, the Thatcher governments believed local government *itself* could be a hindrance to efficient service delivery. In the 1980s a range of radical measures were implemented including (see Elcock *et al.* 1989):

- *Sale of assets* – 'right to buy' legislation gave council house owners the right to purchase their homes at less than the market value. Local authority land was also sold off.
- *Deregulation* – public sector transport providers (e.g. buses) were compelled to convert to private companies.
- *Introduction of Compulsory Competitive Tendering (CCT)* – councils were compelled to allow private contractors to bid to provide public services.
- *Use of special-purpose bodies* (sometimes known as 'quangos', quasi-autonomous non-governmental organizations).

The belief was that local councils should take on a 'regulatory' role in which they would not be responsible for delivering services but rather for arranging contracts and overseeing performance. The Conservatives argued that this would increase accountability to local people as they could influence service provision as *consumers* of particular services. However, critics of the scheme, including the Labour party, argued that standards of service could actually suffer as contractors seek to undercut each other's bids. Moreover critics in local government argued that the democratic link between electors and those responsible for service delivery would be broken. In practice many local councils put up effective resistance to the aims of Compulsory Competitive Tendering, managing to keep many contracts for services 'in-house', i.e. still run by the local authority itself.

Another strategy used by the Conservatives to reduce local authority power was to transfer control of services to special-purpose bodies or organizations to be run by appointees of central government. For example, training services were removed from local authority control and placed in the hands of new *Training and Enterprise Councils*. *Urban Development Corporations* were established with grants to regenerate local areas. The Conservatives came under fire for the 'quango explosion' which occurred between 1979 and 1997 when it was argued a vast new tier of public bodies had been created that were unaccountable to the public. Yet the use of special-purpose bodies was itself hardly new (in fact, in 1979 the Conservatives argued their numbers must be cut). For example, the postwar Labour government established *New Town Development Corporations* and in the 1970s the *Commission for Racial Equality*. Despite the controversy about the lack of democratic control of such bodies they had a longer prefiguration in the history of British government than is sometimes acknowledged.

In summation, centre-local relations in Britain have been underscored by asymmetries of power. Lacking an enshrined place in the constitution, local authorities have remained at the mercy of central government. The general twentieth-century trend was towards greater centralization, a momentum accelerated by successive Conservative governments between 1979 and 1997. Conservative reforms exploited the powers available to them to weaken the role and powers of local government and to expand the use of centrally appointed special-purpose bodies. Despite this, local government has remained important, being in a position to bargain and negotiate with central government over issues and even to circumvent the aims of government policy.

However, when in office, both main parties have resisted demands for greater local autonomy, focusing their efforts on trying to create mechanisms to ensure more effective local service delivery. One can argue that, as government in Westminster is ultimately responsible to the electorate for national economic performance and welfare provision, parties in power are almost *structurally bound* to have a view of the appropriate levels of taxation and service provision within local areas. This creates strong pressures for central constraints on the actions of local government. As we will see in Chapter 6, these pressures have been keenly felt by the new Labour governments.

British Government – European Union relations

During the last three decades few dimensions of British politics have altered quite as dramatically as Britain's relations with other European countries. The relationship between the British Government and the European Union (EU) is now a crucial aspect of British politics (see, for example, Bulmer and Burch 1998; George 1998). Three aspects of the relationship are particularly important, namely: the political relations between British central government and EU institutions; the policy processes involving domestic and EU institutions; and, finally, the issue of to what extent British politics is now 'Europeanized'.

BOX 4.2: *BRITISH GOVERNMENT – EU RELATIONS*

Political relations

- Britain has traditionally been an 'awkward partner', sceptical about European integration beyond economic affairs and free trade.
- Development of 'supra-nationalism' has been at the core of moves to develop EU institutions (to the discomfort of many British politicians).
- Through the Single European Act (1986), the British government agreed with partner countries to extend *qualified majority voting* on key issues.

Policy relations

- The European Commission is the main determinant of policy in the areas of Agriculture, Fishing, Trade and competition policy.
- Strong and complex institutional links between national government departments and EU institutions. Policy competence is shared in areas such as transport, the environment, regional policy and social policy.

Is British politics now 'Europeanized?

Arguments for:

- In practice, British parliamentary sovereignty is now compromised. European law can now supersede domestic law.
- British policy-makers must 'play the game' of participating in EU structures and must have mechanisms in place to implement EU decisions.

Arguments against:

- In key areas British central government is still the determinant of policy, e.g. macro-economic policy, education, health, law and order and foreign policy.
- British politicians and officials can often use EU regulations to their own advantage.
- Participation in the EU is a way for government to promote the British national interest, while also offering a scapegoat for unpopular decisions.

Political relations

As argued in Chapter 3, notions of British nationalism have played an important part in the attitude of British politicians. In the 1950s Britain was invited to join six other European countries to establish a *European Economic Community* (EEC) which would work towards greater economic and political cooperation between nations states in Europe.

Britain declined the offer, viewing it as a threat to British sovereignty. Instead it pursued free trade agreements with other European countries which would not infringe British political autonomy. However, by the 1960s Britain's relatively poor economic performance was becoming evident and government began to turn to the EEC as a possible remedy for economic decline. British governments applied in 1961 and again in 1967 to join the EEC but were vetoed by the French president, Charles de Gaulle, who feared that Britain's island status, as well as its close links with the USA, would make it an 'inappropriate' European partner.Though the elites of both main parties in Britain were generally in favour of integration, both parties were divided on the issue.

Even after eventual acceptance to the European Community in 1973 (subsequently ratified by the public in Britain's first ever referendum on the issue), opinion remained divided. Pro-EC campaigners generally justified the case for entry on *economic* grounds, believing British business and industry would benefit from participation in a common European market. However, on the continent the proponents of the EC viewed the development of 'supra-nationalism', i.e. greater political and institutional cooperation and integration within Europe, as a key goal. This tension persisted into the 1980s when, despite irritation with many rules (such as the Common Agricultural Policy) which disadvantaged British interests, in 1986 the Conservative government agreed the *Single European Act*. Mrs Thatcher viewed the act as a means of promoting economic liberalization and free trade, themes which fitted well with her domestic economic agenda. Yet the act also accelerated the process of European integration on a number of fronts, not least through the introduction of *qualified majority voting (QMV)*. QMV established the principle that on certain issues national governments could be out-voted and forced to implement the policies agreed by the majority of EC states. These developments further polarized British opinions on European integration, with a strong Euro-sceptic body of opinion growing in the Conservative party. Divisions manifested themselves in debates over the Maastricht Treaty (1992) which aimed to further institutionalize cooperation with the creation of the European Union (EU). The British government agreed to the treaty in general, but negotiated 'opt-outs' by which Britain could refuse to participate in the European social chapter and join the new European single currency. Yet the government was continually hampered by anti-EU sentiment among many cabinet members, back-bench MPs and members of the general public. However, as will be later argued (see Chapter 5) a more cooperative, pro-EU stance was eventually adopted with the election of a new Labour government in 1997.

Policy relations

One irony of British relations with the EU is that despite Britain's reputation as an 'awkward partner' in high-level negotiations, on a more practical, day-to-day level British government has worked well with European partners on policy issues. Indeed, Britain has one of the best records for fulfilling its obligations under EU regulations. Many of the working relationships between government departments and EU institutions are strong. The nature of such relations varies enormously according to which departments and policy areas are under discussion. Traditionally departments less affected by EU legislation such as the Department of Social Security or Home Office have a somewhat detached relationship with EU institutions. On the other hand, due to the EU's powerful influence over trade policy, the Department of Trade and Industry has very close relations with the EU (Richards and Smith 2002: 154). The EU now has primary responsibility for setting policy in the areas of trade, competition, fishing, agriculture and consumer protection. Policy competence is shared between EU and national institutions in such areas as the environment, transport, social policy and regional policy. Hooge and Marks (2001) argue that the EU is dispersing power away from nation states such as Britain and that policy increasingly results from 'multi-level governance'. It is argued that the sheer range of authoritative EU institutions, including the European Commission, the Council of Ministers, the European Parliament and the European Court of Justice, makes it difficult for nation states to influence decision-making. The sheer complexity of relations between these bodies and in the processes of policy-making also makes life difficult. Much draft legislation originates in the European Commission and is then forwarded to the Council of Ministers. At this point officials of nation-state governments can have input. However, at the same stage the draft legislation is also forwarded to interest groups and the European Parliament for their views. In order to influence policy, interest groups must organize on an *EU-wide* level in order to ensure they are consulted. Similarly, in the European Parliament national political parties (such as the British Labour party) must usually try and cooperate with similar parties in other countries (e.g. German Social Democrats) in order to make an impact on the policy process (see Baker and Seawright 1996). Thus, in a variety of ways traditional nation-state-based politics is being replaced by more cooperative joint patterns of representation and lobbying.

In addition, in a number of ways, EU institutions impose upon the practices and policies of government departments in Whitehall:

- Department officials must review relevant draft legislation proposed by the European Commission to determine how it may affect departmental policy and practice.
- Mechanisms must be in place to ensure that EU legislation can be accommodated and implemented.
- Bodies such as the European Secretariat, and departments such as the Foreign and Commonwealth Office (FCO), must monitor developments at EU level ensuring that policies are consistent between different departments and that government objectives are made to dovetail with EU policy objectives.

Despite the power of EU institutions, and the complexity of decision-making, it would be a mistake to downplay the power which nation-states retain to affect policy. Much of the actual policy work of the EU is conducted by nation-state officials, whose approach is strongly influenced by their own departmental priorities. Policy promoted at EU level will often be inspired by nation-state political priorities rather than vice versa. In addition, much of EU policy detail is complex and technical, meaning that nation-state officials will often have considerable autonomy in forming such policy. In this sense EU integration may reinforce elitist patterns of decision-making rather than 'Europeanize' them. Importantly, while bodies such as the European Commission have strong powers to set regulations in particular policy areas, they are nonetheless *reliant* on nation-state governments such as Britain to *actually implement* policy. The process of implementing directives can also be complex, affording ministers or officials a good deal of leeway in how they interpret them.

Is British politics now 'Europeanized'?

The development of the EU has prompted many to ponder whether British politics is now 'Europeanized'. As covered in Chapter 2, Rhodes (1997) proposes that the British state is being 'hollowed-out' upwards towards the EU. More generally there are arguments that the autonomy and sovereignty of British government are being incrementally eroded away. There are a number of factors that can be cited as evidence of Europeanization. European law takes precedence over British law and can be enforced by the courts. In practical terms this is a clear break with the traditional principle of parliamentary sovereignty – the EU now clearly places constraints on what the Westminster Parliament may do. In theory, it can still be argued that ultimate sovereignty resides in Parliament as at a future date Britain could withdraw from the EU, thus removing such constraints. However, in the meantime EU laws and regulations remain a powerful influence over key institutions and policy areas in British politics. Government departments must have mechanisms in place to implement EU decisions and officials must prepare and define their 'positions' for negotiation in EU policy processes. Similarly regional government, local government and pressure groups must organize their activities to lobbying concerning EU policy.

On the other hand, there are strong reasons to be sceptical about the notion of 'Europeanization' (see Richards and Smith 2002). Most obviously, British central government is still the main determinant of policy in most key areas. For example, macro-economic policy (including the setting of income tax) is still the preserve of the UK Treasury. Similarly, British government retains general autonomy to determine policy in education, health, foreign policy, defence, welfare benefits and law and order. It is also unclear that the *structure* of British government has been profoundly affected by the onslaught of EU directives and policy activity. Bulmer and Birch (1998) note that European integration has generally been adopted into the traditional 'Whitehall model' of government with its traditional departmental characteristics. As highlighted above, in many circumstances EU mechanisms are used by officials and/or departments as a way of pursuing their own policy goals. More generally British governments still tend to view the EU as a means of promoting British *national* interest and influence. Governments can find political advantage in European integration in both positive and negative ways. For example, Buller (2000) notes how the Thatcher governments were able to use arguments for European economic integration to back up and support their domestic free market policies. In other circumstances British government can offload responsibility for unpopular measures on 'EU bureaucracy'.

KEY DEMOCRATIC RELATIONSHIPS

Government – interest group relations

Chapter 1 reviewed *pluralist* theories of British politics that emphasize the importance of interest groups to the policy-making process. Pluralism views interest group activity as a vital element in British democracy. Indeed, more generally, the right of individuals to self-organize into groups with shared views and interests is considered one of the hallmarks of *civil society*. Civil society in this sense is taken to be those dimensions of society independent of government and the state, involving groups and networks organized autonomously to represent particular interests. Below we consider the changing dynamics of relations between government and interest groups.

Enhancing 'bottom-up' democracy?

To the extent that interest groups are an important part of British politics, their power might be considered a challenge to the *'top-down'* elitist view of British democracy stressed within the British political tradition. It can be argued interest groups facilitate a more *'bottom-up'* approach in five ways:

- Lobby and articulate views on a consistent basis, ensuring that public opinion is not just restricted to input every five years in a general election.
- Offer avenues through which individuals can participate in politics and the policy process.
- Enable minority views and interests to organize and make their voice heard.
- Produce *functional* representation, allowing particular sectors (e.g. industry) to make their voices heard to decision-makers in a collective fashion (Beer 1965).
- Undertake *scrutiny* of government policy, reviewing how decisions will affect particular interests.

Indeed, interest groups have played a crucial role in influencing government, having become involved in relations with government departments, Parliament and political parties in a complex myriad of ways. The Anti-Corn League was formed in 1839 to oppose law which favoured the wealthy and powerful groups in possession of land. The subsequent success of the league marked an important point in British politics, demonstrating the strength that ordinary people could have when they organized collectively to defend their interests. In the nineteenth century trade unions also developed as a means by which workers in industries could promote their own interests on issues such as wages and rights at work. As the British state grew in the twentieth century so it became more embroiled in relations with interest groups relevant to the sectors of policy or the economy (Middlemas 1979). This process accelerated after the Second World War as government began to intervene more directly in the economy through Keynesian ideas and in society through development of the welfare state. Improvement in access to education and developments in communications technology also facilitated the growth of interest groups. These changes made it easier for individuals to form groups and articulate opinions.

A means to central government's ends?

However, while government interest groups relations became a crucial element of British politics it is important not to overstate the extent to which such relations became a constraint on the autonomy or power of central government. Indeed, the development of such relations was to a large extent encouraged by government itself as a means of helping achieve its own aims and purposes. Key interest groups' involvement in the policy process offered government a number of possible benefits, including:

- *Expertise and information* – interest groups often have expert knowledge of a particular field and can therefore be a vital source of guidance and advice for government.
- *Legitimacy* – having the agreement of key interest groups in an area of government policy can afford the policy a legitimacy in the public eye which it may not have if simply the decision of civil servants or ministers.
- *Implementation* – the success of policy often depends on the cooperation of particular interest groups. It can be difficult to ensure effective implementation of policy if the groups responsible are not sympathetic to the policy.

Central government's self-interest in interest group involvement is also indicated in the general types of interest groups that tend to have most influence. In general, particular interest groups have privileged 'insider' status, meaning they have good formal or informal access to departments, civil servants and ministers, being regularly consulted on policy developments. In contrast 'outsider' groups often have little direct access to government and are forced to place pressure on government through less direct channels such as the media or public opinion (Grant 2000). 'Outsider' groups are typically those with smaller memberships, fewer resources at their disposal, or with the views or values out of tune with government and/or 'mainstream' opinion. 'Insider' groups tend to have strong authority or expertise in a particular area, making their views hard to ignore. Alternatively groups may achieve 'insider' status through having aims or goals that are largely compatible with the aims or goals of government. Groups with good access normally maintain this by working within established 'rules of the game' that do not disrupt established patterns of decision-making. On occasions groups may achieve 'insider' status through the potential which such a group has to disrupt policy-making or implementation in a given area. In the postwar period the groups with the most, albeit varying, access to the policy process have been:

- *Professional groups* – groups with large memberships and expertise in particular policy fields, such as the *British Medical Association*, have been important influences on the development of the public sector in the postwar period.
- *Economic interest groups* – groups having a key role in the economy, such as business, play an important role in policy networks. Multinational companies are usually powerful lobbyists in their own right, whilst industry is represented through the *Confederation of British Industry* (see Marsh and Grant 1977). Private sector employers are represented through groups such as the *Institute of Directors*. Employees are represented through individual trade unions and the umbrella organization, the *Trades Union Congress* (TUC).

As was argued in Chapter 2, important policy networks exist between government departments and interest groups that play crucial roles in determining policy in particular policy fields. Yet despite government's dependence on other groups in implementing policy, it retains significant power to reshape, abolish or create new policy networks.

Reinforcing elitism?

The idea that government interest groups' relations enhance 'bottom-up' democratic practice can be further challenged with reference to how such relations can work in practice. Interest groups are usually represented by a limited number of officers of those interest groups who (if they have 'insider' status) develop relationships with government departments and civil servants through consultation and negotiations over policy. A number of factors can mitigate against such officers 'representing' the interests of their particular group:

- The officers of particular groups may not be particularly 'representative' of their organization as many members may be politically passive. Many organizations (e.g. trade unions) have few resources with which to consult members on their opinions and officers may be elected on low turnouts in internal elections.
- The close involvement of interest group officers with civil servants and

officials may make them more sympathetic to the views of government departments than the more general interest group membership.
- Interest groups are often represented by 'peak' organizations with a range of constituent interest groups. Such groups are often not united, leading to weak or ambiguous policies or stances on key issues. Notable 'peak' organizations are the Confederation of British Industry and Trades Union Congress which contain a wide variety of conflicting group interests.
- 'Insider' involvement inevitably involves negotiation and compromise with government. Such interest groups may have to try and sell the deals they have reached to a sceptical constituent membership.

The 'closed', often secretive, character of key policy networks can often make the policy process more remote and less accessible to groups in civil society. For example, in the postwar period agricultural policy was dominated by the close relations between the Ministry of Agriculture and the *National Farmers' Union*.

Though many policy networks are more open and fluid than the above example, central government's privileged access to information and (usually) resources over other groups mean it often exerts a dominant influence.

The 1960s and 1970s – the myth of trade union dominance

As highlighted above, as the state expanded in the postwar period, so interest group activity also grew and became a more important factor in policy-making. In the view of many authors *trade unions* were to achieve a pre-eminent role in British politics, a role that posed a direct challenge to government authority. The role of the unions became one of the most contested issues in British politics in the 1960s and 1970s. Ideas about 'strong government' became widely contested, with many authors arguing that the power of the trade unions meant Britain had become ungovernable, leading to high unemployment, inflation and strikes (Middlemas 1979; King 1975). Despite the prevalence of these kinds of views, it is questionable whether trade unions had anything like the power over government suggested in these accounts. To assess this issue some broad trends in the relations between government and trade unions must be examined:

- *Voluntarism* – following the Second World War relations between government, employers and trade unions were initially conducted on a voluntarist basis. Contact between unions and government was informal and negotiations between unions and employers (often the government itself) were conducted on the basis of 'free collective bargaining'. The unions sought to defend the wages and rights of their members and did not tend to seek any wider political role. In the context of rising national economic prosperity in the 1950s relations between government and unions were generally convivial even with a Conservative government in power.

- *Move to 'corporatism'* – in the 1960s concerns grew about Britain's relative economic decline and the inefficiency of British industry. Government began to look for ways to intervene to modernize production and boost productivity. Unions began to take on a wider political role as government sought to involve both employers and employees in the effort to improve industry. Voluntarist practices were replaced with new corporatist arrangements (see Cawson 1986). Developments included:

- Creation of the *National Economic Development Council* and similar bodies within particular industries. These were advisory bodies with equal representation from the TUC, CBI and government.
- Attempts at *incomes policies* – successive Labour and Conservative governments made attempts to get union agreement to restrain wage demands in return for extension of union rights and consultation on economic planning.

The Labour government led by Harold Wilson (1964–70) was the first to attempt an incomes policy through the *In Place of Strife* proposals. The government hoped that through its strong institutional ties to the unions (the unions contributed most of the party's funding and provided sponsorship to many of its MPs) it could reach agreement on wages in return for extension of employee rights. However, opposition from many unions and members of the parliamentary Labour party defeated the plans.

Through the 1971 *Industrial Relations Act*, the subsequent Conservative government led by Edward Heath (1970–4) also attempted to implement comparable incomes policy. Again unions withdrew support for the policy (as did many employers). The Heath government's defeat over the miners' strike in 1973 played a role in their defeat in the 1974 election, adding to perceptions of the power of the trade union movement. A final attempt at an incomes policy was pursued by the Labour government (1974–9) under the 'Social Contract' which offered unions (for the first time) an active role in policy; however, again the policy collapsed as national economic problems mounted.

These attempts to incorporate the unions, and the fact that each of the incomes policies failed, led many to argue that the unions were exerting excessive power (see Beer 1982). The Heath government fought (and lost) the 1974 general election after posing the electorate the question, 'Who Governs Britain?' However, Marsh (1992) argues that, even at its height, the trade unions' political power was limited, for a number of reasons:

- The unions had significant, but *negative*, power in industrial relations. They had power to block initiatives, but rarely power to impose their own preferred solutions.
- In particular strategic industries (e.g. coalmining) the unions had a strong influence on wage levels. However this influence was not universal.

- The primary goal of incomes policies was to *constrain wages*, i.e. they were a means by which government sought to discipline unions in the claims they made for pay.

Marsh argues that strong evidence of the limitations of union political power is provided by the manner of its demise. In 1976 the Labour government, under pressure from business and international markets, announced cuts in public expenditure and introduced new deflationary economic policies (see section below on the power of business interests). Government economic strategy was then built around reassuring markets that it would protect their interests, while commitments to the trade unions were reneged upon. Thus once the government changed direction towards pursuing a more monetarist economic policy, unions could do little to resist this despite their opposition to such policies. Yet, in the face of cuts in spending and imposed wage constraints, a wave of industrial unrest (famously dubbed the 'Winter of Discontent') ensued with a series of strikes in the public sector during the winter of 1978/9.

'Thatcherism'

If commentators exaggerated the political power of trade unions, there is little doubt that industrial disputes were a recurring problem that played a role in economic problems such as rising inflation in the 1970s. In addition, regardless of the reality, the perceptions that the trade unions held excessive power became politically very important. The Conservative government's election in 1979 owed much to Mrs Thatcher's exploitation of the 'Winter of Discontent' to argue that Britain had become ungovernable due to the power of the unions and the inability (or unwillingness) of a Labour government to face them down. Union power was seen as part of a wider problem of 'overload' in which government was weighed down by the demands of numerous interest groups (King 1975). Thus it was not only unions which were considered a problem but also groups such as professional organizations, and even industrial lobbyists, who also pressured government to promote or protect their own interests. The Conservative government aimed to reassert the autonomy of central government to provide strong leadership, unencumbered by the demands of vested interests. The Thatcher and Major governments reduced interest group involvement in policy in a number of ways:

- *Power of trade unions politically marginalized and restricted* – corporatist organizations such as the National Economic Development Council, the Manpower Services Commission and the wages councils were abolished. Numerous acts of parliament were introduced to limit the powers of unions to take industrial action.
- *Influence of industrialists and professional organizations restricted* – the *Confederation of British Industry* (CBI) was also marginalized from policy-making, while professional organizations such as the *National Union of Teachers* (NUT) and *British Medical Association* (BMA) were excluded from key discussions of radical changes in

education and health policy. Overall, consultation of interest groups was less frequent and more cursory than in the pre-1979 era.

However, while particular interests were sidelined, other groups with values and ideas more favourable to the Conservatives became more influential. For example, the *Institute of Directors*, which favoured privatization and limits on public spending, became favoured over groups such as the CBI. Similarly an array of new right think-tanks such as the *Centre for Policy Studies* and the *Adam Smith Institute* exerted an important influence on the policy agenda of the Conservatives. Again, as in the earlier postwar period, the patronage and preferences of the government of the day are crucial in determining which interest groups have influence and in what ways. In a sense the Conservatives' marginalization of interest groups can be viewed as a reassertion of the British political tradition and the notions that political authority lies with the executive. Yet while the Conservatives undoubtedly provided *strong* government, whether this was fully *effective* government is more debatable. Studies of policy under the Thatcher governments demonstrate that in many areas the government failed to achieve key aims of policy. Marsh and Rhodes (eds, 1992) argue that this failure resulted in significant part from the opposition of professionals responsible for the actual implementation of policy. Similarly, under Major, policies such as the National Curriculum in education floundered at the implementation stage as teachers refused to carry out key-stage examinations. Thus, despite the exclusion of key interest groups from policy-making, they remained important players in the degree to which the goals of policy were or were not achieved.

Political parties – electorate relations

A key aspect of British democracy is the relationship between political parties and the general population. Kavanagh (2001) argues that the main political parties are important to democracy in a number of ways including:

- *Representation* – parties are a means through which views and opinions can be represented in Parliament.
- *Participation* – parties are a means through which individuals can become practically involved in politics at a national or local level.
- *Recruitment* – parties provide the people who will take key decisions in government.
- *Choice* – competition between political parties ensures people have a choice in how they vote and over the policies of government.
- *Accountability* – political parties must contest regular elections, thus ensuring that politicians can be held accountable for their actions.

The discussion below reviews relations between political parties and the electorate with a view to establishing how far these roles are fulfilled in practice.

Representation

Traditionally, the Conservative party was not overly concerned with having politicians who were representative of the broader public. Indeed, a strongly elitist view dominated with the belief that society has a natural hierarchy. The view of many of the landed gentry who dominated the parliamentary Conservative party was that they were 'born to rule'; endowed with inherited wealth and talent, they felt duty-bound to govern society more generally. Thus their rule was justified with the idea that they were naturally the best leaders, therefore decidedly not representative of the less educated masses. Many Conservatives were motivated by fear of 'mob rule' and wished to prevent the general population having too direct an influence on politics. As the franchise was extended and modern party political competition developed, such elitist attitudes became more qualified as the Conservatives sought wide electoral support. However, even in the postwar period most Conservative politicians and candidates were white, male, middle- (or upper-) class and from a business or legal employment background. The Conservatives maintained their strong links with the aristocratic establishment, most obviously manifest in the overwhelming numbers of Conservative-supporting peers in the House of Lords. Under Mrs Thatcher's leadership the party made a more direct attempt to gain the support of sections of the working class. However, the Conservatives still primarily sought to establish themselves as the most competent party to govern, over and above claims to be representative of the general population (Bulpitt 1986).

The Labour party was initially established by the trade unions in order to provide working-class representation in politics (Minkin 1992). The intention was to promote directly the sectional interests of the Labour movement against other established interests. As highlighted in Chapter 3, while Labour MPs were originally envisaged as 'delegates' of the wider party this idea withered in practice as members of the Parliamentary Labour Party came to see themselves as representatives of the nations as a whole rather than merely the Labour movement. In electoral terms, Labour began to pitch itself as more of a 'catch-all' party, conscious of the fact that it would need middle-class support in order to gain a parliamentary majority. Again, the overwhelming majority of Labour politicians and candidates have been white and male with most coming from a trade union or professional background. For the most part, a Burkean attitude has prevailed in both major parties – the fact that the social background of their politicians has been narrow has not been perceived as a barrier to their adequately representing a much more diverse society. However, this view has been challenged and in recent years Labour has moved to introduce all-women shortlists in certain selection procedures, in order to ensure that women are more adequately represented in the party.

Participation and recruitment

The Conservative party conference is formally an advisory body of which the parliamentary leadership is expected to take notice. In practice, the conference operates primarily as a party rally, used to boost morale and provide a platform for party leaders to reach a wider television audience. Delegates to the conference play the role of cheerleaders as the party leader is provided with an obligatory standing ovation for their main speech. The conference does, on occasions, act as a means of communication between members and the leadership in which disquiet over particular policies can be registered. For example, in the 1980s activists made their enthusiasm for the poll-tax proposals known, whilst in the 1990s many expressed strong scepticism about further European integration. Under William Hague's leadership members were consulted over policy agendas in three different internal-party referendums. However, it is questionable how significant such participation was, given that members had to either accept or oppose the policy packages in their entirety.

The limitations to participation in the Conservative party are illustrated in the party's traditional method of choosing its leader. Until 1965 the Conservative leader bizarrely 'emerged' from discussions between senior figures in the party, the so-called 'magic circle'. Subsequently a system was introduced to elect the party leaders, but the electorate was confined to Conservative Members of Parliament. Edward Heath, Margaret Thatcher, John Major and William Hague each became party leader through this method. Conservative party members were only given a say in selecting their leaders for the first time in 2001, when Iain Duncan Smith defeated Kenneth Clarke in a postal ballot. Conservative MPs appeared to regret introducing this democratic element to leadership selection, choosing to depose Duncan Smith through a no-confidence vote of MPs. In a virtual return to the days of the 'magic circle', MPs then rallied round a single candidate, Michael Howard, and the lack of rival candidates ensured his leadership did not have to be ratified by party members.

While the Conservative party has clearly functioned in a top-down manner, the Labour party has been a little more ambiguous. In a constitutional sense, *in theory*, the Labour party has functioned in a 'bottom-up' manner through an array of democratic elections and procedures. Party policy is formed by the party conference which debates ideas forwarded by branches of the party, including local constituencies. Yet as early as 1955 Labour's constitution was condemned by Robert McKenzie as a 'living lie'. McKenzie (1955) argues that, despite appearances, both the Conservative and Labour parties were similarly dominated by the party leadership. He argued that, while the conference was formally the sovereign body of the party, in practice key decisions and policies were decided by the parliamentary elite. McKenzie's view was to receive further vindication in future decades as Labour leaders and (particularly) Labour governments refused to heed the opinions of the conference on key issues (see Chapter 3 discussion of 'socialism'). Moves to increase the power Labour activists in the early 1980s were short-lived and subsequently successive steps were taken to strengthen the power of the leader and shadow cabinet at the expense of the party conference and the National Executive Committee. This said, conference votes and debates have historically been a mechanism for party members or activists to exert pressure on the leadership. Conference votes have retained both a practical and symbolic importance – for example, the 'modernizing' reforms of the Labour party in the 1980s had to go through the conference to take effect.

Choice and accountability

The most direct effect which the general population can have on political parties is through voting in a general election. It is at this point that government is held accountable for its actions. Competition between the political parties ensures that it is always possible to remove a party from power. According to much democratic theory, voting also offers an opportunity to affect the kinds of policies which government will implement. The political parties each put forward a *manifesto*, presenting its aims, goals and policies for government. Furthermore, if elected, a party traditionally claims a *mandate* to implement this agenda. However, there are reasons to question how far these mechanisms offer a means through which the electorate can influence a party in government.

Governments are not bound constitutionally to implement a manifesto. Manifesto pledges are frequently broken, while governments often introduce policies not hinted at in the manifesto. For example, in 1974 Labour was elected on a manifesto committed to achieving an 'irreversible redistribution of wealth'. This did not occur. Also, anyone reading the Conservative manifesto of 1979 would have little clue as to the radical policies which would ensue in the coming years. Arguably, the idea of the electoral mandate acts more as a legitimizing device for government than a means of implementing the popular will. Government can claim that particular aspects of the manifesto have popular support, when they may have played little part in the reasons why people voted for the party. This said, the manifesto can provide an element of accountability and choice. Parties set out broad values and policy aims which can be compared and used to rationalize an individual's vote. Though parties are not bound by the manifesto, any breaches of commitments or failures to implement key policies can be a political embarrassment.

Impact of mass media

Enhancing democracy, or embedding elitism?

In many ways the development of the mass media has contributed to the development of the democratic process in Britain. Before the birth of the mass media an individual's knowledge of the world around them (including political processes) was largely mediated locally through family, church or school. Development of newspapers, radio and television expanded the sources of information available to the general public, giving them more direct access to national political debates and politicians. The BBC has had an expressed commitment to educating the public on public affairs and to presenting political debate in a non-partisan way. Furthermore radio and TV have created new forums allowing the public scrutiny of politicians, for example through interviews with MPs or in the form of debates on programmes such as *Question Time*. Arguably the mass media has reduced the distance between the electors and the elected, with politicians having to appeal directly to voters as 'one of them' (Finlayson 2002). More generally, the freedom of the press in Britain is seen as a linchpin of a democratic society.

However, there are aspects of the mass media with more ambiguous implications for democracy. While the BBC and other TV channels have remained politically non-partisan (a point sometimes disputed by commentators on both the left and right of politics) regarding party politics, newspapers have had no such neutrality. Broadsheets and tabloid newspapers have generally been owned by wealthy individuals who have established editorial lines that favour one of the major parties. Traditionally the majority of newspapers have supported the Conservative party. The weighting towards the Conservatives increased in the postwar period and by 1992 nine million voters read Conservative-supporting newspapers compared to three million reading Labour-supporting newspapers. How far the bias in editorial lines affects perceptions of political parties and voting intentions is a matter of extensive debate. However, the Labour party certainly believed that the hostile coverage of its policies and political leaders played a big role in their election defeats. Under Blair's leadership Labour tried to woo the Murdoch-owned papers such as the *Sun* to become more favourable towards it. It had some success. However, critics argued this came at the expense of making concessions on policy both to favour Murdoch's business interests and to match the right-wing sympathies of these newspapers.

A major consequence of the development of TV is the effective nationalization of party politics. Most of the information people acquire about political parties is now gained through national TV coverage of party leaders and the parliamentary parties. Perceptions of parties and general election results now depend less on local campaigning and more on images projected through the news, current affairs programmes and party political broadcasts. The importance of television has had a number of important implications:

- *'The medium is the message'* – parties devote much attention to image: the appearance, style and message of political leaders is crafted to come across on TV as well as possible.
- *The 'personalization' of politics* – television has led to greater scrutiny

of the personalities and styles of political leaders. In the 1960s Harold Wilson realized the importance of image as he sought to portray himself as a pipe-smoking man of the people on television. Labour's 1983 general election defeat was blamed in part by the unkempt image of the then leader Michael Foot. Meantime Mrs Thatcher transformed both her fashion habits and speaking style on the advice of image consultants.

The focus on image and the personalities of party leaders has arguably led to superficial considerations taking precedence over more substantive debates on policies and political issues. Over time, tabloid newspaper coverage of politics (and news more generally) has been centred more and more on scandals and 'sleaze' stories regarding individual politicians, rather than wider topics. Coverage of politics on television has also decreased in recent years as competition intensifies between channels to provide more high-rating popular entertainment programmes. Arguably, an important effect of these trends in mass media coverage of politics is to *further embed elitist styles of leadership* within the main political parties. This pattern is manifest in a couple of ways:

- *Strong leadership* – the personalization of politics means that the image of the party leader is considered critical to the political success of a party (Foley 2000). There is therefore a premium on projecting the leader as authoritative, competent and capable of strong leadership. In turn this strengthens the hand of leaders to influence policy and to reorganize the structure of their parties. Mrs Thatcher used such authority to dominate her cabinet. Successive Labour leaders – Neil Kinnock, John Smith and Tony Blair – pushed reforms centralizing power in the party and transforming policies making use of an implied 'back me or sack me' threat. The media's search for evidence of 'splits' or scandals reinforces leadership requests for internal party discipline in order that a united party image can be projected.
- *Political marketing and 'spin'* – the importance of image has motivated both political parties to seek professional advice on how to 'market' themselves, almost as products for sale to the electorate. In the 1980s the Conservatives hired Saatchi & Saatchi to do advertizing. Labour countered with the creation of the *Shadow Communications Agency*, bringing in media-savvy individuals such as Peter Mandelson and Philip Gould to revamp the party's image. Such individuals were not elected within Labour party procedures yet worked closely with the leadership in deciding the message that the party would project. Furthermore, Labour party events such as its annual conference became increasingly stage-managed 'pseudo-events' (McNair 1995), designed mainly to maximize public support for Labour rather than provide for an internal party debate. The leader's media aides would devote energy to briefing the media, 'spinning' what the latest speech or policy announcement meant. As we will see in Chapter 5, these were habits Labour learned in opposition that helped shape its subsequent management of government.

CONCLUSION

Key institutional relationships in Britain are underpinned by a constitution based on the principle of parliamentary sovereignty, the main practical effect of which is to bestow the executive with enormous power, an asset which has strongly conditioned the types of relations central government has established with other political institutions. Traditional relations between central government and, respectively, interest groups and local government, are testament to the executive's scope to alter the 'rules of the game' in interactions in ways which tend to favour its own goals. Furthermore, the leadership domination of the main political parties has heavily constrained the impact that the broader parties have had on the policies and goals of particular governments. A top-down, elitist form of government has persisted. However, Britain's entry to the EC/EU introduced *practical* qualifications to parliamentary sovereignty and required government departments to institutionalize relations with supranational bodies. In a number of areas the EU now dominates domestic policy, whilst it has at least a limited impact on many more. However, British central government holds strong powers to influence and interpret EU policy in ways that reinforce its own priorities. More generally, while central government has maintained a dominant position in the British polity, it has also relied on other institutions in order to achieve policy goals. Local government and key economic interest groups possess resources, expertise and powers which have made them important players in the policy process.

As the state expanded, the executive entered exchange relations and processes of negotiation and compromise in the interest of effective policy. The patterns of such relations changed considerably in the postwar period, reflecting the pressure brought by postwar welfare demands, economic problems in the 1960s and 1970s and the politics of 'Thatcherism' in the 1980s and 1990s. The Conservative governments' marginalization of the trade unions (and other interest groups), the reduction of the powers of local government and cuts in the civil service may be understood as a reassertion of the British political tradition. Central government exploited its constitutional authority to reshape institutional relationships in ways that it believed would secure more responsible and efficient government. Thus, it should be remembered that despite the far-reaching nature of many post-1979 Conservative reforms, they were in many ways *with the grain* of the long-standing traditions of strong government and classical Liberal economics.

In Chapters 5, 6 and 7 we examine how the new Labour government elected in 1997 has grappled with the British political tradition, key institutional relationships and the constitution.

CHAPTER 5

New Labour in Power

INTRODUCTION

Previous chapters reviewed influential models of British politics, key institutional relationships and key ideas. The final three chapters of the book are devoted to examining contemporary British politics and the issue of the extent to which British politics may be changing. This chapter looks broadly at the policies, discourse and governing style of the new Labour government elected in 1997. In so doing it seeks to evaluate how far the Blair administration has broken with the trends of British politics established in the postwar period and under 'Thatcherism'. It is argued that despite the 'newness' of parts of new Labour's agenda they are nonetheless working within the parameters of the British political tradition, deploying a generally top-down, elite-centred form of government. This analysis is extended in Chapters 6 and 7 which examine the 'modernization' of government and constitutional reform since 1997.

INTERPRETATIONS OF NEW LABOUR: COMPARISONS WITH THE PAST

There is now a vast literature devoted to interpreting new Labour and its impact on British politics. Most accounts put new Labour in comparative perspective; the actions of the Blair government are evaluated through comparisons with the performance, ideas and policies of previous British governments. Though there is great diversity in the perspectives offered, three general types of interpretation are identifiable. Authors variously view new Labour as:

- A continuation or extension of 'Thatcherism'.
- A renewed type of social democracy, or 'third way'.
- A continuation of 'old' Labour.

This section briefly reviews the arguments in favour of each of these perspectives, drawing attention to the strengths and weaknesses of each.

'Thatcherism' continued?

Given that the Conservatives sustained an 18-year period in government it is hardly surprising that new Labour has been assessed through comparisons with what has become known as 'Thatcherism'. Indeed, some prominent interpretations suggest that new Labour be best understood as the *continuation*, even *extension* of 'Thatcherism' (Hay 1999; Heffernan 2001: viii; Watkins 2004). In this view, far from new Labour's election heralding a new era in British politics, the Blair government has further entrenched the changes enacted by successive Conservative governments. Such accounts argue that Labour leaders have come to believe both that *most* of what the Thatcher-Major governments did was justified and that they have little alternative, practically or electorally, but to continue with similar policies.

For example, Heffernan argues that in the wake of four defeats Labour believed it had to capture the 'middle' ground and hence altered its policy programme to match the preferences of key voters. In so doing, the party betrayed its traditional commitment to social democratic policies. He argues:

> today, New Labour clearly rejects traditional social democratic means (as well as a great number of its ends) and so rules out high rates of progressive taxation and increased levels of social expenditure. Egalitarianism and a redistributive politics, both key tenets of a revisionist social democracy (not to mention radical alternatives to its left), no longer count at all. The revised politics of New Labour is an illustration of a neo-liberal paradigm that characterises the contemporary socio-economic policy agenda.

Thus for Heffernan a dramatic change has occurred, with a traditionally centre-left party now effectively abandoning each of the key elements of left-wing or social democratic belief. Similar arguments are developed by Colin Hay (1999: 42) who argues that between the mid-1980s and mid-1990s Labour engaged in a process of 'catch-up' with Conservative ideas and policies. He suggests that in the key areas of economic policy, social policy, privatization and trade union reform Labour gradually accommodated itself to the Thatcherite agenda. Thus there has been a process of convergence between the ideas and policies of the Labour and Conservative parties. Hay (1997) argues that this has created a 'one vision polity' in which there is perceived to be no alternative to neo-Liberal policies. Two factors have contributed creating this new Thatcherite consensus:

- *Electoral needs* – Labour leaders came to believe that to win they had to attract the votes of 'middle England'. To do so they embarked on a process of finding out the preferences of key voters (e.g. through focus groups) and designing policies to fit with the expressed preferences of these voters (and since these people were often traditionally Conservative voters their preferences were often Thatcherite) (see Hay 1999: 77–103).
- *Perceptions of 'globalization'* – Labour leaders came to accept fashionable accounts of 'globalization'. In particular they believed that in an ever-integrating world market national governments are increasingly powerless to prevent capital moving to areas of the world with low taxes and lightly regulated economies. As such, Labour saw little

alternative but to continue with neo-Liberal policies of tax-cutting, wage restraint and deregulation in order to make Britain as attractive as possible for investors (see Hay 1999: 28–31).

Consequently, for Hay (1999: 136) it is not merely electoral expediency that has led Labour to adopt Thatcherite policies; it is also belief that in a globalizing world there is no alternative to them. Hay, along with other commentators such as Callinicos (2001) and Watkins (2004), argues that it is disingenuous for new Labour to present itself as a real alternative to 'Thatcherism'. For such critics notions of the 'third way' and Labour's new rhetoric of 'inclusion' and 'partnership' are little more than cloaks attempting to put a softer face on what are essentially neo-Liberal policies.

These perspectives are particularly useful in accounting for the large areas of continuity between 'Thatcherism' and the politics of new Labour, in particular continuities in economic policy. However, these accounts have been criticized by others for overlooking important differences. Indeed some argue new Labour can still be interpreted as a centre-left, social democratic party.

A renewed type of social democracy, or 'third way'

Gamble and Wright (1999) point out that throughout the Labour party's history it has 'modernized' its ideas to account for new circumstances and challenges. Similarly, in the view of Fielding (2003), the creation of new Labour marks another modernization of social democratic ideas, one which takes account of the changing context ushered in by 'Thatcherism' and globalization. A stronger version of this view is offered by the Labour party 'modernizers' themselves who argue that Labour has held firm to many of its traditional values but believes that they must be pursued in quite different ways from the past (Gould 1998; Mandelson and Liddle 1996). Hence strategies such as nationalization and Keynesianism are no longer possible or desirable in the modern context. Rather, long-standing goals such as equality of opportunity and social justice must be pursued in different ways. Thus Mark Wickham Jones (1995) argues new Labour acted to 'recast its social democratic commitments' in this new context.

Such arguments have perhaps become most commonly associated with the work of Anthony Giddens and his notion of the 'third way' (see Chapter 2). Rhodes and Bevir argue the 'third way' should be understood as a response to the dilemmas raised by 'Thatcherism'. Whilst influenced by traditional socialist ideas new Labour had to deal with the challenges posed by the apparent failure of Keynesian economics and the issues of globalization and welfare-dependency. As such, it has indeed embraced the need for a dynamic modern economy, rejecting old-style social democratic intervention. However, Giddens argues that new Labour is also critical of neo-liberalism, particularly the way that 'Thatcherism' created large sections of the population who were effectively excluded (through poverty, or lack of opportunities) from the rest of society. Whereas Thatcherite neo-Liberals wanted to let the market operate as free from intervention as possible, new Labour believes that government has a responsibility to regulate markets and ensure that individuals have access to opportunities. This 'third way' perspective wishes to combine commitments to a market economy with the pursuit of social justice. Arguably then there are elements of new Labour's agenda which cannot be straightforwardly linked to neo-Liberal ideas. These include:

- A concern to remould democratic processes in Britain (e.g. devolution agenda).
- An acknowledgement of the need to address problems relating to social exclusion (see below under 'welfare').
- A re-emphasis upon the importance of employment, education and training as a means of addressing social exclusion (e.g. through the 'new deal').
- An acknowledgement of the link between state action and the need to deal with social and economic problems.
- A broad commitment to strengthening core public services, particularly in areas of education and health (e.g. through significant spending increases).

Giddens and Blair view the new Labour project as a transcendence of the two 'old ways' of both old-style social democracy and neo-liberalism. However, Driver and Martell (2002: 222) argue that this is a somewhat grandiose view. For them the 'third way' is not a heroic transcendence of the 'old' ways but rather a middle road between them bringing together parts of each. Thus, elements from the left, such as public services and social justice, are combined with features of the right such as free markets and low taxes. The difficulty is that different values underpin the different policies. As such the third way contains contrasting and even contradictory ideas and policies, meaning new Labour's agenda lacks any clear ideological coherence (ibid: 223). Similarly Smith (2004: 224) argues that new Labour is 'hydra-headed ... difficult to define, because it is full of contradictions and it presents a head to suit the occasion'.

Continuity with 'old Labour'

Another interpretation of new Labour questions how 'new' it in fact is. In contrast to the above accounts which stress differences between the modern Labour party and 'old' Labour, authors such as Coates (2001) argue there is actually strong continuity. Indeed, it is argued new Labour's behaviour is in many ways typical of how Labour has acted in the past, particularly whilst in government. Rubenstein (2005: 165) argues that now, as in the past, Labour are 'moderate social reformers' and that 'In essentials the party's policies have not changed'. He argues that in contrast to the stereotyped notions of 'old' Labour the party had done little since the 1940s to extend public ownership, had usually sought support of centrist 'floating voters' and had avoided electorally damaging large tax increases on the middle classes. It had also frequently disappointed its core supporters and party members in not pursuing a more radical left-wing agenda. Thus understood, new Labour may be viewed as yet another moderate Labour government. Coates (2001) argues there are similarities between 'old' and 'new' Labour, most notably that whilst in power Labour tends to retreat from its more radical commitments, leading to a sense of betrayal on the part of many members and supporters. As in the past Labour leaders have used inter-party mechanisms to attempt to stifle internal dissent and have ignored opposition to their policies. Allender (2001) goes further, arguing that new Labour displays various characteristics shared by all previous Labour governments, including:

- An absence of ideology.
- 'Pragmatism' over principles.
- Emphasis of the national over the 'sectional'.
- A lack of democracy and excessive bureaucracy.

Thus in contrast to those who say new Labour has turned its back on socialist beliefs, Coates (2001) and Allender (2001) argue that Labour has never followed these whilst in government in the past.

These perspectives are particularly effective in deconstructing the simplified 'old' *v.* 'new' versions of Labour as well as some of the more simplified accounts of postwar British politics. However, they may overstate the continuities between old and new Labour. For one thing Labour has now, for the first time, served two terms in power during most of which time it has remained ahead in the polls, and indeed won a third term. In the past disillusion with Labour always led to defeat – this pattern has been broken. Furthermore, as Larkin (2001: 51) argues, there are significant changes in the context by which 'old' and 'new' Labour have governed. Two changes of significance are the fact that there is now a larger gap between rich and poor in comparison with the 1970s and, more generally, the state's ability to intervene in the economy may be more constrained than before. Also 'new' Labour has, until recently at least, been a more internally tranquil party, lacking the organized left wing which featured in the past.

Where's the coherence?

To varying degrees most of the above accounts stress the inconsistencies in new Labour. For example, though Hay sees new Labour as essentially neo-Liberal in approach, he argues that it is nonetheless currently 'labouring under false pretences' in projecting itself as an alternative to 'Thatcherism'. Accounts such as those of Driver and Martell (2002) point to the co-existence of contradictory neo-Liberal and social democratic ideas and policies. Critics such as Coates point to contradictions of Labour adopting more radical ideas in opposition, which are then ditched when in government. In the remainder of this chapter it will be argued that a more coherent interpretation can be provided when evaluating new Labour against some of the wider traditions of government in Britain. The above critiques emerge from comparing new Labour with particular sets of ideas, i.e. 'Thatcherism', social democracy and 'old' Labour beliefs. This chapter will make similar comparisons with more detailed reference to new Labour's performance in government over eight years. However, new Labour will also be compared to the broader ideas and practices of the British political tradition identified in earlier chapters. In turn, the broad areas of economic policy, welfare policy, governing style and governing discourse are considered. This will be conducted with the following questions in mind:

- To what extent are new Labour's policies and ideas identifiably neo-Liberal and/or Social Democratic?
- How far does new Labour's approach break with or develop the elitist, top-down style typical of previous governments?
- To what extent is new Labour reforming or reinforcing traditional institutional relationships in Britain?

In conclusion it will be proposed that more coherence in new Labour's approach can be discerned if new Labour is interpreted more in terms of overall governing techniques and *style*, rather than its espoused ideas.

DIMENSIONS OF NEW LABOUR IN PRACTICE

Economic policy

It is perhaps in the area of economic policy that new Labour has most closely followed the path pursued by previous Conservative governments. Broadly speaking, new Labour has embraced neo-Liberal macro-economic policies with the emphasis on creating conditions in which business and competition will prosper. However, there have been a number of significant developments of policy, some of which diverge from the goals and values of preceding governments. This analysis will focus on four key features of new Labour's economic approach (see Box 5:1) namely: macro-economic stability, 'rules-based' economic management, pro-business/pro-competition policies and micro-level redistributive measures.

BOX 5.1: *NEW LABOUR'S ECONOMIC STRATEGY 1997–2005*

Key features

- *Macro-economic stability* – commitment to fiscal and monetary stability; broad adoption of monetarist policy.
- *'Rules-based' economic management* – adoption of a set of prescribed rules for economic management designed to produce stability and transparency in decision-making.
- *Pro-business, pro-competition* – policies orientated to help business prosper through encouraging competition and decreasing burdens of regulation and taxation on enterprises.

- *Micro-level redistribution* – policies aimed at redirecting wealth towards certain economically disadvantaged groups, e.g. low-paid working families and children in poverty.

Key policies

- *Operational independence for the Bank of England* – government handed over power to set interest rates to the Bank of England, removing the possibility that government could manipulate these for short-term political gain.
- *Commitment to low inflation* – inflation rate monetary authorities are expected to ensure that inflation rate is more than 1 per cent above or below the set target of 2.5 per cent.
- *'Golden rule' on borrowing* – over an economic cycle government may only borrow to *invest,* not to fund public expenditure.
- *Private finance initiative* – extended and expanded policy initiative introduced by Conservatives for encouraging private investment in public services such as education and health.
- *Minimum wage and working families' tax credit* – introduced a minimum wage level for most employees and a guaranteed minimum income for families with at least one working member in the household.

Macro-economic stability

It is important to remember that on entering power the Labour party had never served two full terms in government. Between 1951 and 1997 it had served in government for only 11 of those years. In contrast, the Conservatives had been re-elected four times since 1979 and indeed had dominated twentieth-century British government. A large part of Labour's failure was perceived to be a result of the economic crises that had engulfed it each time in had been in power previously. On a number of occasions Labour governments had significantly boosted public spending on entering office only to be forced to reverse policies and make cutbacks when economic problems emerged. Historically, financial markets had tended to lack faith in Labour governments and its perceived economic failure disillusioned voters, usually helping precipitate a quick exit from government. Consequently, new Labour was very keen to establish *credibility* with the financial markets and to project an image of economic *competence* to voters. However, the Conservatives had also had problems with the economy and the unpopularity of many of its pro-market policies played a significant part in its defeat in 1979. New Labour surmized that (like previous postwar governments) the Conservatives had pursued 'boom and bust' policies in which periods of unsustainable economic growth were followed by inflation, unemployment and recession. Moreover, it argued that the Conservatives had exacerbated the long-term weaknesses of the British economy, including the problems of low investment in British industry, low skill levels and low productivity levels (Brown, pre-budget speech 1999). Low investment in public services such as education and health was also identified as a key weakness of Conservative policy. Nonetheless, under Blair new Labour had explicitly acknowledged that it believed many of the economic changes wrought by the Thatcher-Major governments were necessary (Oborne 1999: 140) and much of new Labour's economic stance represents continuity with that of the Conservatives.

In order to distance itself from the Labour party's traditional 'tax and spend' image new Labour took a number of steps to establish credibility with the money markets whilst in opposition. First, the party pledged to stick to the plans of the previous Conservative government to freeze public spending for two years and focus on cutting national debt rather than increasing public spending. It also committed itself to pursuing low inflation and not to raise the basic rate of income tax. Labour pledged to increase spending on its priority areas of education and health only when economically 'prudent' to do so. On entering office, the new Labour government immediately took the unexpected step of giving operational independence to the Bank of England to set interest rates. This was designed to further boost credibility with financial markets as the change prevented future governments manipulating interest rates in order to boost popularity (e.g. in the months leading up to a general election). More generally, under new Labour the Treasury has had a firm grip on economic policy, with the chancellor, Gordon Brown, actually extending its mechanisms of control. This approach stands in marked contrast to the Wilson government's goal in the 1960s to weaken the power of the Treasury (see Chapter 4). Thus, rather than challenge the 'City-Bank-Treasury' nexus (Ingham, 1984) new Labour has sought to work with and reassure it. In government, new Labour can be interpreted as embedding a type of 'rules-based' economic strategy, which contrasts markedly with that of previous Labour administrations.

Rules-based economic management

A range of authors have described new Labour's economic strategy as 'rules-based' reflecting a shift in the government's approach to managing the economy that may be traced back to around the mid-1970s (Burnham 2001; Watson 2002; Annesley and Gamble 2003). During much of the postwar period governments often employed (relatively speaking) a more 'hands on' approach to managing the economy. Features of this kind of strategy included nationalized, state-run industries; wage incomes policies; and forms of intervention in markets. One difficulty for governments was that the decisions they took on such economic issues were often hotly debated (e.g. setting interest rates) and if economic crisis emerged this often quickly became a political crisis for the government (Burnham 2001: 130). In other words, if things went wrong government would get the blame. The Thatcher governments' reforms, particularly the privatization programme, established a trend towards a more 'hands off' approach to the economy. However, again these changes were politically controversial – the government's pro-business and anti-trade union measures were matters of great political debate. Arguably, since the early 1990s and the government led by John Major there has been an attempt to move towards a 'rules-based' approach which seeks to de-politicize economic management. The idea is to establish a set of rules through which economic decisions should be taken and to distance the government from the effect of those decisions. New Labour introduced such rules, most prominent amongst which were:

- The '*golden rule*' – over an economic cycle government may only borrow to *invest*, not to fund public expenditure. The aim is to stop the government spending more than it can afford on public services while discouraging groups from lobbying the government for more spending.
- An *inflation target* of 2.5 per cent – the monetary policy of the Bank of England ensures that inflation does not deviate from this target by more than 1 per cent above or below. The bank has discretion over how this should be achieved, e.g. by altering interest rates.

Such measures were aimed to establish credibility with financial markets but also served other purposes. They removed immediate responsibility for setting interest rates from government, thus eliminating or reducing the political damage to it if interest rates should rise. More generally the 'rules-based' approach seeks to distance the government from responsibility for the economic problems that may arise from market activity. Furthermore, in theory such rules stabilize the expectations of both interest groups and voters – if people expect the government to stick to rules they may be less likely to make demands on them (e.g. for higher pay) that would lead to a breaching of such rules. Thus the government wishes to project an image of competence (i.e. it can be trusted to set and stick to rules) while distancing itself from decisions that may be necessary to follow such rules.

Pro-business and pro-competition

Labour historically had been associated with an 'anti-business' tag, partly due to its strong ties to the trade union movement. New Labour leaders have been at pains to establish themselves as on the side of British business. They have done so in a number of ways including cuts in corporation tax; reducing the tax burden on business in an effort to make it more internationally competitive; and de-regulation, reducing the legislative restrictions on employer practices. Much of the 'rules-based' approach outlined above is designed to prevent other pressures (e.g. rises in public spending or inflation) undermining the conditions in which business can prosper. In some ways new Labour's pro-business stance is most clearly demonstrated within the European Union in which it resisted certain moves (favoured by other centre-left parties) aimed at improving rights for workers on the basis that it will overburden employers (Clift 2004). Moreover, on a global scale Tony Blair and Gordon Brown have been at the forefront of promoting international financial liberalization to keep state regulation of capital flows to a minimum (Watson 2002: 197).

New Labour's faith in business is also clearly manifest in its pursuit of the *Private Finance Initiative*. This policy was developed by the Conservatives in the early 1990s as a means of encouraging business to invest in public services. Private sector involvement in public services had long been anathema to most in the Labour party, yet on entering office new Labour enthusiastically picked up and expanded the policy. Under the rhetoric of the need for 'partnership' between public and private sectors the Blair government extended the policy to encourage business to invest in projects in the area of education, health and transport. The policy offers the government a quick way to boost investment in key services (e.g. building new hospitals) without adding to public borrowing. However, government incurs the cost of procuring such investment and subsequently effectively 'renting' new buildings from the private sector. The scheme has incurred the wrath of public sector unions concerned that private ownership will lead to poorer pay and working conditions for public sector employees.

Indeed, while new Labour has established pro-business credentials its relationship with the unions is now colder than in the past. The broadly neo-Liberal economic stance of the government has strained relations with the Labour movement generally and some unions have come to question their institutional ties with a party which they no longer see as promoting its interest. However, there are still important relations between new Labour and the unions (Shaw 2004) and the latter have made some gains under new Labour including a commitment to the European social chapter (establishing employees' rights) while more recently public funds have been made available to 'modernize' unions.

If there has been a clear 'loser' in new Labour's economic strategy then it may be Britain's manufacturing sector. While many sections of the economy have prospered under new Labour, manufacturing has continued to suffer from the high value of the pound, making exports expensive. From the outset Labour made it clear that it would not intervene in British industry; indeed it removed decisions on monopolies and mergers from political control. The problems of low productivity, low skills and low investment have persisted and manufacturing has even entered recession. Some efforts at a new industrial policy have been made (e.g. Gordon Brown established new Regional Development Agencies aimed at encouraging investment in regions), but overall new Labour's stance favours the interests of finance capital over industrial capital in much the way Conservative policy did. It remains to be seen whether Labour's policies on education and welfare-to-work can do much to alleviate these problems in the longer term.

Micro-level reform and redistribution

Despite the strong continuities between new Labour's economic policy and that of its Conservative predecessor, there are some significant differences. In particular, Gordon Brown has taken a number of actions, many at a micro-level, which have brought redistributive effects which help certain disadvantaged groups. These include:

- Creation of the national minimum wage – specifies a minimum hourly rate below which people should not be paid.
- Creation of the working families' tax credit – specifies a minimum income that a family with one working member should receive.

Many interpret new Labour as being moderately redistributive by 'stealth'. Through a range of small changes, such as abolition of mortgage tax relief for married couples and pension changes, Gordon Brown has generated tax that can be diverted to aid some of the least wealthy groups. As is argued below, these changes are tied to a welfare policy seeking to encourage people to work and also to reduce child poverty.

Economic record

In many ways new Labour has thus far confounded the sceptics in presiding over an economy that has maintained steady growth, low interest rates, low inflation and falling unemployment. It has had success in establishing credibility with financial markets and projecting an image of economic competence to the electorate. Furthermore, new Labour has surprised many in being able to plan for and (thus far) fund very significant increases in public spending in its key areas of health and education. Despite a broadly neo-Liberal approach some discerned 'new Keynesian' elements to current strategy in which investment in public services is used as a means of boosting economic productivity (Gamble and Wright 1999). Micro-redistributive measures appear to have had an effect in reducing poverty levels and low pay (Pearce 2004). However, such changes stand in tension with Labour's broader commitment to a deregulated economy that has produced a further widening of the gap between rich and poor (Paxton and Dixon 2004).

While previous Labour governments made some attempts to mitigate the power of the Treasury over economic policy, new Labour has actually *strengthened* its role. This is indicative of the influence of classical Liberal economic ideas on new Labour, helping explain why it is now more content to work with the Treasury which has had a long-standing prejudice in favour of monetarist policy (see Chapter 4). Perhaps new Labour's most significant reform of economic management has been to further embed a 'rules-based' approach aimed at depoliticizing much of the decision-making process. Rather than being a simple ceding of power this can be viewed as a deliberate strategy to distance government from responsibility for economic problems or unpopular decisions, hence enhancing its own autonomy. However, whether it can retain such autonomy over the longer term is open to question as demands from public sector workers for improved conditions continue to grow.

Welfare

New Labour has made significant effort to link its economic strategies to its reforms of the welfare state. Once again the influence of neo-Liberal thought on new Labour is clear; however, more social democratic ideas have also played a role.

BOX 5.2: *WELFARE REFORM STRATEGY 1997–2005*

Key features

- Welfare reform presented as necessary to promote both 'social justice' *and* a 'dynamic economy'.
- Tackling 'social exclusion' – reform has emphasized the need to re-engage people who may have become disconnected from the rest of society through unemployment, being a single parent or lacking educational opportunities.
- Welfare-to-work – reform has focused on encouraging/forcing welfare claimants to either find jobs or take up training or educational opportunities to improve their chances in the job market.
- Making work pay – new changes have been introduced with the aim of ensuring that where people work they at least receive an income they can live on and that support is available to help enable people to work.

Key policies

- New deal – young and long-term unemployed people are offered the options of taking a job, a voluntary position or entering education or training for six months. They must take one of these options or benefit will be withdrawn.
- National Childcare strategy – a programme to significantly expand childcare spaces in the public, private and voluntary sectors. A key aim makes childcare available for parents wishing to go out to work.
- Creation of 'Jobcentre plus' – the Employment Service and Benefits agency were merged (2001) with the aim of facilitating the process of moving people off benefits and into work, e.g. all new claimants must have an interview to discuss future work opportunities.
- Pension reform – a range of measures to give pensioners a guaranteed minimum income and to reward people saving for retirement.
- Cutting child poverty – the aim is to cut child poverty by 50 per cent by 2010 through improvements in benefits, childcare and work opportunities for parents.

The Conservative legacy and new Labour's vision

The Conservatives substantially reformed the welfare system in the UK during 18 years in government. Their changes were informed by new right and neo-Liberal critiques of state provision of welfare which emphasize the negative economic and social consequences of universal welfare programmes. Welfare expansion was seen as a drain on the productive sectors of the economy, encouraging growth of a 'dependency culture' in which people lived at the expense of others (Murray

1994). Influenced by welfare reform strategies in the USA, the Conservatives cut benefits and put pressure on claimants to take up any job opportunities that came along. Ironically, under the Conservatives unemployment increased dramatically as, subsequently, did state spending on welfare. Always distrusted by the electorate on welfare issues, consecutive Conservative governments baulked at making the wholesale reform of welfare which many of their ideological gurus advocated.

Historically, Labour had been associated strongly with the development of the welfare state and had championed universal benefits (see Chapter 3). However, new Labour's stance has been different. New Labour has also been influenced by ideas from the USA, but has also adopted ideas associated more with welfare reform within other EU countries. Like the Conservatives, new Labour believes that welfare regimes have been associated with economic and social problems. However, for new Labour, welfare need not necessarily be purely a drain, but can be used positively as a support for people in the transition between jobs and to help tackle social problems. Reform of welfare is seen as necessary not just to reduce the economic burden on the state but also to help tackle 'social exclusion', the problem of groups who are effectively excluded from broader society, e.g. the long-term unemployed. There are a number of ideas and polices involved that can be summarized under the headings of work first, making work pay and anti-poverty strategies.

Work first

New Labour has been heavily influenced by the US policy on 'workfare' in which welfare recipients have to work in return for benefits. Under the banner of the communitarian-inspired notion of combining 'rights and responsibilities', new Labour asserted the idea that people could only enjoy rights to benefits if they also exercised responsibility for looking for work and taking opportunities to gain working experience or training. The guiding principle has been the idea of 'work first' – gaining work is seen as the principal way in which people can escape poverty. Hence the welfare system should be reorganized to encourage people to find work, to offer them support in obtaining it and where necessary offer support to allow them to work. Particular energies should be diverted to aiding particular groups such as the young and the long-term unemployed who may have difficulty breaking into the job market. At the heart of this strategy has been the new deal, which targets such groups.

Welfare claimants are offered four options: work experience, voluntary experience, further education or training. The new deal introduces a new *coercive* element to the welfare system as claimants *must* take up one of the options or lose benefits. The aim of the policy is to offer experience to the unemployed and to create an active labour market in which people are not left without work or training for years on end. More generally, benefit rules have been changed to compel groups such as lone mothers to have interviews with welfare officers to explore opportunities for returning to work. These reforms overlap with new right concerns that many welfare claimants must be urged or forced to alter their behaviour to take personal responsibility for their situation. However, the new deal can also be interpreted as a more social democratic measure, the initiative financed by money raised in a one-off windfall tax imposed upon privatized utilities, with the money subsequently being used to finance the creation of new opportunities for disadvantaged groups.

Making work pay

The strategy of encouraging work has also been supported by measures aimed at ensuring that it is worthwhile for people to take job opportunities. One concern was that some jobs were so poorly paid that people may even end up with less money than they would receive from benefits. More generally there was the fear of the 'poverty trap' where people perceived that they would get little relative reward for working. In response, Gordon Brown established the *Working Families' Tax Credit,* a scheme which guarantees low-paid workers with a family a minimum take-home pay through giving tax credits on what they earn. Low group incomes have received further aid with the creation of a national minimum wage, now at £4.70 per hour, as well as the introduction of a new 10p starting rate for tax. However, new Labour has not only attempted to remove the financial disincentives for people to go out to work, it has also sought to help people overcome other obstacles. Through the National Childcare strategy the government has attempted a major expansion of the provision of childcare across the country. The focus has been on generating affordable and accessible childcare places through public, private and voluntary sectors. In this way it is hoped parents will be able to find the childcare that may be needed in order for them to take up employment. Critics such as Levitas (2001) have argued Labour's focus on 'work first' has drawbacks in that it devalues unpaid or caring work, including many of the roles women find themselves in. Others have attacked the policy as too narrow to deal with the problem of low incomes – while redistributive measures have helped low-*paid* workers, unemployment benefits themselves have merely risen with inflation (Glyn and Wood 2001).

Anti-poverty strategies

New Labour's attitude to tackling poverty has been shaped by concepts of 'social exclusion' which have been shaped by ideas of 'stake-holding' as well as by welfare reform strategies in the EU (Annesley 2003). Traditionally many in the Labour party were motivated by the goal of moving towards equality of income and large-scale redistribution from the wealthy to the less well off. In place of these ideas new Labour views the key problem not to be wealth inequality as such but more to do with particular groups being, in effect, excluded from society, whether through poverty, long-term unemployment, poor education or poor housing. The task of government then is to find ways to generate opportunities for people to reconnect to society with programmes such as the new deal outlined above. However, a particular concern of the government has been the question of child poverty, both in terms of the suffering itself as well as the long-term effect it has on children's life chances. New Labour set the ambitious goal to eliminate child poverty completely within 20 years and to cut it by 50 per cent by 2010. A range of steps has been taken including increase in child benefits, and the 'making work pay' and childcare initiatives outlined above are also intended to contribute to this effort. The government has also been concerned with the issue of pensioner poverty and in the first term introduced a new means-tested Minimum Income Guarantee.

Welfare record

By the time of the 1997 election Labour had abandoned any residual commitments to the aim of income or wealth equality. Like the Conservatives new Labour sees welfare 'dependency' as a significant problem and it has significantly extended efforts to get people into employment. Nonetheless the goal of 'equality of opportunity' and 'social inclusion' (including attacks on poverty, particularly child poverty) held a significant place on the agenda. At the time of writing new Labour appeared likely to meet its target of reducing child poverty by a quarter between 1999 and 2004. The Institute of Fiscal Studies calculates that redistributive measures introduced by Gordon Brown played a large part in this reduction. However, inequality in wage levels has continued to rise, albeit more modestly than under most of the Conservative years in office. At present, government policies look likely to do little to aid those workers stranded in low pay service jobs, reinforcing the polarization of wage levels (IPPR, *State of the Nation*, 2004). Thus the main effect has been the amelioration of some of the worst effects of inequality. Little has been done to alter the overall patterns of structured inequality (Chapter 2) which have been such a core feature of British society and politics (Goodman 2001). Change in welfare under Labour has been less radical in reforming benefits that arch neo-Liberals advocate, whilst also falling well short of the large-scale redistribution agenda which many on the left advocate. While new Labour has continued the Conservative trend to shake up the welfare system to discourage 'dependency', it has also reinforced aspects of the postwar welfare settlement by boosting certain universal benefits.

Governing style and leadership

Previous chapters argued that government in Britain has tended to be conducted in a top-down, elitist manner. However, the styles and tactics of different governments have varied widely. This section examines the governing style and leadership approach adopted by the new Labour government.

BOX 5.3: *NEW LABOUR'S GOVERNING STYLE AND LEADERSHIP 1997–2005*

Key elements

Executive leadership:

- *Strengthening of prime ministerial power base* – new resources have been devoted to increasing the power base of the prime minister at Downing Street, including the creation of new directorates and involving the appointment of a range of political advisers, experts and trusted party loyalists to influential positions alongside the prime minister.
- *'Presidential' approach to leading and representing government* – centralization of power around the prime minister around whom the government's image is focused.
- *Marginalization of cabinet* – cabinet is sidelined as a collective decision-making body as most important work done in bilateral or small group meetings.

External relations:

- *Pro EU stance: lobbying for 'deregulated' EU economic policy* – possibly most pro-European government since Heath. Has pushed for economic deregulation, though credibility damaged by close US ties.
- *Reinvigoration of 'special relationship' with USA* – close relationship established with Clinton and maintained with Bush since 2000.
- *Support for Iraq War* – Blair campaigned for international support for war on Iraq, but gave British backing to unilateral US action when UN refused support.

Party management:

- *Centralization of power* – dissent towards the new Labour government from party members has been stifled through '*Partnership in Power*' apparatus.
- *'Tranquillized' internal relations* – internal conflicts and factionalism less than in the past, though party membership dwindles.

Executive leadership

From the outset, Tony Blair has been keen to assert leadership within government and over its policy agenda (Rentoul 2001). Central to this effort has been the development of the offices of 10 Downing Street to facilitate and extend the prime minister's influence over government. More generally, Blair has pursued a 'presidential' style of leadership, making him one of the most dominant prime ministers in recent history.

Broadening the No 10 power base

Under Blair, the resources directly available to the prime minister have been significantly expanded. Key developments include the creation of three new directorates within Downing Street, namely the Policy Directorate; Communications and Strategy Unit; and Political and Government Relations Directorate. Moreover links between the prime minister's office and the cabinet office have been strengthened, increasing the influence of the former. Spending on such offices has increased from £7 million per year under the Conservatives to more than £11 million under new Labour. Allied to this, Blair has brought in an unprecedented number of special advisers to his offices, experts or political associates who work directly on his behalf. Norton (2003: 277) argues that since 1997 a *de facto* prime minister's department has been created. These offices develop policies and express the prime minister's demands to departments, often engaging in bilateral negotiations with ministers. A key innovation has been the key role given to the prime minister's press secretary – previously this role was always occupied by a civil servant. However, Blair brought in his aide Alastair Campbell (later replaced by David Hill) to the role in which he was given a contract as a special adviser, yet with executive authority over civil servants (Rentoul 2001: 393). So concerned was new Labour with representation in the media that it created a new rule in which all statements by senior figures on policy would have to be cleared through the Downing Street press office. However, despite taking these centralizing steps, Blair and his close advisers were frustrated by the limitations to the grip which they could establish on government departments. Relatedly, they were unhappy at the difficulties in implementing change within policy area (Seldon 2004).

'Presidential' style

As outlined below, new Labour built its public image around Blair's leadership, projecting the idea that he would offer single-minded and strong leadership. This took place in a context in which election campaigns had been becoming increasingly personalized, i.e. ever more scrutiny and attention was being focused on the personalities of the party leaders (see Chapter 4). This has led to what some refer to as the 'presidentialization' of British politics in which the parties themselves are of less importance in determining election outcomes than in the past (Foley 1999).

Many attribute Labour's two landslide victories to the character of Blair himself and his ability to inspire trust in his abilities. In power, Blair has made use of the extended resources of 10 Downing Street to exert leadership in government. Heffernan (2003) argues that through combining use of these with his own personal resources (including popularity and political authority) Blair has developed a *predominant* role within government. A crucial feature of Blair government has been the virtual abolition of cabinet as a collective decision-making body. Most key decisions are now made through *bilateral* discussions between individual ministers and the prime minister rather than at full cabinet meetings. This pattern was established from the outset, with no cabinet ministers other than Blair and Brown being involved in the historic decision to give the Bank of England operational independence in 1997. More generally, Blair has sought to stamp his authority over the direction of government policy, even when under criticism from elements of the party or the public. In a speech to the Labour party conference in 2003 he declared: 'I can only go one way, I haven't got a reverse gear.' However, notions of 'presidentialism' in British politics have limitations. Unlike US presidents, the British prime minister still gains authority through the election of a particular party and he is dependent of the support of that parliamentary party to stay in office. Despite Blair further developing 'presidential' characteristics in his role as prime minister, in spring 2004 speculation rose that colleagues might be prepared to mount a challenge to him in view of unpopularity over issues such as Iraq. Thus, despite Blair's unprecedented dominance over his government, he is still ultimately dependent on the consent of his party colleagues to continue.

External Relations

EU

The Conservative government had been wracked for several years by splits over the issue of European integration. While John Major had maintained a cautiously pro-EU line, the party as a whole became increasingly sceptical, particularly of the idea of a single European currency. New Labour was elected on a platform which was much more enthusiastic about the EU in which it pledged to play a leading role. Furthermore it committed itself in principle to joining the European single currency provided that the economic conditions were right and that the public approved entry through referendum. Labour quickly demonstrated more enthusiasm for European integration by signing up to the social chapter, a commitment to basic rights for employees that the previous government had opted out of. However, Labour's main contribution to debates within the EU has been to push for greater economic liberalization and deregulation. Indeed, Britain was an important player in establishing a new agreement which committed the EU to a ten-year economic liberalization programme. New Labour has been critical of other social democratic parties in Europe for maintaining support for employee-employer relations with more emphasis on workers' rights. Indeed, Blair has made alliances with figures from the right such as Berlusconi of Italy and Anzur of Spain to press for less regulation (Clift 2004: 46). Nonetheless, the contrast between Labour's relatively positive stance towards greater EU integration and the Conservatives' sceptical stance (under Hague, Duncan Smith and Howard) has emerged as one of the major fault lines of British politics in the new millennium. Yet at important moments, as under previous governments, Britain's relations with Europe were subject to strain through its ties with the United States.

Special relationship

The 'special relationship' between the USA and the UK had waned slightly in the mid-1990s due to indifferent relations between President

Clinton and John Major. However, relations were reinvigorated after Tony Blair's election, owing much to the good relations that emerged between new Labour and Clinton's new Democrats. Blair called on Clinton as a source of influence over negotiations in the Northern Ireland problem (due to the large number of Irish Americans) and this played a part in the signing of the historic 'Good Friday' agreement. To a large degree this agreement between the divided communities to share power in an elected assembly owed much to the peace process developed under John Major. The relationship was also crucial to provoking the NATO intervention in the Kosovo crisis in 1999, a move which a number of US commentators disapproved of. Relations became strained in private at the point where Blair and Clinton disagreed on the issue of whether to threaten the use of ground troops (Seldon 2004: 397). However, US support for the intervention had been crucial, and Blair's role was pivotal in coordinating the ultimately successful effort to force Serbian troops out of Kosovo. Against some expectations, the 'special relationship' was sustained strongly following the inauguration of a new Republican US president, George W. Bush, in 2001. Following the shocking terrorist attacks on the USA on 11 September 2001, Blair announced that Britain should stand 'shoulder to shoulder' with the USA in their response to these events. Britain offered military support to the US intervention in Afghanistan and the hunt for members of the Al Qaeda terrorist network. Blair further offered support to the US administration as they developed plans for a military invasion of Iraq to depose Saddam Hussein's leadership. Ostensibly the plans were presented as part of the 'war on terror', on the basis that Iraq possessed weapons of mass destruction that it might use to attack the West or to pass to terrorists to do so. The attempts to link the 11 September terrorist attack and Iraq appeared tenuous and the subsequent war in Iraq proved one of the most controversial issues in world politics over recent years.

Support for Iraq War

While the Bush administration was determined to pursue the war option, Britain initially pushed a more cautious stance. Blair urged the USA to establish a new UN resolution on Iraq threatening the regime and giving authorization for war if its conditions were not met (Baker 2002). This strategy had success, yet fell apart when France, Germany and other countries expressed opposition to US plans. Realizing it could not get a resolution passed, the USA decided to press ahead for war unilaterally. Crucially, Blair then decided to back the US stance and pledge British military support. This immediately alienated Britain from key European partner countries who viewed such action as a violation of the authority of the UN. Public opposition against war plans reached a peak when over a million people marched in London to oppose British support for the USA (opinion polls also showed that a majority of the population opposed the war). Opposition was also large within the parliamentary Labour party with 139 Labour MPs supporting an anti-war amendment when the issue went before the House of Commons.

Blair established an important convention by calling a vote on the issue in Parliament (*constitutionally* he could have taken the country to war without doing so). However, he was unmoved by extra-parliamentary opposition, justifying the war on the basis that it was necessary to protect British national interests. One could scarcely find a better example of the deployment of a *conservative notion of responsibility* as inherent within the British political tradition – in this case Britain was taken into a war its population opposed on the basis that political leaders considered it best for the country's interest (see Conclusion). Blair's stance reinforced the 'special relationship' with the USA yet ultimately cost him considerable domestic political capital. The evidence that Iraq was in a position to launch weapons of mass destruction was hotly debated before the war, before crumbling in its aftermath as inspectors found no such weapons.

Party management

As we saw in Chapters 3 and 4, the broader political party membership has tended to have a limited role in influencing the leadership of the party when in government. However, we also observed that wrangles and animosity between party activists and the leadership have plagued the Labour party in office. Such infighting often proved politically damaging, encouraging perceptions of a divided, squabbling party.

In 1997 the party adopted the document '*Partnership in Power*' with the ostensible aim of encouraging membership involvement in policy formation and encouraging consensus between the mass party and the leadership. However, although party members have new opportunities to offer opinions and submit ideas, the process is mediated through party 'gatekeepers' (Shaw 2004: 56), appointed by and accountable to party leaders. These party managers have numerous organizational techniques through which dissenting opinion can be stifled or mollified. For example, suggested amendments to policy documents can be refused on the grounds that they are inconsistent with existing or planned Labour government legislation (ibid.). '*Partnership in Power*' also reduces the time the party conference spends debating policy areas and gives the leadership more opportunities to press its own 'line' to delegates. Ordinary constituency Labour party delegates have fewer opportunities to speak and there is evidence that those favouring the government view are more likely to be called to speak (ibid: 59). On the very rare occasions where the leadership is defeated in a conference debate (e.g. on the issue of the Private Finance Initiative, 2002), the government has quickly made it clear that it will not change its policy. As in the past, Labour leaders justified ignoring the democratic opinion of the *party* on the basis that they believe they are putting the interests of the *country* as a whole first. Furthermore, as is argued in Chapter 7, Labour leaders have also gone to extraordinary lengths to try and impose their preferred party candidates for devolved institutions on to party members. In summation, there has been a 'drift toward a more powerful control apparatus, greater organisational centralisation, more concentrated patterns of authority and tauter discipline' (Shaw 2004: 67). For many new Labour enthusiasts this centralization is no cause for embarrassment, rather it is a necessity for competent government. Apparatchiks such as Gould and Mandelson have argued that it is essential that party leaders have a tight grip on a party in an age in which the media will exploit any sign of dissent or internal division within a party (Gould 1998; Mandelson 2002). As a result of such tight party management new Labour has thus far avoided the types of public splits which damaged it electorally in the past. However, the stifling of dissent may also help explain a declining membership and low levels of activity in the party.

Governing discourse

As was argued in Chapter 4, the role of ideas in British politics is an important and complex one. At one level ideas and ideologies may shape the way politicians see the world and, hence, the views and policies they promote. At another level ideas are used by politicians to gain votes and popularity even if those ideas do not always fully reflect their personal beliefs. Furthermore, ideas exist in competition with the ideas of other political actors, playing an important role in gaining and sustaining political power. In this section we focus on the ideas and imagery new Labour has *projected* to the public in an effort to recruit people to its vision and to sustain public support. As we will see, while some novel ideas and strategies have been pushed there are a number of key themes with a longer pedigree in the discourse of British politics

BOX 5.4: *GOVERNING DISCOURSE 1997–2005*

Key ideas

- *Neo-liberalism* – e.g. perceived implications of 'globalization', limits it places on state power.
- *Communitarianism* – e.g. notion of 'rights and responsibilities', individuals' obligation to broader community.
- *The third way* – bringing together 'social justice and a dynamic economy'.

Gaining support

- *Strategic use of discourse* – language tailored or 'spun' to appeal to particular audiences.
- *Populism* – projection of policy to appeal to perceived worries of electorate, e.g. on asylum and immigration issues.

Projecting leadership

- *'Presidential' presentation of Blair* – Labour's public image centred on Blair and his strength, empathy and 'feel' for public opinion.
- *'Country' before party or popularity* – decisions justified in name of 'national' interest.

Key ideas

New Labour has been thoughtful, in both the ideas it has projected to the public, as well as the means by which it projects them. Two factors help explain this. First, many argued Labour's defeat in previous elections owed much to it losing the 'battle of ideas' with the Conservatives (Hall 1983). The Conservatives, with the help of a sympathetic tabloid media, had managed to paint Labour as potential dangers to British prosperity. Labour has become aware of the need to plan each encounter between the party and the public in order to maximize support and get its message across (Marshment 2002).

A range of ideas have influenced the governing discourse of new Labour. As highlighted above there are contrasting, even contradictory ideas informing Labour's economic and welfare policies. Similar tensions and paradoxes exist in the discourse Labour has used to justify its reform programme. However, as we will see, new Labour has attempted to use such tensions as strength rather than a weakness. The most significant influences come from ideas associated with neo-liberalism, communitarianism and the third way:

- New Labour draws directly from *neo-Liberal* discourses in much of its analysis of changes in the global economy. Indeed, the concept of globalization has become an important element of new Labour's self-justification. Blair describes globalization as the 'driving force' behind its ideas 'because nobody is immune from the massive change globalization brings' (1999). New Labour appears to adhere to the idea that globalization is an unstoppable force, forcing countries to adopt a deregulated economic approach which makes itself as attractive to market investors as possible (Hay 1999). Thus, traditionally Keynesian and interventionist strategies are viewed as undesirable and unworkable in the context of a globalizing economy.
- *Communitarianism* (Etzioni 1995) has been a significant influence on new Labour, most obvious initially in the new Clause 4 of the Labour party constitution which argues 'the rights we enjoy reflect the duties we owe'. Its most obvious impacts on the governing discourse of new Labour are perhaps in the areas of social policy and law and order. In both of these areas Labour has been keen to promote a renewed sense of *individual* responsibility for both finding work and avoiding criminality. For example, in welfare policy Blair has stressed the need for a 'something for something' approach – benefits and entitlements should only be received in return for individuals taking responsibility to look for work. Fairclough finds that when Blair uses the term 'rights' it is almost always matched by use of the term 'duties' or 'responsibilities'. Work is stressed as fundamental to the moral character of individuals and a decent society. For example, Harman argues work 'brings independence, self-respect ... a sense of order', Blair states starkly, 'if you can work, you should work' (Fairclough 1999: 47, 52). The communitarian themes deployed by new Labour have often had a strongly authoritarian streak stressing the need to be 'tough' on welfare reform and law and order. Famously, Blair

deployed the phrase 'tough on crime, tough on the causes of crime' and has stressed 'zero tolerance' of juvenile delinquency.

- If there is unifying theme to new Labour's ideas it is undoubtedly the notion of the *third way* (see account of third-way perspective in Chapter 3). The concept of the third way incorporates ideas from neo-liberalism, communitarianism and social democracy. It is initially defined in terms of what it is not, i.e. neither old-style state intervention of the left nor the laissez faire of the new right' (Bastow and Martin 2003: 48). Thus it dissociates itself from the ideas of both 'old' Labour and 'Thatcherism'. Perhaps the most outstanding feature of the third way is the manner in which it takes ideas long considered to be opposites or contradictions and attempts to combine them into a relatively coherent discourse. At the core of this is the aim of combining 'a dynamic economy with social justice'. Thus Labour advocates both a globalized deregulated economy and state action to ensure opportunities for people. Similar traditional right-left ideas are combined thus: 'ambition *and* compassion', 'enterprise *and* fairness' (Blair 1999). The aim has been to create an inclusive 'one nation' discourse that people from different backgrounds and occupations can identify with. Jessop (2003: 23) argues that this discourse contrasts markedly with the approach of the Conservatives under Thatcher who promoted a divisive 'two nations' discourse which sought to polarize people.

Gaining support

However, it is not only through promoting inclusive third-way ideas that new Labour has sought to appeal to win the 'battle of ideas' and appeal to the electorate. It has also sought to target and adjust its messages in order to appeal to the pre-existing values and prejudices of groups of voters. There are two main ways it has attempted to do this:

- *The strategic use of discourse* – commentators have pointed to the way in which new Labour tailors its message to appeal to the audience it is addressing. For example, Fairclough (1999) notes the way policies and ideas are summarized and 'spun' to right-wing-leaning papers such as the *Daily Mail*. New Labour stresses the 'toughness' of its welfare-to-work policies which are then presented by editors under headlines such as 'Welfare – the Crackdown' which are designed to appeal to those who believe many welfare claimants are an undeserving drain on taxpayers. Thus new Labour's message is constructed in a way to appeal to a group of people who might not traditionally sympathize with Labour. However, on other occasions (e.g. when addressing the Trades Union Congress conference) similar policies may be promoted in terms of 'tackling social exclusion' or promoting 'equality of opportunity'. In this case the aim is to appeal to the more left-leaning sentiments of a particular audience.
- *Populist appeals* – for many on the left of British politics one of the most regrettable aspects of new Labour's approach has been its

willingness to pander to popular concern over issues such as crime, asylum-seekers and illegal immigrants. Randall (2004: 184) argues that a feature of new Labour's law and order approach has been the pursuit of 'a host of headline grabbing initiatives embodying a populist zeal for punishment'. For example, a new 'three strikes and you're out' rhetoric has been used to support mandatory jail sentences for certain offences. Furthermore, under pressure from Conservative and tabloid concerns about asylum seekers 'swamping' Britain, new Labour has responded with populist initiatives to 'fast-track' and reduce the number of applications for asylum.

Whereas new Labour has sought to shore up key support through populism, there are other parts of its agenda that remain relatively unsung by the party's media managers. Indeed, many of the more progressive measures enacted by new Labour (see section on 'welfare', above) have received very few headlines, perhaps reflecting a fear that they will play badly with 'middle England' voters. As argued above, the redistributive aspects of new Labour's programme have been conducted by 'stealth' rather than as a proudly proclaimed aim (e.g. minimum wage, working families' tax credit, child poverty programme). The former foreign secretary, the late Robin Cook (2003: 344), complained that new Labour 'keep such progressive policies under the counter in a backroom where members who know where to find them can slip in and find them while the spin doctors are not looking'. Consequently, it may be that new Labour is overlooking an opportunity to appeal to its core vote and, more generally, may be passing up the chance to win people over to the virtues of redistribution.

'Presidential' presentation of Blair

There is little doubt that much of new Labour's strategy has revolved around using Tony Blair to personify the new Labour project. General election campaigns have increasingly centred on the issue of which of the main party leaders people believe would make the best prime minister. Foley (2002: 5) argues that in such circumstances political leaders have become 'public commodities that are continually probed, tested and evaluated'. New Labour tailored its pursuit of power with this assumption in mind, placing the cultivation and promotion of Blair himself at the centre of its electoral strategy.

Much of the effort has been focused on presenting Blair as a strong leader yet simultaneously 'one of us'. For example, following the death of Princess Diana, Blair was seen to reflect/shape public reaction with a statement in which he dubbed her the 'People's Princess'. Rawnsley suggests that this phrase:

> is the outstanding example of Blair's ability to entwine emotional vernacular ('utterly devastated', 'our hearts go out to them') with formal ceremonial expressions of regret (we are today a nation in mourning). He imported his reaction like a normal person – 'like everybody else' as he put it – into his role as Prime Minister. (...) The moment confirmed

> Tony Blair as the consummate political actor of his age . . . (he) instantly and accurately divined . . . what a large proportion of the country needed to hear' (Rawnsley 2001: 61, 62)

Finlayson (2002: 593) argues that 'through such linguistic devices Blair simultaneously exudes formal authority and the ordinary "blokeishness" that is so central to his style.' Similarly, Labour party broadcasts have sometimes focused solely on Blair in informal contexts chatting in kitchens or drinking coffee discussing general political themes in relaxed 'common sense' mode (ibid: 595). In this way many of the traditional ways of appealing to voters such as through appealing to ideological stances or party identification are bypassed. Aside from communicating Labour's message this strategy aims at generating a 'presidential' conception of Blair as someone who is in a sense 'above' the more general political affray, yet in touch with people on the ground. Through creating a 'presidential' aura the aim has been to enhance the public legitimacy and hence leadership autonomy of Blair as the custodian of public trust. It was this quality of public trust which was hotly debated during the 2005 general election campaign.

'Country' before party

Relatedly, it has often worked to Blair's advantage to appear distant from his party on issues. Opinion polls (until recently) showed Blair as more popular than his party, and voting studies suggested he was able to attract the support of instinctively Tory voters. Indeed, it can be viewed as part of a conscious strategy to sustain electoral appeal and to bolster his authority. Like previous prime ministers and chancellors (including Labour prime ministers) Blair and Brown have used the idea of the 'national' interest to justify policies and to dismiss critics in the party. In 2000 and 2002 Labour leaders suffered (rare) defeats at the party conference over the issues of pensions and their support for the Private Finance Initiative. In both cases they announced that there would be no change of the policy, reminding critics that they had been democratically elected to take decisions for the whole community rather than the wishes of the conference. Like previous Labour prime ministers such as Callaghan and Wilson, Blair has ignored the conference where it has threatened his policies, invoking the trump card of putting 'country' before party. However, it is not just party opinion which Blair has been willing to defy. On a range of key issues, most notably Iraq as discussed above, Blair has faced down huge public opposition and unfavourable opinion polls. Again though, he appeals to the idea of the 'national' interest, even where current polls suggest the nation's views are different.

CONCLUSION

Across significant areas of ideology, welfare policy and, particularly, economic policy there are strong areas of continuity between new Labour and the approach of its Conservative predecessors. New Labour leaders have been convinced of the need to establish close relations with business in the context of 'globalization' in which the financial markets wield massive power. Consequently, the Blair government has retained neo-Liberal commitments to low inflation and a dynamic market economy. Furthermore, it has further developed and embedded a 'rules-based' system of economic management which aims to 'de-politicize' key economic decisions. However, a number of different sets of ideas, notably those of the 'third way', have been influential on new Labour, inspiring parts of its agenda to break from strict neo-liberalism and contain identifiably social democratic elements. Strategies of economic and welfare reform have bolstered the Treasury's traditionally dominant position in determining economic policy.

Despite espousing a 'third-way' discourse with dimensions emphasizing 'democratic renewal' and 'inclusion' and 'partnership', it may be argued that new Labour has developed a strongly elitist form of government that adheres to many of the key features of the British political tradition. However it has *reconstructed* an elite-centred approach to government by responding to changing economic circumstances and a '24-hour' media. Economic reforms have been concerned with insulating government from direct criticism over unpopular changes, while retaining control over the process by careful prescription of rules. Labour leaders have brought in large teams of their own special advisers to the heart of government while cabinet has effectively been downgraded as a collective decision-making body. An iron grip has been maintained over the Labour party itself, where mechanisms for stifling dissent have been enhanced and used to considerable effect. Meantime, careful attention has been devoted to 'spinning' government actions to the public, including presenting Blair in 'presidential' terms as a strong leader willing to ignore his party and promote the perceived 'national interest'. However, Blair has also been willing to ignore broader public opinion and face down popular revolts over controversial issues. While residual attempts to compromise with public and/or party opinion over key decisions were still discernible in the first term (e.g. over fuel protests or increased state pensions) these were largely abandoned in the second term. Talk of 'partnership in power' has receded as Blair falls back more and more on the British political tradition's government 'knows best' ethos. On both tuition fees for students and foundation hospitals the new Labour leadership pursued policies which for many in the party (and broader public) represented a breach of core Labour values issues about which they care most. However, the elitist character of the Blair leadership was most clearly evident over Iraq in which Blair ignored the views of the public even after the largest ever political demonstration in Britain against the war. Despite taking a more positive attitude to the EU than the Conservatives, on the 'crunch' issue of Iraq the British government once again sided with the USA, seeking to uphold the 'special relationship' and the supposed importance this confers on Britain as a significant player in world politics. However, to evaluate more fully the impact of new Labour it is necessary to consider two of the most significant parts of its agenda, namely the 'modernization' of public services and the constitutional reform agenda.

CHAPTER 6

Modernizing Government

'Modernizing public services is crucial to everything the government wants to achieve for the country.'

Tony Blair (1999)

INTRODUCTION

Having considered a number of crucial aspects of new Labour's strategy over the last six years, it is necessary to look closely at how it has attempted to change the very *process* of British government itself. As highlighted in the last chapter, the concept of 'modernization' has been important within new Labour's governing discourse. In this chapter we review and evaluate what has become loosely known as the 'modernizing government' agenda, initiated by new Labour, but involving a range of groups and actors both within and beyond the public sector. In so doing, we are concerned to examine just how far the reforms associated with this agenda mark a break with the dominant ideas and practices of government in Britain that existed in both the postwar and Thatcher-Major periods. We address the following questions:

- What are the main features of the modernizing government agenda?
- What ideas underpin these reforms?
- How successful have reforms been in achieving their stated goals?
- How far do the changes break with the practices of earlier governments?

THE CONSERVATIVE LEGACY

Before examining these issues it is necessary to put recent change in context. Previous chapters emphasized the importance of the British political tradition and how particular ideas and practices have been maintained within British government over many decades. However, as we also argued, it would be misleading to believe that there have not also been important changes in the processes of government; indeed the state itself is constantly evolving in response to internal and external pressures. Prior to new Labour's election, the British state was subject to very significant changes introduced by Conservative governments over an 18-year period. As was discussed in Chapter 2, the Conservatives were heavily influenced by a new right critique of the practices of British politics. To recap, key elements of this critique included:

- A belief that government should not intervene in the economy. In Britain, the state was too embroiled in economic affairs, leading to poor economic performance.
- The key to economic success is to encourage private enterprise and competition.
- The public sector is likely to be self-interested and will tend look after its own interests above providing quality services to the public.

These beliefs had an important role in shaping the various ways in which the Conservatives reformed the practices of government over four terms in power. Key features of change included (see Box 6:1) the privatization of key public services; the restructuring of the civil service; introduction of 'quasi-market' mechanisms into the public sector; reduction of the powers of local government; and the creation of numerous new regulatory bodies to monitor service provision. For Rhodes (1997), the state had thus been 'hollowed out' (see Chapter 2) with powers being transferred upwards to bodies such as the EU, sideways to the private and voluntary sectors and downwards to special bodies and agencies.

BOX 6.1: *KEY CONSERVATIVE REFORMS OF BRITISH GOVERNMENT*

- **Privatization**

A defining feature of Thatcherism was the privatization agenda in which public assets were sold to the private sector. Key public services such as Gas, Water, Electricity, British Telecom and the Railways were sold through shares issues. Overall, between 1979 and 1997, the state-owned sector of industry was reduced in size by over two-thirds. In addition, the Conservatives 'contracted out' provision of certain public services to the private sector.

- **Reform of the civil service**

Believing that civil servants spent too much time in policy-making to the detriment of efficient management, the Conservatives introduced some radical changes to the structure of Whitehall. The most significant change under the Thatcher governments was the introduction of the 'next steps' agenda. Semi-autonomous agencies were 'hived-off' from the Whitehall centre to undertake executive functions of government. By 1997 around two-thirds of the civil service were agencies.

- **Introduction of 'quasi-market' mechanisms in public sector**

The Conservatives sought to emulate what they considered the efficiency and innovation of free markets within the public sector. To do so, they introduced 'quasi-markets' in areas including education and health. For example, in education schools were made to 'compete' for school pupils, with the incentive of gaining more funding from government for more pupils enrolled. In health a 'purchaser-provider' split was introduced to create a quasi-market in health provision.

- **Reform of local government**

The Conservatives mistrusted local government and in a quite ad hoc manner reduced its powers over a number of years. Caps were placed on the amount of money councils could raise from their local communities and funding from central government was squeezed. Under the Compulsory Competitive Tendering scheme (CCT) local authorities were forced to contract out provision of local services to the private sector if they could provide them more cheaply than the council itself. A range of powers held by local authorities was transferred to unelected special bodies of various sorts. The Conservatives also fostered a bigger role for voluntary (i.e. non-governmental) groups to provide local services.

- **Rise of the 'regulatory state'**

The Conservatives set up a range of bodies to regulate newly privatized industries (e.g. Oftel and Ofgas). They also set up numerous new audit and inspection bodies responsible for reviewing public service provision and empowered to impose changes where they considered these to be failing. One notable example was the creation of OFSTED in education which, among other powers, was given the authority to close schools they considered to be failing.

New Labour's dilemmas

Consequently, the state which Labour inherited in 1997 differed in many important ways from that which it had last worked with in the late 1970s. New Labour faced having to confront a range of issues which emerged from the Conservative reforms of government.These changes can be understood as the development of what many call a long-term shift from a system of government to one of *governance* (see Chapter 2). Over the last three decades many more groups and organizations have become involved in the construction and implementation of public policy. Reforms in the 1980s and 1990s have made the boundaries between the public and private sectors less clear and management of government has become increasingly decentralized and multi-layered. The term governance 'captures a system in which any permutation of government and the private and voluntary sectors provides services' (Rhodes and Bevir 2003: 52). Within this system all organizations exchange resources, and they must develop inter-organizational links in order to achieve their goals. The resultant 'networks' are now seen as the dominant means of coordinating the delivery of public services.

Authors such as Richards and Smith (2002) and Marsh *et al* (2003) caution against overstating the changes associated with 'Thatcherism' and the emergence of 'governance'. For them the state was not so much 'hollowed out' as reconstituted. Despite privatization policies, government actually *increased* state intervention in many areas such as defence and education policy (see also next chapter under 'civil liberties'). Campbell and Wilson (1995) argue more powers were acquired by ministers after 1979 than at any other time in the modern period. While the Conservatives imposed managerial change on the public sector this was imposed on existing structures of welfare provision (Richards and Smith 2002: 234). Furthermore, despite the anti-welfare stance of the new right, the Conservatives were unable to break the welfare state which remained electorally popular and in many ways institutionally robust. Richards and Smith argue that while there has indeed been a shift towards governance, it remains the case that the majority of *key decisions* are made within the core executive which 'possesses greater resources than most other actors in the policy process to protect its status and power' (Richards and Smith 2002: 272).

Nonetheless, there is widespread agreement that on entering office new Labour faced challenges resulting from the institutional fragmentation which undoubtedly occurred under the Conservatives. Rhodes and Bevir (2003) argue that there were four dilemmas thrown up for new Labour by changes under the Conservatives:

Fragmentation

Services were now delivered by a combination of central government, local government, special purpose bodies, the voluntary and the private sector. Public services delivery was more fragmented than ever before.

Steering

One consequence of such fragmentation was a reduced ability for central government to 'steer' public services. Departments and agencies became increasingly disconnected from one another. Arguably, the Conservatives failed to take the steps necessary to strengthen the core executive's ability to lead government.

Accountability

Many feared such fragmentation eroded accountability. Sheer institutional complexity obscures who is accountable to whom for what.

Management change

Reforms of the civil service, particularly the trend to *corporate management*, generated fears that the traditional public sector ethos – including the values of public duty, integrity, impartiality and loyalty – was being eroded. Efficient management was too often taking priority over a sense of duty to the general public.

(Adapted from Rhodes and Bevir 2003: 131–5)

As covered in Chapters 2 and 5, new Labour has been variously influenced by neo-Liberal and third way thinking (including communitarian concepts). Indeed, Labour's response to the above dilemmas has been informed by such ideas. The modernizing government agenda which emerged under new Labour may be regarded as an attempt to build upon, rather than overturn, changes introduced by the Conservatives, yet simultaneously constitutes an effort to restructure the British state in a range of important ways.

A couple of cautionary points must be made here. The modernizing government agenda is not set in stone – it is a constantly evolving programme of change within which there have been numerous twists and turns over the last six years. Nor should it be considered a thoroughly coherent or internally consistent agenda. A vast number of different types of initiative have been brought under the umbrella of 'modernization' and many of these stand in tension with one another. As we will see, the government has had difficulty in managing a series of such complex and often disparate reforms.

MODERNIZING GOVERNMENT AGENDA

The modernizing government agenda was outlined in the white papers *Modernising Government* (1999), *Modern Local Government* (1998), *Strong Local Leadership: Quality Public Services* (2001), *Reforming Our Public Services: Principles into Practice* (2002) and others. These papers variously stress the themes of 'joined-up' government, partnership, performance improvement and innovation, citizen-centred services and local democratic renewal (see Box 6:2).

BOX 6.2: *VISION OF MODERNIZED GOVERNMENT*

Key features

- *Joined-up government*

Different branches of government must work together more closely to deliver public services more effectively. Many policy problems, e.g. poverty can only be addressed by an approach which coordinates activity rather than simply leaving particular departments with responsibility for dealing with aspects of problems. Rather, services must be 'joined-up' and strategic in order to 'cut across organisational boundaries to get to the root of a problem' (*Modernising Government*, 1999, Ch 2, p2).

- *Partnership*

Not only must the different branches of government work together, there should be collaboration and partnership between all groups involved in delivering public services, including the public, private, voluntary and community sectors. In this way 'holistic' solutions to problems can be generated through pooling of ideas, resources and strategies.

- *Performance improvement and effective 'delivery'*

Performance at all levels of government must be assessed in order to drive improvement in service delivery. Though establishing new targets, performance measures and conducting audits and inspections, the work of government can be continually reviewed. The overall aim is to ensure high-quality services are delivered to the public.

- *Performance innovation*

Improvements should be driven in significant part by innovation in policy design and implementation. A modernized public service will, where appropriate, experiment and even take risks to achieve optimal outcomes (*Modernising Government*, 1999, Ch 1, p4). Branches of government will be encouraged to adopt 'best practice', i.e. poor or average performing public services will be encouraged to copy the working practices of the best.

- *'Choice' and high-quality, 'citizen-centred' public services*

The needs of the service user will be given priority over the interests of the service provider. In areas such as education and health consumers should have the kind of choice of service provider they would expect in other areas of life (*Reforming Our Public Services*, 2002: 23). The views of citizens should inform public policy and services should be available to individuals in as integrated and convenient a way as possible.

- *Democratic renewal*

Relatedly, local people should have 'a better say and a better deal' from local councils. Often 'inefficient and opaque' decision-making will be tackled by measures to renew local democracy, including more elections and more dialogue between councillors and local people *(Modern Local Government*, 1998, p36).

We will now examine each of these themes and in each case consider:

- The rationale behind each of the themes.
- Key practical initiatives and reforms undertaken.
- Problems and dilemmas faced in pursuing themes.
- How far changes break with the ideas and practices of pre-1997 period.

Joined-up government

With the publication of the modernizing government white paper in 1999, 'joined-up' government became a prominent goal for Labour and it has remained an important concept since. As Ling (2002: 615) argues, joined-up government is best viewed as a response to the perception that services had become fragmented, and this problem was hindering achievement of policy goals. Consequently, new Labour set out the aim of coordinating activities *across* organizational boundaries such as between central government departments and between branches of central and local government. According to Pollitt, new Labour hopes to gain four benefits from 'joined-up' government:

- *Eliminating situations where policies undermine each other* – for example, policies to improve discipline in schools pursued by local education authorities may conflict with policies to combat youth crime pursued by the local police. Greater discipline in schools may result in more exclusion of disruptive pupils, leading to more young people on the streets who may commit crime. If local service providers collaborate more they may be able to avoid implementing policies which produce this kind of clash.
- *Make better use of scarce resources* – for example, school buildings are often left unused for long periods. Collaboration between different groups could result in other community groups making use of facilities at times when school pupils are not present.
- *Gain synergies through bringing different stakeholders together* – for example, joint working. An 'problem-estates' collaboration between

police, housing departments, schools and residents' associations may generate more effective ways of tackling problems.
- *Offer seamless, rather than fragmented access to services* – for example, well-designed government websites will allow individuals easy link access to the websites of particular service providers.

(Adapted from Pollitt 2003:35)

Measures taken, aimed at fostering coordination, 'joined-up' government and partnership since 1997 include changes in the prime minister's office, the creation of government task forces and units, area-based initiatives and the reform of local government (see Box 6:3).

BOX 6.3: *JOINED-UP GOVERNMENT AND PARTNERSHIP*

- *Changes in the prime minister's office and cabinet office*

Changes to the prime minister's office and the cabinet office have led to their effective fusion (Hennessy 2000). In recent years a range of new units have been established in the cabinet office with the aim of coordinating government policy and ensuring performance improvement (see below).

- *Creation of task forces*

Somewhere in the region of 300 task-forces (Rhodes and Bevir 2003: 92) have been established to facilitate coordination: between central government departments, between departments and the private sector, and between central and local government. These include entities such as the Competitiveness in Europe Task Force, and the New Deal Task Force advisory group (see Platt 1998).

- *Creation of cross-cutting 'units'*

Similarly a range of units have been established with the aim of achieving joined-up working. Most prominent among these is the Social Exclusion Unit (SEU) which was established by Tony Blair with the aim of promoting 'social inclusion'. It was tasked with overseeing work on cross-cutting issues including truancy and school exclusion, street-living and deprived estates. The government also established a Women's Unit to coordinate work on gender issues, and also the Performance Innovation Unit (later renamed the Strategy Unit) responsible for disseminating research findings, particularly information about 'best practice' throughout central and local government.

- *Establishment of area-based initiatives*

The government has taken a vast range of initiatives which seek to establish partnership between relevant local groups, in particular areas concerning particular issues. Prominent among these have been the 'Action Zones' which have been set up to combat problems which may be affecting a particular area in an acute way. For example, health action zones bring together local health and social services as well as a range of other local groups from the voluntary or community sectors. The aim is to provide more seamless health provision for local people through interdependent working relations between local service providers. Action zones have also been established in some areas on the issues of education or employment in which relevant local public, private and voluntary groups collaborate to coordinate strategies.

- *Legislation for 'duty of partnerships'*

The Crime and Disorder Act (1998) introduced a statutory requirement for local authorities and police authorities to establish strategic partnerships to reduce crime and the public's fear of crime (Newman 2001: 110) The Health Act (1999) made forms of partnership between health and social services obligatory.

- *Local government reform*

The government stipulated a new requirement for local authorities to consult with all relevant local groups concerning decisions they make. Legislation also empowered local authorities to engage in partnership agreements with other local groups such as private or voluntary sector service providers, allowing them to pool budgets and resources *(Modern Local Government*, 1998, Ch 8, p4). Furthermore the government gave local authorities a new corporate responsibility for ensuring the 'economic, social and environmental well-being of the whole community' (ibid: p3).

How innovative is the joined-up government agenda?

There is no doubt that new Labour has placed heavy stress on the themes of joined-up government and partnership. Government papers, speeches and policy guidelines have certainly been permeated by a 'collaborationist discourse' (Clarence and Painter 1998) stressing the themes of cross-organizational working and partnership. Jupp (2000) finds that the word partnership was used 6,197 times in Parliament during 1999 compared to just 38 ten years earlier. In this way, the rhetoric of joined-up government fits with new Labour's broader discourses of inclusiveness and stake-holding.

However, it is important to consider just how innovative the joined-up government agenda is in practical terms. Historically, the idea is not as new as it first seems – previous governments had made attempts to deal with cross-cutting issues, notably with the 'overlords' experimented by the Churchill government and in the *Re-organisation of Central Government* white paper, which sought greater inter-governmental coordination, under the Heath government. According to Rhodes the coordination of public services has long been a 'holy grail' for government, always just out of reach. Nevertheless, at the very least the joined-up government agenda does mark a re-invigorated attempt to provide such coordination in the context of increasing institutional fragmentation.

The scale of the challenge of 'joining-up' became quickly apparent. In early 2000 the Performance Innovation Unit published two reports which highlighted difficulties of achieving joined-up government citing:

- The continued dominance of departmental agendas in the policy decisions.
- A lack of skills necessary for 'joined-up' working in departments and lack of capacity for cross-cutting initiatives (*Wiring it Up* 2000: 14).
- Lack of clear lines of accountability and responsibility within cross-cutting initiatives (*Wiring it Up* 2000: 17).
- Too *many* government initiatives, causing confusion, not cooperation (*Reaching Out* 2000).

Nonetheless, the government has persisted with the joined-up government agenda. In order to facilitate joined-up working it sought to increase leadership skills in the public sector and to provide financial and resource incentives for collaborative working. The outstanding problem for the government is likely to be the continued prevalence of 'departmentalism'. For example, Richards and Smith (2002) point to the failure of government to act in a coordinated manner during the foot-and-mouth crisis during 2001. The Ministry of Agriculture, Fisheries and Food (MAFF) and the Department for Environment, Trade and the Regions (DETR) battled over government policy. The former defended the conflicting interests of the agricultural industry (which opposed a cull of animals to beat the disease), the latter defended the interests of the tourist industry (who supported a cull) (Richards and Smith 2002: 9). Consequently, the government's handling of the issue was confused and arguably contributed to the scale of the crisis. Richards and Smith (2002: 8) question whether joined-up government is possible in the context of the existing parliamentary system. Certainly, as long as government remains primarily structured around different departments, with ministers primarily responsible for looking after 'their patch', then moves to encourage 'joined-up' working face an uphill struggle.

Performance improvement and effective 'delivery'

New Labour's pledge to improve public services was a key factor behind its election wins in 1997 and 2001. Providing high-quality public services has long been a goal of the Labour party, one which remained intact despite the transition to 'new Labour'. The government has been acutely aware that it is likely to be judged on how well it is perceived to have delivered improved public services.

Consequently, at the heart of the modernizing government agenda is the desire of government to improve public services and deliver on its key goals for reform. One of the main ways government believes this can be achieved is by creating a culture in which public bodies are continually reflecting on the services they provide and how they may be improved. To foster such reflection it is believed public bodies must be accountable for the decisions they make and must generate, or be given, targets against which their performance can be measured. A range of reforms since 1997 have focused on driving up performance (see Boxes 6:4 and 6:5).

BOX 6.4: *PERFORMANCE: CENTRAL GOVERNMENT*

- *Introduction of the Comprehensive Spending Review (CSR)*

Every three years a review is carried out of all spending across all government departments. Departments are required to carry out comprehensive spending reviews of everything they do. The Treasury then lays out a detailed plan of how much spending each department will have over the subsequent three years. One aim is to encourage departments to think about how most wisely to spend their budgets in the longer term rather than on a year-to-year basis.

The CSR also results in *Public Sector Agreements*, which are reached between the Treasury and departments about performance targets. The targets are very detailed and if not met the Treasury will 'claw back' funds they would otherwise release to departments. Through Public Sector Agreements the Treasury now has unprecedented powers of scrutiny and influence over individual departments.

- *Creation of prime minister's 'delivery unit'*

In June 2001 the prime minister announced the creation of a new 'delivery unit' which would operate within the cabinet office. The task of the unit is to ensure that the government achieves its priority goals in reforming the public sector across all key areas including health, asylum, education and crime. It works with departments in an attempt to make sure service delivery plans are in place and to strengthen departments' capacity to meet aims. Furthermore, it monitors progress against the targets laid out in Public Sector Agreements and keeps the prime minister informed of progress. Approximately every two months a 'stock-taking' exercise is held between officials of a given department and either the head of the delivery unit, Michael Barber, or the prime minister himself. Where targets are not being met agreement is reached about appropriate action.

- *Creation of new audit and inspection bodies*

The Conservative governments greatly increased the number of bodies devoted to externally reviewing the performance of key public services. Labour continued with this trend and has created a massive range of new audit and inspection bodies. For example, in health it has established the *National Institute of Clinical Excellence* (NICE) and the *Commission for Health Improvement* (CHI), in higher education it has created the *Quality Assurance Agency* (QAA) and the *General Teaching Councils* (GTCs).

BOX 6.5: *PERFORMANCE: LOCAL GOVERNMENT*

- ***Best value***

Much reform of local government over the past six years has been based around the promotion of 'Best Value', a scheme introduced to replace Compulsory Competitive tendering enacted by the Conservatives. The scheme seeks to ensure that local services are both high-quality and cost-effective, providing 'best value' for local people. Over a five-year period local councils are required to review how they provide each of their individual services to set targets for improvement by promotion of the 'four Cs' – challenge, comparison, consultation and competition *(Modern Local Government*, 1998 Ch, 7, p6). Reviews involve considering how and why services are being provided, analysing how they compare with the performance of others, consulting with service users, opening service provision for competition between suppliers and collaborating with the private and voluntary sectors. Each of the reviews is subject to inspection by central government inspectors who are empowered to impose changes if dissatisfied with the review. More generally, councils must publish an annual performance plan setting targets for performance. These are also subject to external audit inspection. Where inspectors deem local councils to be 'failing' they have the power to take responsibility for providing particular services away from the council. They may, for example, hand control of local services over to the private sector.

- *Comprehensive performance assessments*

In 2002 a new scheme to assess the *overall* performance of councils was introduced. Through the comprehensive performance assessment councils are designated in one of the following categories: 'high performers', 'strivers', 'coasters' or 'low performers'. The assessment involves an inspectorate drawing together the different inspection and audits carried out regarding a council's services and coming to a judgement about how they are performing overall. Those councils deemed to be performing well are subsequently subject to less regulation and inspection by central government. Councils deemed to be performing poorly are subject to tougher scrutiny and may even have responsibility for running certain services removed from them. The scheme is supposed to ensure 'continuous improvement' in local services, freeing the best-performing councils to innovate, while focusing attention on poorly performing authorities to drive standards up. Local authorities are also allowed, indeed encouraged, to establish Public Sector Agreements with central government regarding particular parts of service provision.

Performance targets: innovation or obsession?

Overall, the government's stress on competition, target-setting and inspection marks continuity with trends pursued by previous Conservative administrations. In many ways the changes accelerate that trend. Indeed, critics argue that new Labour has become target obsessed. The government has been criticized for failing to meet its own targets in certain areas and also for quietly scrapping certain targets when it appeared unlikely that they would be met. Nonetheless, the government can claim success in meeting a range of targets in key areas such as education, health and crime as well as in making very substantial progress toward them in others (see Toynbee and Walter 2005 for review). However, the 'target-culture' that has been created has been criticized on a number of grounds:

- Too much focus on achieving targets as opposed to assessing whether services really are improving for users. Some have associated new Labour's focus on targets with the culture of 'spin' in which an exaggerated impression of improvement is created. It is argued that 'targets' do not always reflect real improvement in services provided. This view is backed up by opinion poll surveys indicating many people perceive there to be no clear improvement in areas such as health and education, despite the impressive figures presented by government.
- Setting tough targets can be counter-productive. If energies are focused heavily on achieving one target, other parts of service provision may be neglected.
- National targets for performance improvement may clash with targets set by local authorities.
- Powerful inspection bodies can lead to perverse outcomes. For example, local authorities may start behaving in ways they believe will

satisfy external inspectors, rather than what they believe is best for the local people in an area.
- Public sector workers are spending too much time form-filling and satisfying the bureaucratic demands of inspectors. This increases stress levels and detracts from the core aim of providing quality services to the public.

Despite giving some acknowledgement to such criticisms (e.g. introduction to *Strong Local Leadership: Quality Public Services*), the government is determined to press ahead with its agenda to improve public sector performance. 'Delivery' was very much the key theme of Labour's second term. The main concern critics have is that such reforms are too driven by *central* government and consequently public sector employees do not have enough opportunity to improve services through their own initiatives.

Performance innovation

Achieving the goal of improved public service delivery is to be accomplished in substantial part by innovations in performance practices and service quality. Part of the government's vision of 'modernizing' public services is that where appropriate public services will experiment and even take risks to achieve greater efficiency *(Modernising Government*, 1999 Ch 4, p4). Additionally, public services must learn lessons from successes elsewhere. The drive for innovation has a number of interlinking elements (see Box 6.6).

BOX 6.6: *INNOVATION*

- *Strengthening leadership powers, incentives and skills*

Another cabinet office unit, the Office of Public Service Reform, was established in 2001 and given a key task of enhancing the capacity and skills of civil servants and others to provide innovative leadership. It was also tasked with reducing bureaucratic rules where they may be stifling innovation. More generally, reforms have created more scope for leaders to receive financial rewards where they have had successful results.

- *Promoting 'earned autonomy'*

Measures such as Comprehensive Performance Assessments and other reforms work with a principle of 'earned autonomy'. Where public services are considered by central government to be performing well they 'earn' the right to have less regulation and interference from the centre. Consequently they will have more power to pursue innovative ideas.

- *Promoting 'evidence-based' policy*

One of new Labour's favourite slogans has been 'what counts is what works'. This means that changes in policy ought to be driven not by abstract theory, or political ideology, but by evidence of what actually works in practice. To this end, the government has increased sponsorship of academic research into policy change and has appointed many academics and policy experts on to policy commissions, task forces and working teams. The idea is to draw upon available individual expertise and research evidence when forming policy.

- *Dissemination of 'best practice'*

Where evidence of successful policy practice comes to light, the government has been keen to disseminate such information to relevant groups via bodies such as the Strategy Unit.

The 'best practice' philosophy: new, old or smokescreen?

Though new Labour's rhetoric around promoting innovation may be new, the drive for increased efficiency is clearly not. Successive governments have been driven by different 'fashions' as to how this may be achieved. New Labour seems to accept much of the new right understanding of the public service as tending to be risk-averse and self-interested. By continuing to promote plans to give pay incentives for individual success the government, like its predecessor, appears ready to challenge the traditional 'ethos' of the public sector (Richards 1997). The stress on 'best practice' arguably offers wider scope for innovation than the Conservatives' ideological promotion of market mechanisms. In other words, it is not necessarily assumed that the private sector will offer the most efficient solutions. However, the 'what works' philosophy is less original than it may appear. In fact, as is argued in Chapter 3 (see subheading 'Pragmatism and Empiricism'), policy-makers in Britain have traditionally been sceptical of abstract ideas or ideology in forming policy. There has been a long-standing distrust of theory and a preference for forming policies on the basis of empirical evidence as to what will work most effectively within the circumstances of the time. Pragmatism in policy-making is the norm.

However, critics suggest that the government's use of 'evidence' is highly selective. In other words evidence is quoted where it is convenient for government, overlooked where it is less useful. For example, while he was education secretary, David Blunkett condemned much research into education policy which he said was 'seemingly perverse' and unconnected to 'the reality of many people's lives' (2000: 1). Meanwhile, he pushed through a policy of performance-related pay for teachers with a distinct lack of empirical evidence that such a scheme was likely to work. Janet Lewis of the *Joseph Rowntree Foundation* expressed the fear that 'evidence-based' policy may be a pseudonym for 'what we want for our own political purposes' (*Guardian*, 15 Feb. 2000).

Choice and citizen-centred services

Echoing 'third way' philosophy, the modernizing government agenda has a stress on the notion of citizenship. It is argued that the needs of citizens should be at the heart of public sector change. Importantly, consideration of the demands of citizens should take priority over the interests of the public sector provider. Related to this, a strong theme of Labour's second term was the emphasis on 'choice' for consumers of services in areas such as education and health. More generally it is argued services should be organized to maximize benefit and convenience for those who use them. Citizens should also have a direct input into policy decision-making: their views and opinions must be taken into account. Steps taken towards 'citizen-centred' public services include 'one-stop shops' and consultation exercises (see Box 6.7).

BOX 6.7: *CITIZEN-CENTRED SERVICES*

- *Commitment to make all state schools 'specialist'*

Government has expanded the number of schools with a 'specialism' in areas such as technology, languages, arts, sport and science. In 2003 it announced its intention to make all state schools specialist and to increase parental choice over the type of education their children receive.

- *Creation of Foundation hospitals*

In 2004 the first tranch of Foundation hospitals was launched. The hospitals have relative freedom from central government control with their income related directly to the number of patients they manage to treat. Consumers have new rights to choose the hospital they are treated at.

- *Promotion of 'one-stop' shops and IT*

Linking to the theme of 'joined-up' government, efforts have been made to ensure that services are as convenient and accessible to their users as possible. For example, some local councils have sought to create 'one-stop' shops where citizens can access a range of services, rather than be forced to visit several different offices to obtain these. Some of these initiatives link to the government's 'social inclusion' agenda where, for instance, education and welfare services are made easier for those needing to access these by integrating them into one-stop shops. Additionally, the government has set out the highly ambitious goal of making all government services accessible online by 2005.

- *Large-scale public consultation exercises*

In 1999 the government established the 'people's panel', a group of 5,000 people brought together as a representative sample of the population according to characteristics such as age, gender, race, occupation and class. Several waves of research were conducted with the panel to assess people's views about public services on a range of issues. Views obtained were fed into the creation of government performance targets. For example, the panel was asked which services it wished longer and more convenient service hours for – the government then set targets for improvement in the top five service areas as voted on by the panel. Subsequently individual departments such as the home office and NHS began to make use of large-scale consultation exercises with sample groups from the general public. The people's panel was wound up in 2002 as the government argued consultation had become an integrated part of what individual departments do, removing the necessity for a general panel.

- *Pressure-group consultation*

The new Labour government has been much more willing than its Conservative predecessors to consult with pressure groups before decision-making. In addition, representatives of a range of interest groups and relevant organizations have been invited to serve on many of the cross-cutting task-force bodies mentioned above.

Citizens: served or subsumed?

For some, new Labour's promotion of 'choice' in areas such as education and health represents one of its most clear adoptions of the language and beliefs of the new right. In contrast, authors such as Giddens (1998) argue that a centre-left conception of choice is required to meet realities of a modern society which has become more individualized through economic and technological change (see also arguments of post-Marxist 'new times' authors Hall and Jacques 1989). However, a key element of the philosophy underlying specialist schools and foundation hospitals is that competition between service providers for customers will drive up standards. The policies themselves build upon the direction pursued by Conservative governments to promote diversity and internal markets in the public sector. It is too early to evaluate properly the impact of such measures, but critics argue there is every prospect that they will foster further inequalities in service provision. The fear of many, particularly on the left of the Labour party, is that schools and hospitals with a predominantly middle-class intake will benefit while those with a lower-class clientele will end up with fewer resources.

Government white papers such as *Modernizing Government* and *Modern Local Government* express enormous faith that public services can be made much more widely accessible through the use of information technology. Though a range of services has gone online in recent years there have been a great many problems in implementing new IT systems. A particular problem has been continuing tendencies to 'departmentalism' where different wings of government are unprepared for the kind of integrating demands involved in implementing IT systems (Organ 2003).

The concept of the 'citizen' was introduced into British government with the unveiling of the Citizens' Charter under John Major. In some ways new Labour's rhetoric on citizenship overlaps with the new right's belief in the danger of 'producer' interests dominating those of the public. However, arguably Labour's concept of citizenship is somewhat broader than that offered by John Major. Whereas the Citizens' Charter conceived of the citizen as being primarily a *customer*, new Labour's stress on partnership and collaboration provides an acknowledgement of individuals and groups as 'stakeholders' in public policy.

However, despite greater consultation with individuals the influence of 'citizens' in the policy process is still a very limited and mediated one. 'Consultation' does not necessarily imply influence and it is unclear to what extent the views obtained by government departments in consultation exercises actually impact on government priorities. Marsh *et al* (2001) report that Labour has grown increasingly immune to the influence of pressure groups during its time in office. Perhaps the most significant attempts to involve citizens in the process of government have been at a local level within the agenda for democratic renewal.

Local democratic renewal

Under Conservative administrations local government had been stripped of many of its powers and public interest and confidence in local authorities had dwindled. Drawing on 'third way' notions of democratic renewal, new Labour took the view that in order to gain the confidence and trust of local citizens local government had to become more open and responsive to their needs. Local elections were seen as just one way of being held accountable by the public – more attempts to keep in touch with local views between elections were required. Furthermore, local government should be made more readily accountable to local people through new forms of citizen involvement in public decision-making. In this way the aim was to shift power away from local service providers towards local service users. Initiatives include local consultation exercises and new political management structures (see Box 6.8).

BOX 6.8: *LOCAL DEMOCRATIC RENEWAL*

- *Local consultation*

As mentioned above, under best value local authorities are now required to consult with local businesses, voluntary and community groups. They must also consult the general local population for their views on local services. The views of local people are intended to feed directly into the targets and performance indicators which local authorities set. In recent years (and not just in response to best value) many local authorities have introduced new forms of local consultation, including 'citizens' panels', a sample of people taken to be representative of the local population. Other initiatives include the use of citizen 'juries' and focus groups which ask groups of local people to consider particular issues 'in-depth'. Views of particular sections of the population have also been sought and used in initiatives such as the *Better Government for Older People* initiative.

- *New political management structures*

The 2000 Local Government Act required all councils in England to change the way they were managed. All were to establish a clear separation between the executive and scrutiny functions of the council. They were given a choice of three models of political leadership to choose from: a directly elected mayor with a cabinet, a cabinet with a leader and a directly elected mayor with a council manager. The aims of these reforms were to clarify accountability within councils, revive public interest in local politics and promote dynamic leadership.

- *Citizen participation in special local initiatives*

Some of the special initiatives and partnership bodies tasked by the government to improve particular services or areas have sought the direct participation of local people whom the initiatives affect. As well as consultation exercises there have been elections to partnership boards.

Local democracy: renewed, or in further decline?

Moves to greater consultation have arguably done much to 'open up' the process of government at local level. Reforms introduced under new

Labour have accelerated the trend (which emerged in the mid-1990s) for councils to adopt new and diverse ways of consulting and engaging with the public. New and productive forms of partnership and collaboration have been forged and a range of new consultative and participative initiatives have been embraced (to varying degrees) by local councils (Lowndes, Pratchett and Stoker 2001). The initiatives are significant as in principle they offer citizens direct forms of democratic input into political processes. Such measures are innovative within a British political system that has traditionally relied virtually exclusively on representative forms of democracy, i.e. we elect people to consider and take decisions on our behalf.

However, difficulties have been encountered. Local groups and individuals have sometimes complained of 'consultation fatigue', that they are being asked for views on too many occasions to be practically useful or convenient. Furthermore some councils have been concerned that consultation exercises sometimes raise people's expectation of what can be delivered to unrealistic levels, particularly as councils are so heavily constrained by limited finances, resources and regulation by central government. At a more fundamental level, it is questionable just how far such consultation exercises have increased the influence of citizen opinion in the work of local councils. Research by the DETR and Audit Commission suggests that participation and consultation exercises have had only a limited impact upon the final decisions taken by councils.

The new political management structures have certainly not generated any significant revival in public interest in local government. There has been only very limited interest from either the public or councils themselves in moving to the government's preferred option of having a directly elected mayor. Most councils have adopted the cabinet and leader option as their new political management structure, the option which offers most continuity with previous council structures. Lowndes and Wilson (2003: 292) suggests recent changes may be little more than 'window dressing', while the overwhelming picture in local government is one of 'business as usual'.

More generally, there is a growing consensus that over time Labour's commitment to local democratic renewal has become the poor relation of its drive (outlined above) to improve performance and service delivery (Lowndes and Wilson 2003; Lowndes, Pratchett and Stoner 2001; Pratchett 2002). Such is the energy required by local authorities to both meet the performance targets set by central government and satisfy central government inspectorates that other dimensions of reform are being squeezed. Indeed, the recent implementation of Comprehensive Performance Assessments and the fostering of local Public Sector Agreements are arguably making local government ever more accountable to *central* government for their decisions, rather than local citizens or service users.

Possibly the most significant local democratic innovation is the use of participative mechanisms, including elections, within some of the government's special projects to revive local communities. Both the

Conservatives and new Labour have been sometimes criticized for their use of partnerships and special-purpose bodies to provide local services as these are usually unelected and not directly accountable to local people (unlike local authorities). However, the use of participative mechanisms potentially gives such projects a new democratic legitimacy as they directly involve those affected by the project. As such they represent a challenge to the political sovereignty of local councils, i.e. they establish rival (arguably in some ways superior) democratic institutions within local areas. Whether such exercises in direct democracy become a more widespread feature of the British political system remains to be seen.

EVALUATING THE MODERNIZING GOVERNMENT AGENDA AS A WHOLE

The above discussion of the different elements of the modernizing government agenda testifies to the influence of a variety of ideas on new Labour. The agenda has clearly been variously influenced by new right and third way thought. As indicated earlier, it would be a mistake to regard the modernizing government agenda as a fully coherent, consistent programme for change. Indeed, the above review reveals a range of tensions within the modernizing government agenda. These include:

'Top-down' versus 'bottom-up' approaches

Many of the reforms are driven by central government with a clear vision of the types of changes it wishes to see. Yet significant elements of the agenda aim to encourage local government, partnerships and networks to collaborate to generate 'bottom-up' solutions to problems.

Performance innovation versus local democratic renewal

As highlighted above, the government's predilection for target-setting and driving up standards in service delivery stand in tension with local democratic renewal initiatives aimed at empowering local citizens and service users.

Evidence-based policy versus centralized-prescription

The government's commitment to promoting 'best practice' and 'what works' stands in tension with its regular willingness to impose its own agenda for change whether supported by research evidence or not.

'Joined-up' government versus creation of multiple new government initiatives

A great deal of effort has been invested in attempting to 'join-up' an increasingly fragmented system of government. However, government has also created a vast range of new initiatives that in some ways arguably make coordinated government even harder to achieve.

These tensions appear likely to persist and pose a challenge for those studying the modernizing government agenda. In the face of such tensions, how are we to characterize the operation of contemporary British government? Where do the reforms to date leave us?

In Chapter 2, we outlined two important contemporary models of the British political system, namely the differentiated polity model and the asymmetric-power model. In this section we make use of these models, exploring to what extent they can accommodate the types of change associated with the modernizing government agenda. As discussed earlier, these models differ in which factors they emphasize as being the most fundamental features of British politics. For instance, the differentiated-polity model stresses intergovernmental relations, power-dependence and the segmented nature of the executive. In contrast, the asymmetric-power model stresses the British political tradition, asymmetries of power and the continued strength of the core executive. We now consider which set of features can best account for the changes introduced under the modernizing government agenda.

Governance and intergovernmental relations (differentiated-polity model) and the British political tradition and 'government knows best' (asymmetric-power model)

The differentiated-polity model is known for promoting the idea of 'governing without government'. In Rhodes's view (1997) it is self-organizing networks which shape policy rather than central government. All 'players' are viewed as dependent on one another for resources, therefore no particular group can dominate. Government is only one player among many. In contrast, the asymmetric-power model stresses that government is still very much committed to centralized and elitist forms of decision-making and believes that in the end 'government knows best'.

The emphasis on 'best practice', 'what works' and evidence-based policy has produced an enhanced role for policy experts, academics and practitioners to make a contribution to policy-making. The current enthusiasm for expert opinion may be taken as evidence of central government's recognition of their dependence on the cooperation and expertise of actors within particular policy fields and their associated networks. In a sense government is showing greater willingness to defer to other bodies during the policy-making process. However, as indicated above it is debatable how thoroughly the government is committed to evidence-based policy. In any case, as Walker points out, 'the short-term horizons of policy-making will always outpace those of research' (quoted in Sanderson 2002: 11). New Labour, like previous governments, is keen to promote 'trail-blazing' reforms of its own which rest on a belief in the capacity and duty of governing elites to initiate and implement ideas effectively.

The agenda for 'citizen-centred' government promises a greater say for ordinary people in decisions that govern them. In principle this does mark a departure from the 'government knows best' philosophy. Indeed, some of the practical measures introduced such as new consultation exercises, participation initiatives, citizens' panels and focus groups do introduce new instruments of democratic input into the British political system.

However, the initiatives are still limited in scope, operating primarily at the local level. As highlighted above, the scope for involving citizens in decision-making may actually be reduced by central government's increasing demands for performance improvement. Indeed, it is clear that as time goes by the democratic renewal is slipping down the government's agenda. In this sense, the values of the British political tradition may be regarded as reasserting themselves.

Power dependence (networks dominant) *v.* Asymmetrical patterns of power (government dominant)

At one level, initiatives such as area-based initiatives and the best value regime can be seen as further embedding the type of power dependent and exchange relations outlined in the differentiated-polity model. There is considerable evidence of greater 'partnership' working between different policy 'players'. Generally, local councils do appear willing to embrace a less central role in service provision and have an understanding of their dependence on other groups. In initiatives such as *Better Government For Older People* central government has been happy to encourage networking between different organizations and innovative relationships between different groups. However, central government has also played a crucial role in *shaping* the *types* of relationship that develop. For example, in the case of best value and the comprehensive performance assessment, while local partnership has been encouraged, central government has actually *increased* its powers of scrutiny and intervention in local affairs. The creation of new performance targets and forms of inspection are (in some respects at least) reducing the scope for local autonomy. Consequently, policy outcomes are more likely to be favourable to the goals of central government. It is also clear from experience of area-based initiatives and best value that different organizations (public, private or voluntary) still regard central government as a dominant 'player' to whom they look to provide key resources, guidance and often leadership (Clarence and Painter 1998). Therefore, there are clear 'asymmetries of power' in operation that largely favour the core executive.

A segmented executive *v.* A strong, segmented executive

Both the differentiated-polity model and asymmetric-power models emphasize the segmented nature of the executive. Indeed, it is clear that despite recent 'joining-up initiatives' segmentation remains a key characteristic of the British executive. However, the recent reforms do demonstrate the continuing strength of the executive to assert its authority across different branches of government. Furthermore restructuring of the cabinet, prime minister's and Treasury offices have had the effect of further centralizing decision-making in particular areas. The implementation of the Comprehensive Spending Review and associated Public Sector Agreements have compromised some of the traditional autonomy held by different departments. Nonetheless, the stress within both the differentiated-polity model and asymmetric-power models on the continuing strength of individual departments remains vindicated, with some reports of supposed 'joining-up' initiatives becoming dominated by individual departments (Taylor 2000). However, the new initiatives, perhaps particularly the area-based initiatives, are testament to the strength of the core executive to set the agenda and assert involvement in government policy at all levels.

On balance, it can be argued that the changes and policy trends associated with the modernization programme lend more support to the asymmetric-power model. The differentiated-polity model is indeed a useful perspective with which to examine the agenda, particularly with its emphasis on networks and partnership. However, the asymmetric-power model's stress on the strength of central government and asymmetries of power mean it can more easily accommodate the modernization process. Indeed, as we have seen, the modernizing government programme is in respects extending the power of the core executive and developing new mechanisms to enhance central influence.

Further still, one may suggest that under the modernizing government agenda a new defining 'feature' of the British polity is emerging, namely:

A Centralized, if segmented, regulatory state

There is nothing new about the idea of a regulatory state. Governments have always used types of regulation, monitoring and inspection. However, the Conservative governments between 1979 and 1997 greatly extended the types and forms of public audit and inspection (Hood *et al* 1999). This trend has been amplified with the creation of so many new audit and inspectorate bodies under the modernizing government agenda. However, the present government's reforms have arguably brought a qualitatively new dimension to the regulation of public bodies with the promotion of *enforced self-regulation* (Hood *et al* 2000). For example, before councils are externally reviewed under the best value regime they are compelled to conduct their *own* reviews of services. Councils are thus forced to self-regulate. The likelihood is that when they self-regulate they will try and anticipate what government inspectors will be looking for. Thus the expectations, values and demands of central government are likely to weigh heavily in the minds of local actors even in the process of 'self-regulation'. Faced with the threat of central government intervention where they deem services to be 'failing', the government hopes local councils will adjust and self-monitor their behaviour to meet goals defined by central government. Thus central government may be considered to be exercising new powers of control over other actors.

It should also be noted that the sheer number of different audit and inspection bodies now in place means that regulation is highly segmented. Despite recent efforts to 'join up' the different regulatory branches of government, the bodies still have significant autonomy to decide the targets and values they employ. This can further burden local authorities who have to satisfy many different auditors who may place different, even conflicting, demands upon them.

CONCLUSION

The modernizing government agenda builds upon changes in the British polity during the 1980s and 1990s. It does not reverse the reforms introduced by the Conservatives, indeed in many respects it extends them. However, the agenda is informed by a vision of public services which can be distinguished from that of the new right. Joined-up government marks an attempt to reassert coordination at the heart of central government as well as to foster networking between governmental and non-governmental organizations. There is no *automatic* assumption that the private sector is always the best provider of public services, though the government has been very keen to extend private sector involvement in service provision. The modernizing government programme seeks to drive up performance standards through target-setting and increasing regulation of service providers. The reforms open up more spaces for citizens, experts and interest groups to make their voice heard. However, how far such opinions impact on decision-making varies considerably and is often limited.

Clear tensions persist within the modernizing government agenda, particularly between initiatives promoting centralization and those facilitating decentralization. As matters stand, tendencies towards centralization appear to be increasingly strong with projects such as local democratic renewal becoming more marginalized. Local government experts speak increasingly of the 'new centralism' in local public service provision (Pratchett 2002). Public services have been subject to greater levels of regulation, scrutiny and inspection than during any previous period. Thus the British political system continues to be characterized by asymmetries of power and in many ways central government is developing further ways of extending its dominant role within the policy process. In such a context the idea of 'governing without government' appears at best dubious. Indeed it is striking that for all the apparent (and in some ways genuine) novelty of the modernizing government agenda, the assumptions informing change are largely compatible with the British political tradition. 'Modernized' government still believes it knows best!

CHAPTER 7

Constitutional Reform

'... the United Kingdom's constitution changed more between 1970 and 2000 and especially between 1997 and 2000 than at any comparable period since at least the middle of the 18th century.'

Anthony King (2001: 24)

INTRODUCTION

There is general agreement that the constitutional reforms introduced by new Labour represent the most clearly radical dimension of their agenda. In this area new Labour differs from not only its Conservative predecessors but also previous postwar governments. In fact, over the space of just a few years the British constitution has arguably undergone its most extensive shake-up for centuries. In this chapter we seek to evaluate both how significant these reforms are and what the likely consequences of recent change will be.

As discussed in Chapter 4, the British constitution has long been a curiosity to observers both at home and abroad. De Tocqueville (1832) famously argued 'the British Constitution has no existence'. This kind of argument has carried weight inasmuch as Britain has always lacked the kind of codified, written constitution found in many other democracies such as the United States. There is no single document which we can refer to as 'the British constitution'. Rather, the British constitution has evolved as a combination of common law, statute law and (crucially) convention. As such, the constitution is founded not on a rationalized set of rules (such as securing individual rights) but rather on the long-standing principle of parliamentary sovereignty. The Crown-in-Parliament is the supreme authority – Westminster has (theoretically at least) unconstrained power to make or unmake any law it wishes. Beyond this, constitutional rules in Britain have developed through particular conventions becoming established and then carried on by tradition. Consequently the constitution has remained relatively stable over many centuries – change has tended to be evolutionary and incremental, rather than revolutionary.

Furthermore, for most of the twentieth century the constitution was not generally an area of hot political debate. Both Labour and Conservative parties tended to see debates around constitutional change as at best a distraction from more weighty issues. Both parties battled to gain the right to exercise the untrammelled powers offered by the majoritarian Westminster system. Arguments for constitutional change tended to remain at the margins.

However, in the 1970s and 1980s a number of factors combined to put constitutional reform firmly on the political agenda. Factors include: the rise of Celtic nationalism; European integration; and the experience of 'Thatcherism'.

Rise of Celtic nationalism

In the 1970s the Scottish National Party began to garner unprecedented levels of support in Scotland, arguing that Scotland should become independent from England. Nationalist sentiment grew as many in Scotland became increasingly unhappy about the country's treatment within the existing Westminster political system. There was a sense that too many decisions affecting Scotland were being taken without sufficient regard to the views and interests of those living there. Similarly, in Wales support for the nationalist party Plaid Cymru grew as many in Wales became concerned that Welsh culture was under threat. In response to this the Labour government (1974–9) offered to create devolved government in Scotland and Wales, which would enable more decisions affecting Wales and Scotland to be made within those respective countries. However, the Labour party was divided over the issue of devolution, as was the electorate. A referendum among the Welsh produced a large majority against devolution. While a majority voted in favour of Scottish devolution voting numbers were insufficient for the change to be enacted. However, as is covered below, despite these defeats the devolution debate was to come back on the agenda in the 1980s.

After the onset of the 'troubles' in Northern Ireland in 1968 the British government struggled to find an answer to the political and religious sectarianism dividing communities and producing violence. In fact a range of constitutional changes such as proportional representation and power-sharing arrangements were experimented with in Northern Ireland. The effort to find a solution to the troubles meant governments were willing to consider the kinds of constitutional change which they ruled out in the rest of Britain, such as power-sharing arrangements and methods of proportional representation. However, campaigners for constitutional reform were subsequently able to use the Northern Ireland case to argue alternative systems were workable.

European integration

In 1975 Britain held its first national referendum on the issue of whether Britain should remain part of the EEC (which it had joined in 1973). This established a new precedent – for the first time the population at large had been asked to decide a specific issue. Moreover, entry to the EEC had important constitutional implications – powers were transferred upwards to Brussels and European law given priority over British law wherever these may conflict. The process of European integration was deepened in the 1980s with the Single European Act, a measure which introduced Qualified Majority Voting (QMV). QMV effectively 'pools' sovereignty between all members of the European Union on a range of issues. Consequently, the British government can now be forced to implement policies which it has opposed. The Maastricht Treaty (1992) extended the use of QMV and the powers of the EU over domestic policy. Perhaps the most significant constitutional implication of European integration is that it represents a challenge to the principle of parliamentary sovereignty. In effect there is now a 'higher' authority than Westminster – European law constrains what the British Parliament may decide.

'Thatcherism'

The Conservative governments of 1979–97 had no sympathy with the measures for constitutional reform being proposed by various pressure groups (see below). However, the Conservatives did take a range of steps which had constitutional implications. These included:

- *Stripping powers from local authorities* – 'caps' were placed on the amount of money local authorities could raise from local taxpayers. Control of many services and functions provided by councils were handed over to unelected special purpose bodies appointed by central government. In addition, the Labour-controlled *Greater London Council* (led by Ken Livingstone in the mid-1980s) and *Metropolitan County Councils* were abolished. Critics argued these measures demonstrated contempt for local democracy, placing ever more power in the hands of central government (see Chapter 3).
- *Radical reform of the civil service* (see Chapter 4).
- *Centralization of power* – reforms in areas such as education gave government ministers more powers to intervene directly in particular policy areas. For example, establishment of the National Curriculum in the late 1980s gave the secretary of state for education new powers to decide what subjects were taught within schools. The Conservatives were also willing to push through policies even when clearly unpopular. Despite the hostility of the Welsh and Scottish electorate to 'Thatcherism' they were willing to pursue such policies in the teeth of overwhelming opposition. For example, the poll tax was introduced a year earlier in Scotland than in the rest of the UK, leading to perceptions that the Scots were being used as 'guinea-pigs' for the policy.
- *Restriction of civil liberties* – a range of legislation on terrorism and law and order issues placed new restrictions on individual liberties, with the police gaining more power to detain and interrogate criminal suspects. For example, in the early 1990s outdoor 'rave' parties, newly popular among young people, were effectively made illegal by the Criminal Justice Act. The Act also compromised the traditional 'right

to silence' held by those accused of criminal acts. A detainee's silence could now be used *against* them in a court of law. Critics argued such measures amounted to an unjustifiable extension of the power of the state at the expense of the rights and liberty of the individual.

For many constitutional reform campaigners the Conservatives' period in office illuminated the dangers of the British constitution, enabling a government to push through unpopular policies which threatened democratic procedures and infringed individual rights. Certainly, campaigns for constitutional reform grew strongly during the period. In particular, devolution came back on to the political agenda as many people in Scotland and Wales grew tired of having policies foisted on them by a Conservative party which had gained very little electoral support in those respective countries.

ADVOCATES OF CHANGE

Having considered the context in which debates around constitutional reform emerged it is necessary to consider briefly which actors and groups have been involved in pressing for constitutional change in recent years. As we will see, changes since 1997 are not merely the achievement of the present new Labour government – a range of groups and organizations have been involved in the process (see also Foley 1999).

Pressure groups

When constitutional reform was still at the margins of political debate in Britain the flame for change was kept alive by pressure groups interested in pushing for particular types of constitutional reform. Groups such as *Liberty* and the *Electoral Reform Society* maintained low-level pressure on government to consider changes to the electoral system and enhancement of civil liberties respectively. However, the most influential pressure group in recent years has been *Charter 88*, which was formed to present a uniquely comprehensive case for across-the-board constitutional reform represented in a ten-point plan for change. Charter 88 played a crucial role in influencing the Labour party's debates on the constitution and during the 1990s links between the organizations grew.

Think-tanks

As mentioned in Chapter 5, Labour has had ties with a range of centre-left 'think-tanks' over a number of years. Such groups exist to generate and develop ideas for political change. Organizations such as *Demos*, the *Fabian Society* and the *IPPR* have had the ear of many influential centre-left politicians and policy-makers. One theme stressed by such think-tanks has been the need for *democratic renewal*, reform of the political system to try and re-engage a public who have become marginalized from or disinterested in politics. Such groups have produced numerous pamphlets and briefings on possible constitutional changes based on research of the likely practical benefits and difficulties likely to be encountered in implementing them. Such research has provided an important resource for those arguing for change.

Centre and centre-left media

Ideas for constitutional reform have also been promoted amongst centre and centre-left political opinion by sections of the media. Newspapers such as the *Guardian, Observer* and *Independent* have adopted editorial lines favouring constitutional reform and given space to those arguing for change to make their case. Moreover, some influential journalists have become well-known champions of constitutional change. For example, both Andrew Marr and Will Hutton have written book-length pieces on the need for Britain to alter its political system to adapt to the modern world. Will Hutton's *The State We're In* (1995) became a bestseller in which he argued that constitutional reform was an important part of his vision of a 'stakeholder' (see Chapter 6) society.

Opposition political parties

Traditionally, opposition parties have been more enthusiastic about constitutional reform than incumbent governments. However as debates around the constitution developed in the 1980s and 1990s the division between government and opposition over constitutional matters became a chasm. As outlined above, the rise of nationalist parties in Scotland and Wales added a new dimension to political debate in Britain, raising the prospect that at some future date the UK system may actually break up should the Celtic countries vote for independence. The Liberal party had been the longest-standing advocates of constitutional change, particularly PR, and the alliance (later merger) of the Liberals and the Social Democratic party in the 1980s became powerful advocates of constitutional reform. Though never quite succeeding in their aim of 'breaking the mould' of the two-party system in Britain, the alliance made a much stronger political force than the Liberals had been for most of the postwar period. They continued to make a robust case for constitutional reform and the overhaul of the British political system in a climate which was becoming ever more steadily warm for such ideas. In 1996 the Liberal Democrats and the Labour party agreed to unprecedented cooperation on the issue of constitutional reform forming a joint consultative committee aimed at reaching consensus between the parties on the need for a broad range of constitutional changes (Blackburn and Plant 1999: 468). Such links were bolstered by close personal relations between the respective party leaders, Tony Blair and Paddy Ashdown. Ashdown was apparently successful in persuading Blair of the need to seriously consider electoral reform (Rawnsley 2001: 204). In 1997 the Liberal Democrats had their most successful ever election in terms of seats won, thus establishing a significant group of opposition MPs lobbying for radical constitutional reform.

It was during the 18-year period of opposition that the Labour party became increasingly sympathetic to many of the various campaigns for constitutional change. The 'modernization' of the party's policies and values led by Neil Kinnock in the mid 1980s to early 1990s offered proponents of change a unique window of opportunity to influence the Labour party. Indeed, rarely has a political party been so open about the need to reconsider its whole programme and (ostensibly at least) to be open to new ideas. The Conservatives' use and arguably abuse of the powers available to them in the 1980s focused many minds on the idea that Britain required not only a change of government but changes in the political system itself. Though still regarded by many in the party as something of a side show from 'bread-and-butter' issues such as education and health, by the time of the 1992 general election the Labour party had become an advocate of a range of radical constitutional changes. Despite the crushing blow of defeat in 1992 the party's commitment to reform was if anything bolstered by the election of John Smith who raised the profile of proposed constitutional changes such as devolution which he declared 'unfinished business'. Subsequently, Tony Blair kept the momentum for constitutional reform going:

> We can continue with the over-centralised, secretive and discredited system of government that we have at present. Or we can change and trust the people to take more control over their own lives. (Tony Blair, June 1996)

For many, Labour's commitment to constitutional reform represented the most radical part of its programme. The Conservatives sought to portray such proposals as 'constitutional vandalism' and issued dire warnings about the possible end of British politics should Labour be elected. Though constitutional reform was not a central campaign theme for new Labour in England, the party remained committed to change and won the 1997 election on a manifesto which included radical pledges on reforming the constitution.

CONSTITUTIONAL REFORMS SINCE 1997

One of the key questions for political commentators following new Labour's win was: would the agenda for constitutional reform formed in opposition be implemented once in government? Sceptics were able to point to a long history of the Labour party (in particular) backtracking on constitutional reforms it had proposed in opposition. Moreover, a number of the changes advocated by new Labour in principle appeared to challenge the political culture associated with the British political tradition (see Chapter 3). Pledges on devolution and electoral reform posed a clear threat to the dominance of Westminster and the centralized unitary state. Meanwhile, commitments on freedom of information and human rights appeared likely to challenge the secretive and elitist character of the British state.

In this section we review the constitutional changes implemented under new Labour. We draw attention to the main features of change and the implications of such reforms. Furthermore, we seek to evaluate just how significant the changes have been and whether they constitute substantial change to the practices of British politics. In turn we consider: devolution; House of Lords reform; freedom of information; human rights; electoral reform; and abolition of the Lord Chancellorship.

Devolution

Scotland

As promised, new Labour offered people in Scotland the opportunity to vote in a referendum for the re-creation of a Scottish Parliament. It also asked voters whether the Parliament should have limited powers to adjust personal tax rates from the national rate. The electorate answered 'Yes' to both questions and in 1999 the first elections were held for the new Scottish Parliament (74 per cent in favour of the Parliament, 64 per cent on tax-raising powers). The Parliament can pass legislation on health, education, local government, transport and other issues. It may also increase or decrease personal rates of taxation by up to 3p in the pound. However, Westminster retains control over macro-economic policy, defence, social security and constitutional issues.

The Scotland Act transfers to the Scottish Parliament full powers over the domestic functions previously carried out by the Scottish Secretary of State and the Scottish Office. One of the most significant features of Scottish devolution is that it breaks with the principle of (Westminster) parliamentary sovereignty. The Scottish Parliament can pass primary legislation on a range of key areas without reference to Westminster. This creates the possibility that the Scottish Parliament may adopt different policies from those passed at Westminster. Indeed in the first few years there have been some notable cases. For example, the Scottish Parliament decided that Scottish students would not have to pay up-front tuition fees for their university degree courses. However, English students must now pay tuition fees according to legislation passed at Westminster.

Creation of the Scottish Parliament also has the effect of leaving Scottish MPs elected to the Westminster Parliament in an unusual position. They do not have involvement with what is passed in the Scottish Parliament yet can vote at Westminster on matters (e.g. education and local government) which affect only people living in non-Scottish parts of the country. This raises the 'West Lothian' question about whether it is fair for Scottish MPs to vote on matters which do not directly affect them or their constituents. The issue has begun to become, as many expected, an issue of controversy. In May 2003 Tony Blair appointed John Reid, a Scottish MP, as health secretary for England and Wales. The Conservatives and others heavily criticized the appointment as well as the fact that Labour's controversial plans for Foundation hospitals were only passed in the House of Commons by virtue of Scottish MPs voting for the measure. Though there are plans to reduce the number of Scottish MPs at Westminster the controversy over whether they should be allowed to vote on purely English matters looks likely to continue.

Wales

As highlighted above, there was less enthusiasm for Welsh devolution in comparison to Scotland. Nevertheless, new Labour legislated to create the promised Welsh Assembly following a 'Yes' vote carried by the tiniest of margins in a referendum of the Welsh electorate. The Assembly only has powers of secondary legislation (the rule-making necessary to implement Acts passed at Westminster). It also has a number of committees on issues such as transport, housing, environment and economic development.

The Assembly does not challenge the principle of Westminster sovereignty in the way that the Scottish Parliament does – it does not have the power to avoid or overturn legislation passed at Westminster. The legislation concerning the Assembly is much more prescriptive than that of the Scottish Parliament and constitutionally its status is similar in respects to that of a local council (Johnson 2001: 336). Its power very much depends on how much flexibility is contained within legislation passed by Parliament – the more flexible it is the more opportunity the Assembly has to decide how an act is implemented. This has led to political battles concerning just how prescribed primary legislation affecting Wales has been. For example, Assembly members recently appear to have won a concession from the government which will mean that under new education legislation the Assembly will have the power to prevent Welsh students from paying tuition fees.

Creation of the Assembly has created other tensions for new Labour in terms of party management. Against the wishes of most party members in Wales the Labour leadership promoted Alan Michael as party leader in Wales against the locally preferred candidate Rhodri Morgan. Effectively the London leadership was able to impose its candidate by gaining trade union block votes, despite a majority of Welsh Labour party members voting for Morgan. This caused great resentment in Wales leading in the end to the Welsh Assembly itself forcing Alan Michael to resign, to be replaced by Morgan. The incident demonstrated the difficulty of maintaining the top-down 'control-freak' party management approach in the context of devolution.

Northern Ireland

The Northern Ireland Assembly is similar to Scotland, and unlike Wales, in that it has powers to make primary legislation. It has full legislative control of agriculture, education, economic development, health, social security and environment. Westminster retains powers over police, security and criminal justice and the Assembly has no tax-raising powers. What is particularly unique about the executive in the Northern Irish Assembly is that it must be power-sharing, i.e. the minority parties will always have people on the executive. This is to ensure that neither Unionists nor Nationalists can dominate.

This system adopted is very unusual in that it dispenses with the idea of majority rule, the principle which guides almost all democratic systems (Johnson 2001: 338). It is designed to ensure that those actors across sectarian divides in Northern Ireland must work together to try and achieve effective government. The Assembly is only part of a wider 'peace process' which includes the release of political prisoners and cease fires from the major terrorist groups in Northern Ireland. Yet, it is wider issues, such as the decommissioning of terrorist weapons, which have proved the biggest obstacle to the success of the institution. The Assembly is currently suspended, with all powers being held by the secretary of state for Northern Ireland. It remains to be seen if compromise can be reached to enable re-establishment of the Assembly and whether (in particular) Unionist support for the Good Friday Agreement can be maintained.

Certainly, whilst in operation the Assembly did achieve cooperation between groups whom it would have been inconceivable to even have in the same room just a few years ago. Most strikingly, the executive included members of Sinn Fein. Previously the Thatcher governments had banned Sinn Fein from having its voices played on TV or radio owing to its alleged links to the IRA terrorist group. Owing to its particular political circumstances Northern Ireland is again the one area which Westminster elites appear thoroughly keen to devolve power to. Whether it can do is a matter which lies principally in the hands of the political groups in Northern Ireland itself.

English regions

Labour moved quickly to legislate to create a mayor and elected Assembly for London. The Assembly is designed with various purposes in mind including promotion of economic development and wealth creation, promoting social development and improving the environment in Greater London (Barnett 2002: 239). The mayor has duties to prepare and revise strategies relating to transport, the future development of London and environmental issues. The powers of the mayor are constrained – all strategies must be consistent with national policies and s/he must consult the Assembly and London borough councils. Overall, the powers of the Assembly are limited in comparison to the Greater London Council which existed before 1986.

While creation of a London mayor and Assembly does not represent a radical form of devolution, it has proved a political headache for its architects. To the horror of Tony Blair the left-wing former leader of the GLC, Ken Livingstone, emerged as the favoured candidate among Labour party members in London for party candidate for mayor. As in Wales, the party leadership gerrymandered the selection process to ensure its favoured candidate, Frank Dobson, was selected. However, Livingstone then chose to stand as an independent and won an easy electoral victory over Dobson. The headache has continued as Livingstone, fortified with independent electoral legitimacy, has opposed the government's unpopular plans to privatize the London Underground, even taking it to court in an unsuccessful attempt to overturn the policy. Once again, Labour paid the price of clinging to top-down 'control-freak' tendencies in preference to letting devolution run its natural course.

The Government has been reluctant to extend regional devolution, with ministers being divided on the issue. In May 2003 it was announced that referendums would be held in four areas concerning the creation of elected regional assemblies. This was done after a consultation exercise which sought to highlight areas where there may be a groundswell of opinion favouring a regional assembly. However, the powers on offer were limited.

Unlike in parts of Europe such as Catalonia there is no history of democratic regional government in England. Campaigners argue that a strong democratic voice at regional level would do much to challenge the centralized British state and might well produce more effective government (McQuail and Donnelly 1999: 264). It could also redress the imbalances being created by Scottish and Welsh devolution, allowing forms of English alongside Celtic forms of regional self-government. However, there is no great momentum for devolution in the English regions and little sign that the government as a whole has much belief in the idea. As we will see, this is just one area in which campaigners for extensive constitutional reform feel badly let down by new Labour.

House of Lords

The 1997 election manifesto committed new Labour to abolishing hereditary peers in the House of Commons. Previous Labour governments had failed to achieve this, coming up against trenchant opposition from the Lords themselves. However, new Labour found a way round critics in the Lords, reaching a deal whereby all but 92 of the hereditary peers would be abolished with the remainder elected by the peers themselves.

However, since this move, reform of the House of Lords has stalled. In 1995 Tony Blair had called for a 'proper directly elected chamber'; by 2001 this had been downgraded somewhat in a call for a 'democratic second chamber'. However, in 2003 Blair himself opposed options for reform which proposed that significant proportions of the Lords be democratically elected. In fact, the House of Commons voted on a choice of seven different models for the House of Lords. In the end all were rejected and further reform of the Lords now looks unlikely for the foreseeable future.

Nonetheless, abolition of the hereditary peers is itself a radical step which brings to an end a practice which had been in place for several centuries. It eradicates from the political system the idea that an individual is deemed worthy of sitting in Parliament merely by virtue of the family they were born into. In this sense it strikes at an important branch of elitist government in Britain.

However, it is also important to consider the net outcome of Lords reform to date. Labour's retreat from the idea of an elected second chamber leaves a House of Lords that will continue to be chosen, ultimately, by the prime minister. In a sense then reform to date actually *strengthens* the power of the executive within Parliament. The changes introduce no new 'checks and balances' into the system and, though the Lords have been willing to oppose the Blair government on numerous occasions, the institution does not yet have the new public legitimacy and independence which many constitutional reformers want. There are few clearer-cut examples of new Labour's perspective on democratic renewal regressing in government from the stance adopted while in opposition.

Freedom of information

Another area where the government has clearly backtracked is on the issue of freedom of information. Freedom of information was a priority issue for many constitutional reform campaigners. It is the belief of many campaign groups that strong freedom of information regulations are necessary to ensure that individual rights are protected. As Chapter 3 argues, governing elites in Britain have traditionally viewed secrecy as an essential part of efficient government. However, campaigners take the opposite view. They argue that information held by government is in effect held in trust on behalf of the general population. As such, the government can have no legitimate interest in keeping the information it gathers and uses private. The only exception would be in cases where release of information would clearly harm the public interest. It is argued that without freedom of information government is likely to become incompetent, partisan and corrupt. During the mid-1990s new Labour leaders became sympathetic to such arguments and Tony Blair spoke of the need to end the 'obsession with secrecy within government' (Tony Blair speech to Charter 88, 17 July 1996). Furthermore, the Labour party included plans for a Freedom of Information Act in its 1997 general election manifesto.

Campaigners were further delighted when the newly elected government published the white paper *Your Right to Know* which set out proposals for a Freedom of Information Act which guaranteed individuals access to all public information unless release would 'substantially harm' the public interest. However, the government subsequently stalled on the issue and the minister responsible for the white paper, David Clark, was sacked. Under Jack Straw's guidance in 2000 the government passed a Freedom of Information Act of a much weaker kind than that proposed in 1997. The government would only have to demonstrate that release of information would 'prejudice' public interest. Consequently the Act fell well short of the aims of campaigners, leaving the government plenty of scope with which to block release of public information. The transformation of Labour's perspective on the issue from opposition to government was dramatic. Such a retreat is surely testament to the enduring powers of ideas central to the British political tradition within governing circles. In the end, the Freedom of Information Act was a pale imitation of the radical new rules that most constitutional reform campaigners wanted.

Human Rights Act

Of much more significance was Parliament's passing of the Human Rights Act in 1998. The Act enshrined the *European Convention on Human Rights* into British Law. The Convention bestows individuals with a range of fundamental human rights including: right to life; prohibition of torture; prohibition of slavery; freedom of thought; freedom of expression; and freedom of assembly (Barnett 2002). The Human Rights Act prescribes that all Acts of Parliament must be passed in accordance with the Convention. Individuals can appeal to the courts where they believe their rights as laid down in the Convention are being breached. Significantly, the British judiciary is empowered to ensure that both government legislation, as well as the rulings and procedures implemented by public authorities, do not contravene the Act. Judges are thus able to challenge government decisions if they believe human rights may be being compromised.

Constitutionally the Act is very significant in a number of ways. It is important in establishing, for the first time, a coded set of individual rights for citizens in the UK. Though it is not the full Bill of Rights which some constitutional reform campaigners wish to see implemented, it is nonetheless historic in giving constitutional guarantees to individual citizens against the power of the state. The Act is also important in that it further 'Europeanizes' the British political system, giving British judges the powers to implement European Law. In so doing, it represents a challenge to the doctrine of parliamentary sovereignty. The Act gives priority to upholding the Convention over the traditional ability of Westminster to introduce whatever legislation it wishes. The implications of the Act began to be felt when in February 2003 a judge ruled that David Blunkett's attempt to restrict asylum-seekers' right to claim state benefits breached the Convention. Blunkett was furious as in his opinion a democratically elected government was being thwarted in pursuing its agenda by judges. However, many supporters of the Act saw it as demonstrating the benefits of the legislation, namely offering protection to vulnerable people against government misuse of power. Despite the radicalism of the Act, it does not do away with parliamentary sovereignty as judges may challenge but *not overturn* acts of legislation. In such circumstances government may have to push a 'remedial order' through Parliament to amend offending legislation.

Electoral reform

In opposition, some sections of the Labour party became sympathetic to the calls of many constitutional reform campaigners for a change to the first-past-the-post (FPTP) electoral system. Support grew for changing to some form of proportional representation (PR) as favoured in most other European countries. Despite this, many in the Labour party remained implacably opposed to PR. Perhaps as a consequence of this internal split the party entered the 1997 general election committed to holding to a referendum over whether to change the electoral system. Hopes of reformers were raised when Tony Blair appointed Lord Jenkins to head a committee to investigate which type of voting system might be preferable. Moreover, some Liberal Democrats, particularly their leader, Paddy Ashdown, were increasingly confident that Blair was moving in favour of their support for PR (Rawnsley 2001).

However, as it turned out the Labour leadership grew cold on electoral reform. The Jenkins Commission Report (1998) recommended a system combining FPTP and PR systems, but the report was shelved. As new Labour increasingly became accustomed to the benefits of governing with a 179-seat majority under FPTP, support for change within the party drained away considerably. The promised referendum never materialized and the commitment to holding one was dropped from the party's 2001 manifesto.

Despite new Labour's continued commitment to one-party majoritarian rule at Westminster it has in fact introduced PR systems for a range of public elections. Over the last six years PR has been introduced for European elections as well as the new devolved institutions in Wales, Scotland, Northern Ireland and London. This has had implications for both the type of governments formed and for the levels of representation of different parties. It has resulted in coalition governments in Scotland and Wales (always likely under PR as parties would need over 50 per cent of the vote to achieve a majority). Consequently political parties have been placed in the unusual position of having to cooperate with one another to ensure legislation is passed. This has led parties to seek to compromise and negotiate with one another to a far greater extent than typically occurs in the Westminster Parliament. An early example of such compromise occurred when new Labour in Scotland agreed to Liberal Democrat calls to scrap its plans for up-front tuition fees for students in Scotland. In return, the Liberal Democrats agreed to support Labour in a coalition government for the first term of the Scottish Parliament.

Another consequence of PR is that parties often receive more representation than they would receive under first-past-the-post. Nationalist parties in Wales and Scotland have achieved high enough representation to form the main opposition parties in Scotland and Wales. Under PR the Conservatives now have MPs in both these countries when they had failed to win a single Westminster seat in 1997. In addition, minority parties (such as the Greens and Scottish Socialist party) and independents have won seats in the Scottish Parliament as a consequence of PR.

At *present* there appears little chance that either new Labour or the Conservatives are likely to change the FPTP system for Westminster elections. By and large both remain seduced by the opportunity that such a system offers them to yield strong one-party majoritarian government within an adversarial system. However, the introduction of PR for many important elections is significant. If the devolved institutions are perceived to be operating effectively in the medium to long term within parts of Britain then campaigns for electoral reform at Westminster may be reinvigorated.

A striking feature of British politics over the last few years has been the use of referendums. Referendums have been used to establish the devolved institutions as well as, within certain local councils, to create new political structures (see previous chapter). Furthermore, the government is committed to holding a referendum on whether Britain should enter the Single European Currency should its 'economic tests' for entry be met. Arguably, a new convention is being established in which large-scale constitutional change is considered to need the direct consent of the people. Bogdanor (1997: 144) argues that referendums do two things other instruments do not. First they give every voter an equal say. This is in contrast to voting in electoral constituencies in which an individual vote, say for the Conservatives, has relatively little weight in a constituency with a large Labour majority. Secondly, referendums allow voters to decide without reference to party interests. Individuals can have a direct say on an issue rather than be limited to choosing who will take decisions on their behalf. Increased use of referendums could thus be interpreted as introducing a notion of *popular* sovereignty into a hitherto elitist system. However, in our view as yet the use of referendums do not represent a major qualification of the principle of parliamentary sovereignty. For one thing, referendums are still only held if the government of the day chooses to hold them. Secondly, to date one can convincingly argue that referendums have been held on issues where the governing party itself has been divided, or where it may suit it to give direct responsibility to the general public for a controversial decision. As long as referendums can be used in such a selective and convenient way for governing parties then their role as an instrument of popular sovereignty will always be a limited one.

Abolition of the Lord Chancellorship

In June 2003 the government initiated a far-reaching constitutional reform when it announced that the 1,400-year-old post of the Lord Chancellor was to be abolished. Bizarrely, the change was announced during a cabinet reshuffle, leading to the impression that the change was ill thought through. However, though presentation was botched, the proposed changes are very significant. The post of the Lord Chancellorship involves being Speaker of the House of Lords; occupying a place in the cabinet; and acting as head of the judiciary. It therefore involves mixing being a member of the legislature, executive *and* judiciary. As such it embodies exactly the type of blurring between different branches of government which so irritates campaigners for constitutional reform. The reforms involve the creation of a new post of Speaker of the House of Commons and replacement of the Lord Chancellor's department with a new department of constitutional affairs. Furthermore, the Law Lords are to be scrapped and replaced by a new Supreme Court to be appointed by an independent committee of judges. The most important effect of these changes is to establish new 'checks and balances' by separating the political and judicial dimensions of government. In particular, this will mean greater autonomy and independence for the judiciary to self-regulate. At the time of writing many of the details of change have still to be clarified, but in principle the change will reduce the possibility of an over-mighty executive to improperly put political pressure on the judiciary.

EVALUATING THE CONSTITUTIONAL REFORM PACKAGE

Having considered many of the different aspects of reform of the past six years it is necessary to consider the significance of the changes as a whole. In this section we seek to examine just how significant these reforms are – do they fundamentally alter the British political system, or are they merely adaptations of past practice? We first draw attention to general features of change to date, before going on to consider what the longer-term consequence of constitutional reform may be. In our view there are four major features of recent reform as a whole: piecemeal and pragmatic reform; 'irreversible' changes; qualification of parliamentary sovereignty; and lack of a clear 'destination'.

Piecemeal, pragmatic change

Though the constitutional reform package introduces important change to the British political system, the *process* by which such reform has been enacted is arguably very much in keeping with the traditions of British politics. Constitutional reform has been pursued in a piece-by-piece manner and the form of changes owe much to the balance of political forces at the time. In other words, the reforms are based less on any grand plan for constitutional reform (of the type laid out in Charter 88's ten-point plan) and more on pragmatic changes pursued with a 'case by case' approach. Even devolution, which preoccupied the government during its first two years, was more about addressing a range of distinct cases for change, rather than rolling out a theorized vision for a newly devolved British political system. Since 1998 changes have come in a more sporadic pattern and government has tended to justify changes on the perceived merits of individual reforms, rather than as part of a wider package.

'Irreversible' changes

However, if change has tended to be piecemeal in nature then this does not detract from the significance of the different 'pieces'. Indeed, while one must always be cautious about describing political change as 'irreversible', one can argue that many of the changes are unlikely to be reversed by future governments of the left or right. For example, it is inconceivable that any party will seek to reinstate the now abolished hereditary peers. Whilst in theory Westminster could scrap the devolved institutions in Wales and Scotland it is difficult to see this as practically possible without gaining the consent of the resident populations of those nations. Dunleavy, Margetts and Smith (2001: 414) found that support for further powers to devolved institutions is strong while there is little support for any recentralization. Similarly, unless Britain completely withdrew from the European Union, it is unlikely that changes associated with implementing European Law and the Human Rights Convention could be dispensed with. As such, Britain is now committed to several different constitutional 'paths' on which there is little possibility of turning back.

Qualification of parliamentary sovereignty

Perhaps the most outstanding cumulative effect of these changes is the way in which they practically qualify the long-standing principle of parliamentary sovereignty (Flinders 2002: 31). Westminster's ability to dominate the British political system has been challenged in quite unprecedented ways. The challenge is quite explicit in devolution to Scotland which clearly establishes a new centre of legislative and executive power in Edinburgh. The Human Rights Act clearly places new limits on executive and legislative power, providing protection of individual human rights against possible abuse by political authorities. Human Rights legislation, as well as current plans to create a Supreme Court, give judges new powers to act as a 'check' on executive power and hence also qualify parliamentary sovereignty. Increased use of referendums introduce an (albeit, limited) notion of popular sovereignty into the system and freedom of information legislation places at least a minor dent in the culture of secrecy in central government.

Cumulatively, such changes do mark substantial reform of the British political system, achieved in historically a very short space of time.

However, it may be a mistake to view such change as more than a *qualification* of parliamentary sovereignty. Apart from the Scottish (and potentially Northern Irish) cases, only quite limited, non-primary legislative powers have been devolved to the regions of Britain. For the vast majority of the UK, even including Wales, Westminster is still the key political centre of power. Though Human Rights legislation places a check on executive and legislative power, Westminster and Whitehall remain the key day-to-day decision-making bodies. The limitations of reform to the House of Lords, as well as freedom of information legislation, ensure that changes do not seriously challenge the power of the executive. Hence, despite the flurry of changes, the traditional notions of parliamentary sovereignty remain central to the functioning and practices of the British political system.

Lack of clear 'destination'

The piecemeal yet in many ways radical nature of recent constitutional change means it is not entirely clear what the longer-term consequences of these reforms may be. The issue is further complicated by the fact that constitutional reform is likely to be an ongoing process, fuelled by a range of tensions and competing visions of the constitutional future. For example, there now several different types of system in use (FPTP and various types of PR) each of which are underpinned by different theories of what constitutes 'fair' representation and what systems make for effective government. It is unclear what the consequences may be of introducing PR for a range of important elections – can different systems for different elections coexist or will logic dictate pressure for uniformity in the electoral process? There is a lack of agreement on what a fully reformed House of Lords would look like and uncertainty over how far devolution in England should go. Currently the future of constitutional reform is unclear and commentators are divided over what the long-term impact of recent changes will be.

Looking to the future

The discussion below briefly considers where the constitution may 'be going'.

Towards a codified constitution?

As we remarked earlier Britain's constitution has often been considered peculiar as it lacks a single written document which could be considered 'the British Constitution'. It has been a particular concern of campaigners that without an explicit constitution individual rights are always under threat. However, one can argue that recent constitutional reforms move Britain more towards the kind of codified constitution which is common elsewhere. Adoption of the Convention of Human Rights effectively 'codifies' a clearly laid out set of individual rights in British law. Scottish devolution legislation is significant not only in formally describing the powers of a Scottish Parliament but also laying out the powers of the Westminster Parliament. Hennessy argues that the British constitution is moving 'from the back of an envelope to the back of a code'. Similarly, Bogdanor contends that the system is moving gradually from one based on 'convention' to one based on 'code' via a halfway series of codes. What does appear to be emerging is a constitutional *awareness* – changes are compelling actors and institutions to reflect on their relative significance within British and European political systems. Indeed, the need to address anomalies and practical conflicts generated by processes such as devolution appears likely to provoke the development of more specific written guidelines and rules regarding the different roles and functions of government. The current debate over adoption of a codified European constitution is likely to place yet further pressure for constitutional clarity in Britain.

Toward incoherence?

However, commentators such as Anthony King (2001: 100) argue that recent changes make the British constitution *less* clear and actually more incoherent. He argues that prior to changes that have been enacted since the 1970s the British constitution was relatively coherent. It was not consciously designed according to a particular plan but was based around the clear principle of parliamentary sovereignty. However, changes over the last 30 years have brought in practices that sit uneasily with this principle, leading to a confusion over what constitutional principles are being embraced. He argues that the British constitution lacks both a 'plan and planner', whereas previously it at least had a coherent plan. Foley (1999: 286) warns of the increasing tensions between two 'constitutional cultures' in Britain. These are the cultures of traditional parliamentary sovereignty versus the newer culture of 'constitutional sovereignty' (ibid: 279). As in cases such as introducing PR (see above), reforms are injecting new types of practice and constitutional values into a general system for which such ideas are (both literally and metaphorically) foreign. The contradictions and imbalances in the current constitution have prompted some to question whether the British political system can even survive in the longer term.

The break-up of Britain?

In the 1997 general election the Conservatives warned that Labour's constitutional reforms would bring the end of the Britain as we know it. A range of political commentators made similarly apocalyptic predictions. In particular, some people were concerned that constitutional reform could lead to the break-up of Britain, with devolution being merely a stepping stone before Wales and Scotland claimed full independence from England. They predicted the emergence of tensions between different centres of power and, in particular, English resentment at the apparently favourable institutional and financial arrangements secured by the Scots. Other commentators foresaw radical change, but viewed possibilities more positively, arguing for the emergence of a new decentralized 'federal' political system. According to this vision power would be devolved not just to the Celtic regions but to powerful regional assemblies in England as well.

Six years on, neither of these visions has yet come to pass. There has thus far been no 'chain reaction' whereby regions of England flock to demand regional assemblies to match the institutions in Scotland and Wales, nor has new Labour demonstrated enthusiasm for such a task. Despite this there have been embryonic moves towards creating English regional assemblies and one cannot discount the possibility that in coming years a critical mass of grassroots support for devolution may grow in at least some English regions. Certainly, devolution has generated both demands for more powers in the Scottish and Welsh institutions as well as some concern in England about the continued ability of Scottish and Welsh MPs to influence purely English affairs. However, there is as yet little evidence that these nations are likely to move to seek independence – in fact support for the pro-independence Scottish National Party declined significantly in the 2003 Scottish general election. There are also limited signs so far of the backlash against devolution among the English general public which some commentators predicted. Whilst institutional tensions appear likely to persist they do not as yet appear likely by themselves to precipitate either the radical devolution some constitutional reform campaigners wish or the constitutional apocalypse that some Conservatives fear.

CONCLUSION

The British constitution has indeed undergone historic and important change over the last few years. In particular, Scottish devolution and the Human Rights Act constitute significant qualifications of traditional Westminster sovereignty. Furthermore, the Human Rights Act, abolition of the Lord Chancellorship, and the promised creation of a Supreme Court confer the judiciary with more autonomy and resources with which to scrutinize the actions of the executive. There have been meaningful steps toward 'codifying' Britain's constitution and most of the reforms implemented are likely to prove irreversible.

Nonetheless, it is clear that much of the original reforming zeal held by new Labour for constitutional reform has dissipated. Retreats on issues such as freedom of information, English devolution, electoral reform for Westminster and democratizing the House of Lords are all pertinent cases. They point to the enduring power of the British political tradition with its stress on centralized and elitist forms of decision-making and the view that (central) government knows best. Despite human rights legislation, the fragile status of civil liberties in Britain was underlined again recently in the wake of the 11 September 2001 tragedy in the USA. The government rushed in new rules empowering it to detain, arrest and interrogate people on the supposition that they may be connected to terrorism. New Labour has been just as willing as the Conservatives to exploit the opportunities afforded to it in the British constitution to infringe civil rights in the ostensible interests of national security or the 'war against crime'.

However, new Labour has enacted various key pledges on constitutional reform and despite the back tracking over particular issues some ministers still appear keen on pursuing further change. Consequently, there is much for those constitutional reform campaigners seeking more radical change to play for. For as the discussion above highlights, whether consciously or not new Labour's constitutional reform changes do inject new constitutional instruments and values into the British political system. Features of change such as Welsh devolution or the Freedom of Information Act may have disappointed reformers but they also offer a base and a platform from which cases for more radical change can rationally be constructed (Marinetto 2001:419). The British political tradition and the covering doctrine of parliamentary sovereignty still dominate, but they can no longer accommodate or explain all the features of the modern British constitution. The constitution has been 'politicized' over the last few years and is likely to remain so in the foreseeable future.

CONCLUSION

New Labour and the Study of British Politics

REFLECTIONS ON THE ROLE OF THEORY

In the introduction it was argued that theories of British politics offer students three potential benefits:

- Act as a starting point for study – a set of assumptions or ideas to guide analysis.
- Act as a simplifying device – abstract from a mass of detail to draw out points of fundamental importance.
- Assist in explanation – help us move beyond mere description of events, assist in accounting for why they happened in a particular way.

However, it was argued that there has been a general neglect of theory in the study of British politics. Philosophical and conceptual assumptions are often implicit rather than explicit. To reiterate, a key consequence of this pattern is to create a tendency towards empiricist and descriptive accounts of British politics rather than analytical or theoretical pieces. However, it was argued that, strictly speaking, scholars of politics couldn't fully avoid theory as all inevitably bring a set of assumptions to bear on the way they study British politics. This can be of benefit if authors can make these explicit, indicating how it informs and shapes their interpretations. Thus this volume has attempted to make its own theoretical sympathies clear, not just by declaring these in early chapters but by deploying concepts and ideas in later analyses of traditional and contemporary British politics.

In so doing a number of other influential perspectives were rejected. It was argued that the image of the Westminster model has loomed large over many decades, shaping the assumptions of scholars regarding the nature of the British political system. It was suggested that this model struggled to accommodate many of the changes in British politics in the postwar period and perpetuated an unrealistic conception of power as concentrated in the hands of ministers or prime ministers. However it was also suggested that alternative pluralist models overstated the extent to which power was diffused amongst different groups, failing to acknowledge the enduring strength of the executive to agenda-set and exert an (often) dominant role within policy networks. Similarly pluralism in its postmodern guise and the notion of the 'differentiated-polity' were questioned. It was argued that ideas such as 'governing without government', and 'the hollowed-out' state, risk obscuring the many ways in which the British state has further centralized decision-making and perpetuated asymmetries of power.

In contrast this volume has offered support to two perspectives, namely the

- Asymmetric-power model, and the
- British political tradition.

These perspectives have informed analysis of both the traditional dynamics of British politics as well as contemporary developments. Arguably such perspectives have advantages over other key models for two main reasons:

- Both give a prominent role to the importance of *ideas*, the way in which particular beliefs and value-systems shape political action.
- Both explicitly acknowledge that key institutional relationships are *structured* in ways which advantage certain groups over others.

Thus in contrast to many positivist, empiricist and pluralist accounts of British politics it is argued that we must 'take ideas seriously' (Hay 2002) and recognize that particular sets of ideas play a causal role in politics. In addition, in contrast to some mainstream perspectives it is argued that key relationships in politics are structured in ways that are crucial, yet may be unobservable. Thus in explaining politics we should examine how particular structural relationships and sets of ideas condition the activity of particular actors. Change in British politics results form the manner in which political actors react to these inherited circumstances.

Chapter 7 indicated that the 'asymmetric-power' model was an effective way to frame new Labour's modernization agenda. The remainder of this concluding chapter reflects on the continuing influence of the British political tradition under new Labour.

THE ENDURING ROLE OF THE BRITISH POLITICAL TRADITION

Past meets present

The early chapters of this volume expressed sympathy with perspectives that stressed the importance of the British political tradition. This concept informed subsequent analysis both of the traditional dynamics of British politics as well as contemporary developments. This conclusion reflects on how the British political tradition helps account for and explain political change and continuity under new Labour.

Core features

To recap, key features of the British political tradition include:

- A 'top-down' or leadership view of democracy.
- A liberal notion of representation – members of parliament are elected to exercise their own judgement, not necessarily to reflect opinions of their constituents.
- A conservative notion of responsibility – to act responsibly government must be prepared to take action that may be unpopular, or even opposed strongly by the electorate.
- Emphasis on secrecy – in order to be efficient much of the decision-making process should be conducted in secrecy.
- A belief that (central) government 'knows best'.

As Chapters 5, 6 and 7 indicated there have been numerous ideas and policies promoted under new Labour which represent a challenge to the British political tradition. The influential 'third way' discourse has championed ideas such as democratic renewal, devolution and decentralization (Giddens 1998, 2000). This rhetoric has informed citizenship initiatives in the public sector as well as some far-reaching constitutional changes. More generally, the promotion of concepts such as 'partnership' acknowledge that traditional hierarchical styles of decision-making are often ineffective in a polity with many governmental and non-governmental bodies. As we have seen, the core principle of *parliamentary sovereignty* has effectively been qualified by Scottish devolution and European integration. Practical power has indeed been ceded from Westminster in important ways. However the zeal for devolving power expressed by new Labour in opposition pre-1997 has increasingly dissipated whilst in office, leading to the watering down of commitments on reforming the House of Lords and securing freedom of information. In the area of local government, commitment to a 'new localism' always sounded a little hollow, linked as it was to a set of reforms many of which further centralize power. Over time then, the core ideas of the British political tradition have exerted a powerful influence over new Labour, in general winning out over the more radical strands of thought in the party. In other respects these ideas have been influential from the outset, informing Labour's belief in notions such as strong centralized leadership, and a 'government knows best' philosophy. It is clear that Tony Blair believed he had to be seen as at the 'heart' of government; driving change and projecting an image of strength has been key to Labour's strategy for re-election.

Reconstructing elitism

Thus considerable aspects of new Labour's strategy can be accounted for in terms of quite traditional ideas and practices of British government. However, the *means* which the new Labour government has deployed to sustain a centralized style of government have novel dimensions. A modern version of elite government has been fashioned with a number of innovations, including:

- The increased use of advisers and spin-doctors – ministers (not least the prime minister) have brought in a unprecedented number of 'special advisers' to the heart of government, individuals appointed through their own patronage.
- Extension of the prime minister's office, increased policy role of the Treasury and the effective end of cabinet government. Policy now predominantly agreed in 'bilateral' discussion between prime minister, ministers and (sometimes) selected others.
- Strategic deployments of governing discourse, careful attention to 'spinning' government policy. In particular, use of inclusive 'third way' rhetoric.
- 'Control freak' media management, new techniques to ensure new Labour politicians state 'on message'.
- Establishing a strong leadership grip on the Labour party's policy-making process.
- Creating new mechanisms of (central) control over public service performance through new audit and inspection bodies.
- Fostering forms of *enforced self-regulation* in the public service – rewards and punishments established to perform in ways prescribed by the centre.

Thus, in many ways new Labour has not so much challenged the traditional elitist style of government but rather *refashioned* it to take account of external and internal changes in the British state and civil society. Furthermore, it has taken advantage of new techniques to exert influence over lower levels of government. However, the enduring importance of the British political tradition can perhaps best be illustrated with reference to the issue that has dominated Labour's second term, namely the Iraq War.

Iraq War

A number of controversies relating to the war are indicative:

- There was massive public opposition to the war in 2003. Prior to the war opinion polls showed a narrow majority of the British public opposed war. Over a million people marched in London, by far the largest demonstration in British political history. However, Tony Blair resisted this unprecedented opposition, arguing that as prime minister it was his duty to protect British national interests even when unpopular. The British military was subsequently sent to war despite the views of a large section of the general public.
- Opposition to the war was even stronger within the ranks of Labour party members. Yet the membership had no means by which to compel or even influence the prime minister in taking the decision to go to war. Opposition was also strong within the parliamentary Labour party. Government whips worked hard to persuade a majority to toe the 'line' emphasizing that a vote against might bring down the government. Despite using all the mechanisms available to force its

will, 121 still voted against it. Yet, this enormous backbench rebellion was also insufficient to provoke a change of heart by the leadership.
- Many argued that going to war without a new UN resolution was a breach of international law. After much controversy the attorney general eventually advised cabinet that the war was, in his view, legal. Despite many demands the advice he gave regarding grounds for war has not been made public and constitutionally the government cannot be compelled to release them.
- The failure to find weapons of mass destruction in Iraq after the war led many to question both the intelligence used and, more importantly, the interpretation or 'spin' put on it by government. Government consistently resisted calls for an independent enquiry into the decisions leading to war. More limited enquiries were established, first (under Lord Hutton) to investigate the death of weapons inspector David Kelly who had become wrapped up in allegations that the government had 'sexed-up' intelligence reports. The second, conducted by Lord Butler, was into the generation of intelligence before the war. In both cases the government set the remit for the enquiries (in both setting far narrower terms than opponents of the war had wished) whilst also choosing who would chair the enquiries.

In Britain no independent enquiries into the war were conducted as they were in the USA. The Iraq issue illustrates the strength of the executive within the British political system and the relative lack of checks and balances. Yet, despite massive opposition to the war and concern over lack of accountability for it, the government's actions are fully consistent with the top-down leadership view of democracy found in the British political tradition. However, although there was nothing unconstitutional about the decision to go to war (at least nothing as yet proved) there have been significant political repercussions. Tony Blair's personal ratings plummeted following the war and new Labour suffered bad defeats in the local and European elections. The Iraq War threw key aspects of the British political system into sharp focus with many frustrated at the lack of means by which the government could be held accountable for its actions and reasons in taking the country to war. The fallout from the war and related controversies may continue to have repercussions in the coming years.

The role of traditional and modern ideas

In Chapter 3 it was suggested that along with belief in top-down 'strong government' there are other cross-cutting sets of ideas which might be considered elements of a wider British political tradition. These dominant ideas included notions of a liberal economy, pragmatism and empiricism, and British nationalism. It can be argued that these have remained important ideas under new Labour, again being appropriated and adapted according to new circumstances and the government's agenda:

- *A Liberal economy* – in some ways new Labour's economic policy may be understood as the final triumph of broadly classical Liberal economic ideas. Having been challenged by the emergence of Keynesian economics in the postwar period (yet remaining important) the Thatcher governments restored them with fervour. Labour continued to be influenced (at least to an extent) by Keynesian ideas during much of its 'modernization' in the 1980s, yet had abandoned these by the time it entered office in 1997. Third way ideas openly celebrate the goal of a flexible 'dynamic market economy' and new Labour has strengthened the power of the Treasury that has had a long-standing preference for 'sound money'. Notions of 'globalization' and the idea that there may be no realistic alternative to neo-Liberal economics have helped further embed macro-economic policies, to the extent that they are rarely challenged within the mainstream political arena.
- *Pragmatism and empiricism* – a clever aspect of the notion of the 'third way' is that it is presented as 'post-ideological', concerned with 'what works' rather than abstract theory. In this way the values and assumptions which shape the third way can sometimes be obscured by the idea that what new Labour offers is a common-sense response to the realities of the time. Yet, as discussed in Chapter 3, British governments have frequently attempted to promote their policies in pragmatic terms, appealing to a national psyche which is traditionally sceptical of abstract reasoning. New Labour has made use of notions of pragmatism and empiricism, e.g. in calls for 'evidence-based' policy. However these have sat somewhat uneasily alongside a notable zeal for promoting the use of the private sector in the public service provision, often with limited evidence of how successful it may be (e.g. in the case of Public Private Partnerships in the NHS). Like a number of previous governments, new Labour may be charged with making use of the rhetoric of pragmatism to mask its own ideological preferences.
- *British nationalism* – new Labour's stance towards the EU is more enthusiastic regarding further integration than under the Conservatives. However, this position is justified firmly in terms of British national self-interest rather than in terms of the possible virtues of a more federal Europe. It has adapted the long-standing belief that Britain should be a world player, counteracting the Euro-sceptics by arguing Britain must be 'leading Europe, not leaving Europe'. Yet in the second term the Iraq issue caused problems with European partners as Tony Blair made Britain's 'shoulder to shoulder' support of America after 11 September 2001. This led to an extraordinary reinvigoration of the 'special relationship' with new Labour risking a great deal of political capital by associating itself with the United States despite widespread opposition. As on previous occasions in the postwar era a British prime minister calculated that Britain could ensure influence in the world and over the USA by giving it unstinting

public support. Whether it achieved this, or once again made Britain an American poodle (Nelson Mandela famously remarked that Tony Blair was effectively the US foreign secretary) continues to be hotly debated. Unlike the US government, Tony Blair staked his whole case for Britain's support for military action on the basis that Iraq posed weapons of mass destruction that could threaten British interests.

However, despite the enduring influence of traditional ideas on new Labour, and its adaptations of them, a range of more modern ideas have also been important. As discussed in Chapter 5, new Labour has been variously influenced by the ideas of 'Thatcherism', communitarianism and the third way. These help account for some complex patterns of continuity and change in public policy.

One of the clearest differences between new Labour and its Thatcherite predecessors has been its willingness to address demands for constitutional change. While the Conservatives espoused a rhetoric of minimal government new Labour has actually established new tiers of devolved government which pose a direct challenge to the traditional Westminster model. The rhetoric of constitutional change, so long excluded from political debate, entered the mainstream as a by product of Labour's internal modernization and the impact of a range of pressure groups. Significant changes on devolution, human rights and even electoral reform have been implemented over a very short period of time. Whilst enthusiasm for constitutional reform has waned within the Labour leadership, the changes have released forces which could yet serve to provoke further change. These may prove the most far-reaching legacy of the new Labour government. However, much of the agenda for constitutional reform has been deradicalized, most evidently manifest in the new Freedom of Information Act. The rhetoric of devolution has chimed with much of the discourse invoked in the modernization of public services. Third way ideas regarding empowerment, community involvement and enhanced democracy have been common currency. However, in areas such as the reform of local government the reality has much more clearly fallen short of the rhetoric than in the case of constitutional reform. Changes such as best value and comprehensive performance review have been experienced much more as exercises in centralization rather than enhanced local autonomy. Over time, the focus has become stronger on improving service delivery and performance, driven by a new set of demanding audit and inspection regimes. In this sense new Labour has further accelerated the centralizing trends established by the Conservatives. The audit/inspection culture has become such an institutionalized feature of the public sector that it now merits recognition as a core feature of a British polity characterized by asymmetries of power. While there has been a shift from emphasis on market solutions (under the Conservatives) to the idea of networks and partnership (under new Labour) in practical terms new Labour has become a strong advocate of the benefits of private sector involvement in the public sector. Neo-Liberal themes are deployed alongside social democratic rhetoric, a mix that is also found in new Labour's reform of welfare. 'Tough' neo-Liberal influenced ideas such as 'work first' agenda build on directions charted by the Conservatives, while the social inclusion agenda introduces some genuinely new (and arguably social democratic) dimensions to welfare reform, steps which include some redistributive measures. However, as a whole, the 'mix' is weighted in favour of neo-liberalism with the emphasis on individual self-help, managerial and market-based solutions to rationalizing public services. The driving influence of neo-Liberal ideas is most clearly manifest in new Labour's macro-economic policy that is designed to keep financial markets on side and keep a grip on inflation. While provision has been made for significant increases in public spending in priority areas such as health and education, Labour has further embedded 'rules-based' economic strategies which seek to depoliticize macro-economic management.

Thus, despite clear lines of continuity between new Labour and its Thatcherite predecessors the above summary is testament to the continuing *conflict* of ideas within British politics. Thus despite the dominance of neo-liberalism, and the enduring power of the British political tradition, there is still an important contest of ideas in British politics. We cannot understand or explain the impact of new Labour simply with reference to these latter ideas. A complex mix of ideas is in play, and there is little sign that we are in a genuinely 'post-ideological' era.

EXPLAINING THE SURVIVAL OF THE BRITISH POLITICAL TRADITION

However, we may ask *why* the British political tradition survives under new Labour, particularly as elements of its discourse would justify breaking with it. A number of factors have contributed towards this paradox:

- While some of new Labour's discourse challenges a top-down view of democracy there are other ideological influences on new Labour which may help sustain it. As argued in Chapter 3, Fabian ideas regarding paternalistic government have historically been influential on Labour, as have instrumental views of the state, i.e. the state is viewed as an instrument government can use to enforce the changes it desires. There are differing and shifting strands of opinion on, for example, constitutional reform within the party. Despite the radical reform agenda, many have retained an 'old Labour' disinterest in or antagonism towards constitutional change.
- As argued in Chapter 1, the British political tradition should be thought of not just as a set of ideas about democracy, but also an embedded set of practices within government and the state. A top-down and secretive style of decision-making is in many ways written into the 'wiring' (Hennessy 1988) of British government, creating practical obstacles for any government wishing to reform it.

- The existing structure of government creates sets of vested interests, where particular groups may be reluctant to change for fear of losing influence, resources and/or political capital. For example, though many key public services are run locally, central government still tends to be held responsible by voters for poor services. Thus there is an incentive for central government to exploit its powers to keep a grip on local government services, in the knowledge that it is likely to get the credit or blame for service standards.
- Relatedly, the traditional model of 'strong, responsible government' has come to be considered 'the' model for successful government. The Conservative party's success in twentieth-century elections owed much to an ability to project an image of governing competence, i.e. to foster perceptions that it was handling the economy and affairs of state authoritatively and effectively. Having failed to ever govern successfully for two full parliamentary terms new Labour has looked to the Conservatives' strategies for maintaining power and learned from them.

The latter point may help explain some of the difficulties new Labour has had in defining its direction. Historically the Conservatives have preferred an elitist, top-down style of government which is somewhat insulated from public opinion. This chimes with the ideology of conservatism, the need for elite rule and a gradual and cautious approach to change. While there is a congruity between the structure of the British state and traditional conservatism, the terrain is much less hospitable for political forces aimed at democratization and empowerment. Thus there is a conflict for new Labour which may be regarded as torn between pursuing radical democratic reform on the one hand and trying to successfully 'play the game' of retaining power through projecting images of strong leadership and elite governing competence. At the moment, the latter tendency is the dominant one, but it begs the question of how far a Labour government can realize the reforming goals of many of its supporters without a bolder challenge to the existing structures and practices of government.

However, constitutional changes such as Scottish devolution and the Human Rights Act have already made a significant impact, releasing pressures and demands which may yet provoke further change. At a more minor level, new constitutional conventions are affecting political debate in some telling ways. For example, when the issue of adopting a new constitution for the EU emerged in 2004, the government firmly ruled out holding a referendum on the issue. However, under pressure from the opposition by the Conservatives and others Blair dramatically 'u-turned' on the issue – only, since June 2005, to 'u-turn' again! Eurosceptics were able to play on the fact that recent constitutional change (e.g. entry to the EC/EU and devolution) had been ratified by referendums, to lobby that the same logic should apply to an EU constitution. There is some reason to speculate that elements of the British political tradition could become dissolved by stealth as political groups and civil society argue for the logics of recent reform to become more widespread. Whether new Labour has re-styled an elitist form of government for the twenty-first century, or hastened its long-term erosion, will not become apparent for a number of years.

Bibliography

Addison, P. (1975) *The Road to 1945: British Politics and the Second World War*, London: Jonathan Cape.

Affairs, 1989.

Allender, P. (2001) 'What's New about New Labour?', *Politics*, 21 (1), 52–62.

Anderson, P. (1964) 'Origins of the Present Crisis', *New Left Review*, 23, 26–53.

Anderson, P. (2000) 'Renewals', *New Left Review*, 1, Jan.–Feb., 5–26.

Annesley, C. and Gamble, A. (2004) 'Economic and Welfare Policy' in Ludlam, S. and Smith, M. *Governing as New Labour: Policy and Politics under Blair*, Cambridge: Polity Press.

Annesly, C. (2003) 'Americanised and Europeanised: UK Social Policy since 1997', *British Journal of Politics and International Relations*, 5 (2), 143–65.

Bagehot, M. (2001) *The English Constitution* (1867), Oxford: Oxford University Press.

Baker, D. (2002) 'Britain and Europe: More Blood on the Euro Carpet', *Parliamentary Affairs*, 55 (2), 317–30.

Baker, D. and Seawright, D. (1996) *Britain: For and Against Europe*, Oxford: Oxford University Press.

Barnett, C. (1986) *Audit of War: The Illusion and Reality of Britain as a Great Nation*, London: Macmillan.

Barnett, H. (2002) *Britain Unwrapped: Government and Constitution Explained*, London: Penguin.

Bastow, and Martin, (2003) *Third Way Discourse*, Edinburgh: Edinburgh University Press.

Beer, S. (1965/1982) *Modern British Politics*, London: Faber & Faber.

Beetham, D. and Weir, S (1999) 'Auditing British Democracy', *Political Quarterly*, 70(2), 128–38.

Bevir, M. and O'Brien, D. (2001) 'New Labour and the Public Sector in Britain', *Public Administration Review*, 61, 53–4.

Bevir, M. (2001) 'Prisoners of Professionalism: On the Construction and Responsibility of Political Studies', *Public Administration*, 79 (2), 469–89.

Birch, A. H. (1964) *Representative and Responsible Government*, London: George Allen & Unwin.

Blackburn, R. and Plant, R. (1999) *Constitutional Reform: The Labour Government's Constitutional Reform Agenda*, London: Longman.

Blair, T. (1996) Speech to Charter 88, 14 May 1996.

Blair, T. (1999) 'Modernising Public Services', speech to the Charter Mark Awards, Central Hall, Westminster, 26 Jan. 1999.

Blunkett, D 'Influence or Irrelevance: Can Social Science Improve Government?', speech delivered to the Economic and Social Research Council, 2nd February 2000.

Bogdanor, V. (1997/1999) *Devolution in the United Kingdom*, Oxford: Oxford University Press.

Brivati, B. and Bale, T. (1998) *New Labour in Power*, London: Routledge.

Budge, I., Crewe, I., McKay D., and Newton, K. (1998) *The New British Politics*, Essex: Longman.

Buller, J. (1999) 'A Critical Appraisal of the Statecraft Interpretation', *Public Administration*, 77(4), 619–712.

Buller, J. (2000) *National Statecraft and European Integration*, London: Pinter.

Buller, J. (2004) 'Foreign and European Policy' in Ludlam, S. and Smith, M. *Governing as New Labour: Policy and Politics under Blair*, Cambridge: Polity Press.

Bulmer, S. and Birch, M. (1998) 'Organising for Europe: Whitehall, the British State and the European Union', *Public Administration*, 76, 601–28.

Bulpitt, J. (1983), *Territory and Power in the United Kingdom: An Interpretation*, Manchester: Manchester University Press.

Bulpitt, J. (1986) 'The Discipline of the New Democracy: Mrs Thatcher's Domestic Statecraft, *Political Studies*, 34, 19–39.

Burch, M. and Wood, B. (1997) 'From Provider to Enabler: The changing role of the state', in Robins, L. and Jones, J. (eds), *Half a Century of British Politics*, Manchester: Manchester University Press.

Burke, E. (2001) *Reflections on the Revolution in France* (1789), ed. J.C.D. Clark, Stanford, CA: Stanford University Press.

Burnham, P. (2001) 'New Labour and the Politics of Depoliticisation', *British Journal of Politics and International Relations*, 3(2), 127–9.

Butler, D. (2004) 'Electoral Reform', *Parliamentary Affairs*, 57 (3), 734–43.

Butler, D. and Kavanagh, D. (1992) *The British General Election of 1992*, London & Basingstoke: Macmillan.

Byrd, P. (ed.) (1988) *British Foreign Policy Under Thatcher*, Philip Allan.

Cabinet Office (2002) *Reforming Our Public Services: Principles into Practice*, London: Central Office of Information.

Callinicos, A. (2001) *Against the Third Way: An Anti-Capitalist Critique*, Cambridge: Polity Press.

Campbell, C. and Wilson, G. (1995) *The End of Whitehall: Death of a Paradigm?*, Oxford and Cambridge, MA: Blackwell.

Cawson, A. (1986) *Corporatism and Political Theory*, Oxford: Blackwell.

Cerny, P.G. (1990) *The Changing Architecture of Politics: Structure, Agency and the Future of the State*, London: Sage Publications.

Clarence, E. and Painter, C. (1998) 'Public Services Under New Labour: Collaborative Discourses and Local Networking', *Public Policy and Administration*, 13 (3) 8–22.

Clarke, M. and Stewart, J. (1988) *The Enabling Council*, Luton: Local Government Training Board.

Clarke, S. (1988), *Keynesianism, Monetarism and the Crisis of the State*, Cheltenham: Edward Elgar.

Clift, B. (2004) 'New Labour's Second Term and European Social Democracy' in Ludlam, S. and Smith, M. *Governing as New Labour: Policy and Politics under Blair*, Cambridge: Polity Press.

Cm. 1599 (1991) *The Citizens' Charter: Raising the Standard*, London: HMSO.

Cm. 4014 (1998) *Modern Local Government*, London: Stationery Office.

Cm. 4310 (1999) *Modernising Government*, London: Stationery Office.

Cm. 4506 (1970) *The Reorganisation of Central Government*, London: HMSO.

Cm. 5237 Department for Transport, Local Government and the Regions (2001) *Strong Local Leadership – Quality Public Services*, London: Stationery Office.

Cm. 5511 (2002) *Your Region, Your Choice: Revitalising the English Regions*, London: Stationery Office.

Cm. 6404, 6405 (1942) *Social Insurance and Allied Services* (Beveridge), London: HMSO.

Coates, D. & Lawler, P. (eds) (2000) *New Labour into Power* Manchester: Manchester University Press.

Coates, D. (1989) *The Crisis of Labour*, London: Philip Allan.

Coates, D. (2001) 'Capitalist Models and Social Democracy: The Case of New Labour', *British Journal of Politics and International Relations*, 3 (3), 284–347.

Coates, D. (1999) 'Placing New Labour', in B. Jones (ed.) *Political Issues in Britain Today*.

Coates, D. (2002), 'The New Political Economy of Postwar Britain', in C. Hay (ed.) *British Politics Today*.

Coates, D. and Lawler, P. (eds) (2000) *New Labour in Power*, Manchester: Manchester University Press.

Cook, R. (2003) *The Point of Departure*, London: Simon & Schuster.

Cowley, P. and Stuart, M. (2001) 'Parliament : A Few Headaches and a Dose of Modernisation', *Parliamentary Affairs*, 54(2), 238–56.

Coxall, B. and Robins, L. (1998) *Contemporary British Politics*, Basingstoke: Palgrave Macmillan.

Coxall, B., Robins, L. and Leach, R. (2003) *Contemporary British Politics*, Basingstoke: Macmillan.

Cronin, J. (1991) *The Politics of State Expansion*, London: Routledge.

Crosland, A. (1956) *The Future of Socialism*, London: Jonathan Cape.

Crossman, R. (1963) 'Introduction' to Walter Bagehot, *The English Constitution* (1867), London: Fontana.

Crossman, R. (1972) *Inside View: The Lectures on Prime Ministerial Government*, London: Jonathan Cape.

Crossman, R. (1977) *The Diaries of a Cabinet Minister*, London: Hamish Hamilton and Jonathan Cape.

Dahl, R. (1967) *Pluralist Democracy in the United States*, Chicago: Rand McNally.

Davies, J. (2000) 'The Hollowing-Out of Local Democracy and the "Fatal Conceit" of Governing Without Government', *British Journal of Politics and International Relations*, 2 (3), 414–28.

Dearlove, J. and Saunders, P. (2000) *Introduction to British Politics*, Cambridge: Polity Press.

Dearlove, J. and Saunders, P. (1991) *Introduction to British Politics* (2nd edn), Cambridge: Polity Press.

De Tocqueville, A. (1832) *Democracy in America*, Chicago: University of Chicago Press.

Dicey, A.V. (1995) *Introduction to the Study of the Law of the Constitution*, London: Macmillan.

Driver, S. and Martell, L. (1998) *New Labour: Politics after Thatcherism*, Cambridge: Polity Press.

Driver, S. and Martell, L. (2002) *Blair's Britain*, Cambridge: Polity Press.

Driver, S. and Martell, L. (2002) 'The New United Kingdom' in Driver, S. and Martell, L. *Blair's Britain*, Cambridge: Polity Press.

Dunleavy, P., Margetts, H. and Smith, T. (2001) 'Constitutional Reform, New Labour and Public Trust in Government', *Parliamentary Affairs*, 54 (3), 405–24.

Elcock, H. (1987) *Budgeting in Local Government: Managing the Margins*, London: Longman.

Etzioni, A. (1995) *The Spirit of Community*, London: Fontana.

Evans J. and Tonge, J. (2003) 'The Future of the Radical Centre in Northern Ireland After the Good Friday Agreement', *Political Studies*, 51 (1), 26–50.

Fairclough, N. (1999) *New Labour, New Language?* London: Routledge.

Fielding, S. (2003) *The Labour Party: Continuity and Change in the Making of New Labour*, Basingstoke: Palgrave Macmillan.

Finlayson, A. (1999) 'Third Way Theory', *Political Quarterly*, July, 271–79.

Finlayson, A. (2002) 'Elements of the Blairite Image of Leadership', *Parliamentary Affairs*, 55 (1), 586–99.

Flinders, M. (2002) 'Shifting the Balance: Parliament, the Executive and the British Constitution', *Political Studies*, 50 (1), 23–42.

Foley, M. (1999) *Politics of the British Constitution*, Manchester: Manchester University Press.

Foley, M. (2000) *The British Presidency*, Manchester, Manchester University Press.

Foley, M. (2002) *John Major, Tony Blair and a Conflict of Leadership*, Manchester: Manchester University Press.

Forman, F.N. (2002) *Constitutional Change in the UK*, Oxford: Open University Press.

Freeden, M. (1999) 'The Ideology of New Labour', *Political Quarterly*, 70, 42–51.

Friedman (1953) *The Methodology of Positive Economics*, Chicago: University of Chicago Press.

Gamble, A. (1990) 'Theories of British Politics', *Political Studies*, 38, 404–20.

Gamble, A. (1994) *The Free Economy and the Strong State*, Basingstoke: Macmillan.

Gamble, A. and Wright, T. (1999) 'Introduction: The New Social Democracy' in Gamble, A. and Wright, T. *The New Social Democracy*, *Political Quarterly*, London: Blackwell.

Gamble, A. (2004) *Between Europe and America: The Future of British Politics*, London: Palgrave Macmillan.

George, S. (1998) *An Awkward Partner: Britain in the European Community* (3rd edn), Oxford: Oxford University Press.

Giddens, A. (ed.) (2001) *The Global Third Way Debate*, Cambridge: Polity Press.

Giddens, A. (1998) *The Third Way*, Cambridge: Polity Press.

Giddens, A. (2000) *The Third Way and its Critics*, Cambridge: Polity Press.

Glyn, A. and Wood, S. (2001) 'Economic Policy under New Labour', *Political Quarterly*, 72 (1), 50–60.

Goodman, A. (2001) 'Income Inequality', *New Economy*, 8 (2), 92–7.

Gould, P. (1998) *The Unfinished Revolution?: How the Modernisers Saved the Labour Party*, London: Little Brown.

Grant, W. (2000) *Pressure Groups and British Politics*, London: Macmillan.

Grant, W. (2003) 'Economic Policy', in P. Dunleavy, *Developments in British Politics*, 7, 261–81.

Green, T.H. (1901) *Lectures on the Principles of Political Obligation*, London: Longmans, Green.

Greenleaf, W. H. (1983) *The British political tradition, Volume One: The Rise of Collectivism*, London: Methuen.

Greenleaf, W. H. (1983) *The British political tradition, Volume 2: The Ideological Heritage*, London: Methuen.

Greenleaf, W.H. (1987) *The British political tradition, Volume 3: A Much Governed Nation*, London: Methuen.

Hall, S. (1983) 'The Great Moving Right Show' in Hall, S. and Jacques, M. (eds) *The Politics of Thatcherism*, London: Lawrence & Wishart.

Hall, S. (1988) *The Hard Road to Renewal: Thatcherism and the Crisis of the Left*: London: Verso.

Hall, S. and Jacques, M. (eds) (1989) *New Times: The Changing Face of Politics in the 1990s*, London: Lawrence & Wishart.

Harling, P. (2001) *The Modern British State: A Historical Introduction*, Cambridge: Polity Press.

Hay, C. (1997) 'Blaijorism: Towards a One-Vision Polity', *Political Quarterly*, 68 (4), 372–9.

Hay, C. (1999) *The Political Economy of New Labour: Labouring Under False Pretences?* Manchester: Manchester University Press.

Hay, C. (1996a) *Re-Stating Social and Political Change*, Buckingham: Open University Press.

Haydon, C. and Boaz, A. (2000) *Making a Difference: Better Government for Older People Evaluation Report*, Warwick: Local Government Centre, University of Warwick.

Hayek, F. (1944) *The Road to Serfdom*, London: Routledge & Sons Ltd.

Hazell, R. and Sinclair, D. (1999) 'The Constitution 1997–98', *Parliamentary Affairs*, 52 (2), 161–78.

Hazell, R. (ed.) (1999) *Constitutional Futures: A History of the Next Ten Years*, Oxford: Oxford University Press.

Heath, A. *et al.* (2001), *The Rise of New Labour*, Oxford: Oxford University Press.

Heclo, H. and Wildavsky, A. (1981) *The Public Government of Private Money* (2nd edn), London: Macmillan.

Heffer, S. (1999) *Nor Shall My Sword: The Reinvention of England*, London: Orion.

Heffernan, R. (2001), *New Labour and Thatcherism*, Basingstoke: Palgrave Macmillan.

Heffernan, R. (2003) 'Prime Ministerial Predominance? Core Executive Politics in the UK', *British Journal of Politics and International Relations*, 15 (3), 347–72.

Hennessy, P. (2000) *The Prime Minister: The Office and its Holders since 1945* London: Viking Penguin.

Heywood, A. (1997) *Politics*, Basingstoke: Macmillan.

Hirst, P. and Thompson, G. (1996) *Globalisation in Question*, Cambridge: Polity Press.

Hitchens P. (1999) *The Abolition of Britain*, London: Quartet.

Hobhouse, L.T. (1922) *The Elements of Social Justice*, London: Allen and Unwin.

Holliday, I. & Peele, G. (eds) *Developments in British Politics*, 5, London: Macmillan.

Holliday, I. (2000), 'Is the British State Hollowing Out?', *Political Quarterly*, 71, (2), 167–76.

Hood, C. *et al* (2000) 'Regulation in Government', *Public Administration*, 78 (2), 283–304.

Hood, C., *et al* (1999) *Regulation Inside Government: Waste-Watchers, Quality Police and Sleaze-Busters*, Oxford: Oxford University Press.

Hood, C., James, O. and Scott, C. (2000) 'Regulation in Government: Has it Increased, is it Increasing, Should it be Diminished?', *Public Administration*, 78, (2), 283–304.

Hood, C., James, O., Jones, G., Scott, C. and Travers, T. (1998) 'Regulation Inside Government: Where the New Public Management Meets the Audit Explosion', *Public Money and Management*, 18 (2), 6–8.

Hooge, L. and Marks, G. (2001) *Multi Level Governance and European Integration,* Oxford: Rowman and Littlefield.

Hume, D. (1748) *Enquiries Concerning Human Understanding*, Oxford: Oxford University Press.

Hutton, W. (1995) *The State We're In*, London: Jonathan Cape.

Ingham, G. (1984) *Capitalism Divided*, London: Macmillan.

Irvine, D. (2004) 'The Human Rights Act', *Parliamentary Affairs*, 57 (3), 744–53.

James, O. (2004) 'The Core Executive's Use of Public Service Agreements as a Tool of Governance', *Public Administration*, 82 (2), 397–419.

Jessop, B. (2003) 'From Thatcherism to New Labour: Neo-Liberalism, Workfarism, and Labour Market Regulation' in H. Overbeek, (ed.) *The Political Economy of European Unemployment: European Integration and the Transnationalization of the Employment Question*, London: Routledge.

Jessop, B. *et al* (1989), *Thatcherism*, Cambridge: Polity Press.

Johnson, N. (1980) *In Search of the Constitution*, London: Methuen.

Johnson, N. (2004) *Reshaping the British Constitution*, Basingstoke: Palgrave Macmillan.

Johnson, R.W. (1985) *The Politics of Recession*, London Macmillan.

Jones, B. *et al* (2000) *Politics UK*, Harlow: Pearson.

Jones, G. W. (1969) 'The Prime Minister's Power' in A. King, (1969) *The British Prime Minister: A Reader*, London: Macmillan.

Judge, D. (1993), *The Parliamentary State*, London: Sage Publications.

Jupp, B. (2000) *Working Together: Creating a Better Environment for Cross-Sector Partnerships*, London: Demos.

Kavanagh, D. (1987) *Thatcherism and British Politics: The End of Consensus*, Oxford: Oxford University Press.

Kavanagh, D. (1990) *British Politics: Continuity and Change* (2nd edn), Oxford: Oxford University Press.

Kavanagh, D. (2000) *British Politics: Continuities and Change*, Oxford: Oxford University Press.

Kavanagh, D. and Seldon, A. (1994), *The Major Effect*, London: Macmillan.

Kay, A. (2003) 'Evaluating Devolution in Wales', *Political Studies*, 51 (1), 51–66.

Kerr, P. (2001) *Postwar British Politics: From Conflict to Consensus*, London: Routledge.

Keynes, J. M. (1936) *The General Theory of Employment, Interest and Money*, London: Macmillan.

Kickert, W. J. M. (1993) 'Autopoiesis and the Science of (Public) Administration: Essence, Sense and Nonsense, *Organisation Studies*, 14, 261–78.

King, A. (1975) 'Overload: Problems of Governing in the 1970s', *Political Studies*, 23 (3), 284–96.

King, A. (1985) 'Margaret Thatcher: the Style of a Prime Minister' in A. King, (ed.) *The British Prime Minister* (2nd edn), London: Macmillan.

King, A. (2001) *Does the United Kingdom Have a Constitution?* London: Sweet & Maxwell.

Kingdom, J. (2003) *Government and Politics in Britain*, Cambridge: Polity Press.

Kingdom, J. (1999) *Government and Politics in Britain: An Introduction*, Cambridge: Polity Press.

Kingdom, J. (2003) *Government and Politics in Britain: An Introduction*, 3rd Edition, Cambridge: Polity Press.

Larkin, P. (2001) 'New Labour in Perspective: A Comment on Rubenstein', *Politics*, 21 (1), 51–55.

Levitas, R. (1998) *The Inclusive Society?: Social Exclusion and New Labour* London: Macmillan.

Levitas, R. (2001), 'Against Work: A utopian incursion into social policy', *Critical Social Policy*, 21 (4), 449–65.

Lewis, M. and Hartley, J. (2000) 'Evolving forms of quality management in local government: lessons from the Best Value pilot programme', *Policy and Politics*, 29 (4), 477–96.

Leys, C. (1983) *Politics in Britain*, London: Heinemann Educational.

Ling, T. (2002) 'Delivering joined-up government in the UK: dimensions, issues and problems' *Public Administration*, 80 (4), 615–42.

Locke, J. (1690) *An essay concerning humane understanding : in four books*. London : Eliz. Holt, for Thomas Basset.

Lownders, V. and Wilson, D. (2003) 'Balancing revisability and robustness? A new institutionalist perspective on local government modernisation', *Public Administration*, 81(2), 275–98.

Lownders, V., Pratchett, L. and Stoker, G. (2001) 'Trends in public participation Parts 1 and 2: Local Government Perspectives/citizen perspectives', *Public Administration*, 79, (1/2) 205–22, 445–55.

Ludlam, S. and Smith, M. (2001), *New Labour in Government*, Basingstoke: Palgrave Macmillan.

Ludlam, S. and Smith, M. (2004) *Governing as New Labour: Policy and Politics under Blair*, Cambridge: Polity Press.

Luhmann (1982) *The Differentiation of Society*, New York: Columbia University Press.

McIntosh, J. P. (1962) *The British Cabinet*, London: Stevens.

McIntosh, J. P. (1974) *The Government and Politics of Britain*, London: Hutchinson.

McIntosh, J. P. (1977) *British Prime Ministers in the Twentieth Century*, London: Stevens.

McKenzie, R. (1955) *British Political Parties*, London: Heinemann.

McNair, B. (1995) *An Introduction to Political Communications*, London: Routledge.

McQuail, P. and Donnelly, K. (1999) 'English Regional Government' in R. Blackburn and R. Plant, *Constitutional Reform: The Labour Government's Constitutional Reform Agenda*, London: Longman.

Maer, L. (2004) 'The Constitution', *Parliamentary Affairs*, 57 (2), 237–52.

Mandelson, P. (2002) *The Blair Revolution Revisited*, London: Politico's Publishing.

Mandelson, P. and Liddle, R. (1996) *The Blair Revolution*, London: Faber & Faber.

Marinetto, M. (2001) 'The Settlement & Process of Devolution: Territorial Politics and Governance', *Political Studies*, 49 (2) 306–32.

Marquand, D. (1988) *The Unprincipled Society: New Demands and Old Politics*, London: Jonathan Cape.

Marr, A. (2000) *The Day that Britain Died*, London: Profile Books.

Marsh, D. (1980) *The British political tradition*, unpublished paper (mimeo).

Marsh, D. (1992) *The New Politics of British Trade Unionism*, Basingstoke: Macmillan.

Marsh, D., Richards, D. and Smith, M. (2003) 'Unequal Plurality: Towards an Asymmetric Power Model of British Politics', *Government and Opposition*, 38 (4), 306–32.

Marsh, D. (2002) 'Pluralism' in C. Hay, (ed.), *British Politics Today*, Cambridge: Polity Press.

Marsh, D. and Grant, W. (1977) 'Tripartism: reality or myth?' *Government and Opposition*, 12, 194–211.

Marsh, D. and Rhodes, R.A.W. (eds) (1992) *Implementing Thatcherite Policies: Audit of an Era*, Buckingham: Open University Press.

Marsh, D. and Smith, M. (2000) 'Understanding Policy Networks: Towards a Dialectical Approach', *Political Studies*, 48, (1), 4–21.

Marsh, D. and Tant, T. (1989) 'There is No Alternative: Mrs Thatcher and the British Political Tradition', *Essex Papers in Politics and Government*, 69.

Marsh, D. *et al* (1999), *Postwar British Politics in Perspective*, Cambridge: Polity Press.

Marsh, D. and Rhodes, R. (1992), *Policy Networks in British Government*, Clarendon.

Marsh, D. and Rhodes, R. A. W. (1992), *Implementing Thatcherism*, Oxford: Open University Press.

Marsh, D., Richards, D. and Smith, M. (2001), *Changing Patterns of Governance in the UK*, London: Macmillan.

Marshment, J. (2002) *Political Marketing and British Political Parties*, Manchester: Manchester University Press.

Martin, S. (2000) 'Implementing "Best Value": Local public services in transition', *Public Administration*, 78 (1) 209–27.

Marx, K. and Engels, F. (1848) *The Communist Manifesto*, London: Pelican.

Marx, K. (2004) *The Communist Manifesto* (1848), London: Penguin.

Middlemas, K. (1979) *Politics in Industrial Society*, London: André Deutsch.

Miliband, R. (1967) *The State in Capitalist Society*, London: Weidenfeld & Nicolson.

Miliband, R. (1970) *Parliamentary Socialism*, (2nd edn), London: Merlin.

Miliband, R. (1982) *Capitalist Democracy in Britain*, Oxford: Oxford University Press.

Mill, J.S. (1859) *Dissertations and Discussions: Political, Philosophical, and Historical*, London: John W. Parker & Son.

Minkin, L. (1992) *The Contentious Alliance: the Trade Unions and the Labour Party*, Edinburgh: Edinburgh University Press.

Mitchell, A. (1999) *Farewell My Lords* London: Politico's Publishing.

Mitchell, J. (2002) 'Towards a New Constitutional Settlement?' in C. Hay, (ed.), *British Politics Today*, Cambridge: Polity Press.

Mitchell, J. (2004) 'Devolution: Comparative Development and Policy Roles', *Parliamentary Affairs*, 57 (2), 329–46.

Murray, C. (1994) *Losing Ground: American Social Policy*, 1950–1980, New York: Basic Books.

Nairn, T. (2000) *After Britain*, Granta Books.

Nairn, T. (1976) 'The Twilight of the British State', *New Left Review*, 101/2, 3–61.

Newman, J. (2001) *Modernising Governance: New Labour, Policy and Society*, London: Sage Publications.

Norton, P (1984) *The British Polity*, London: Longman.

Norton, P. (2000) 'Barons in a Shrinking Kingdom: Senior Ministers in British Government' in R. Rhodes, (ed.) *Transforming British Government*, New York: St Martin's Press.

Norton, P. (2003) 'Review: The Presidentialization of British Politics', *Government and Opposition*, 34 (4), 274–78.

Nozick, R. (1974) *Anarchy, State and Utopia*, Oxford: Blackwell.

Oborne, P. (1999) *Alastair Campbell, New Labour and the Rise of the Media Class*, London: Aurum Press.

Office of Public Services Reform (2002) *Reforming Our Public Services: Principles into Practice,* London, OPSR.

O'Leary, B. (2002) 'The Belfast Agreement' in C. Hay, (ed.), *British Politics Today*, Cambridge: Polity Press.

Oliver, D. (1991), *Government in the UK: The Search for Accountability*, Buckingham: Open University Press.

Oliver, D. (2004) 'Constitutionalism of the Abolition of the Lord Chancellor', *Parliamentary Affairs*, 57 (3), 754–66.

Organ, J. (2003) 'The Co-ordination of E-government in Historical Context', *Public Policy and Administration Journal*, 18 (2), Summer.

Paxton, W. and Dixon, M. (2004) 'The State of the Nation, Audit of Injustice', *Institute of Public Policy Research*, London: IPPR.

Paxton, W. and Dixon, M. (2004) *The State of the Nation: An Audit of Injustice in the UK*, London: Institute for Public Policy Research (IPPR).

Pearce, N. (2004) 'Asset-Stripping' in *Prospect*, Sep., 00–0.

Peck, E. (2004) 'New Labour's Modernisation in the Public Sector', *Public Administration*, 82 (1), 83–108.

Performance and Innovation Unit (2000) *Leadership in Delivering Better Public Services*, London: Central Office of Information.

Performance and Innovation Unit (2000) *Reaching Out: The Role of Central Government at Regional and Local Level*, London: Central Office of Information.

Performance and Innovation Unit (2000) *Wiring It Up: Whitehall's Management of Cross-cutting Policies and Services*, London: Central Office of Information.

Platt, S. (1998) *Governing by Taskforce*, Catalyst paper 2, London: Catalysts.

Pollitt, C. (2003) 'Joined-up government: a survey', *Political Studies Review*, 1 (1), 34–49.

Poulantzas, N. (1973) *Political Power and Political Classes*, London: New Left Books.

Prabhakar, R. (2004) 'New Labour and the Reform of Public Services' in S. Ludlam and M. Smith, (2004) *Governing as New Labour: Policy and Politics under Blair*, Cambridge: Polity Press.

Pratchett, L. (2002) 'Local Government: From modernisation to consolidation', *Parliamentary Affairs*, 55 (2), pp. 331–46.

Randall, N. (2004) 'Three Faces of New Labour' in Ludlam, S. and Smith, M. *Governing as New Labour: Policy and Politics under Blair*, Cambridge: Polity Press.

Rawnsley, R. (2001) *Servants of the People*, London: Penguin.

Redwood, J. (1999) *The Death of Britain?* London: Macmillan.

Rentoul, J. (2001) *Tony Blair: Prime Minister*, London: Little Brown.

Rhodes, R. and Bevir, M. (2003) *Interpreting British Governance*, London: Routledge.

Rhodes, R.A.W. (1994) 'State-Building Without a Bureaucracy: The Case of the United Kingdom' in Budge, I. and McKay, D. (ed) *Developing Democracy*, London: Sage.

Rhodes, R.A.W. (1997) *Understanding Governance*, Buckingham: Open University Press.

Rhodes, R. (2002), 'The New Public Administration of the British State', in C. Hay, (ed.), *British Politics Today*, Cambridge: Polity Press.

Rhodes, R. *et al* (eds) (2003) *Traditions of Governance*, special edition of *Public Administration*, 83 (1).

Richards, D. (1997) *The Civil Service under the Conservatives 1979–1997*, Brighton: Sussex University Press.

Richards, D. & Smith, M. (2002) 'New Labour, the Constitution and Reforming the State', in Richards, D. and Smith, M. (2002) 'Governance and New Labour', in *Governance and Public Policy in the UK*.

Richards, D. and Smith, M. (2002) 'Interpreting Governance' in Richards, D. and Smith, M. *Governance and Public Policy in the UK*, Oxford: Oxford University Press.

Richardson, J.J. and Jordan, A.G. (1979) *Governing Under Pressure: The policy process in a post-parliamentary democracy*, Oxford: Robertson.

Rubenstein, D. (2000) 'A New Look at New Labour', *Politics*, 20 (3), 161–8.

Sanderson, I. (2001) 'Performance management, evaluation and learning in "modern" local government', *Public Administration*, 79 (2), 297–313.

Sanderson, I. (2002) 'Evaluation, Policy Learning and Evidence-Based Policy', *Public Administration*, 80 (1), 1–22.

Savage, S. & Robins, L. (2001) *Public Policy under Blair*, London: Macmillan.

Seldon, A. (2004) *Blair*, London: Free Press.

Seldon, A. (ed.), (2001) *The Blair Effect: The Blair Government 1997–2000*, London: Little Brown.

Seyd, P. (1998) 'Tony Blair and New Labour', in King, A. *et al New Labour Triumphs: Britain at the Polls 1997*, London: Chatham House.

Shaw, E. (1996) *The Labour Party Since 1945*, London: Blackwell.

Shaw, E. (2004) 'The Control Freaks? New Labour and the Party' in S. Ludlam, and M. Smith, *Governing as New Labour: Policy and Politics under Blair*, Cambridge: Polity Press.

Skidelsky, R. (ed.) (1988) *Thatcherism*, London: Blackwell.

Smith, A. (1776) *An inquiry into the nature and causes of the wealth of nations*. Dublin : Whitestone, Chamberlaine [*et al*].

Smith, M. (1999) *The Core Executive in Britain*, Basingstoke: Macmillan.

Smith, M. (1994) 'Understanding the "politics of catch up": the Modernization of the Labour Party', *Political Studies*, 42 (4), 708–15.

Smith, M. (2004) 'Conclusion: Defining New Labour' in S. Ludlam, and M. Smith, *Governing as New Labour: Policy and Politics under Blair*, Cambridge: Polity Press.

Smith, M. (2003) 'The Core Executive and the Modernisation of Central Government' in Dunleavy, P. *et al. Developments in British Politics*, 7, Basingstoke: Palgrave Macmillan.

Starmer, K. and Weir, S. (1997) 'Strong Government and Weak Liberties: An Overview of Political Freedom in the UK', *Political Quarterly*, 68(2), 135–42.

Stoker, G. (ed.) (2000) *The New Politics of British Local Governance*, London: Macmillan.

Stoker, G. (1988) *The Politics of Local Government*, London: Macmillan.

Sutherland, K. (ed.) (2000) *The Rape of the Constitution*, London: Thorverton.

Tant, A. P. (1993) *British Government: The Triumph of Elitism*, Dartmouth: Dartmouth Publishing.

Taylor, A. (2000) 'Hollowing out or filling in? Taskforces and the management of cross-cutting issues in British government', *British Journal of Politics and International Relations*, 2 (1), 46–71.

Taylor, G. R. (1997) *Labour's Renewal? The Policy Review and Beyond*, London: Macmillan.

Taylor, G. R. (1999) *The Impact of New Labour*, London: Macmillan.

Theakston, K. (1995) *The Civil Service Since 1945*, Oxford: Blackwell.

Tivey, L. (1988) *Interpretations of British Politics*, London: Harvester Wheatsheaf.

Toynbee, P. and Walker, D. (2005) *Better or Worse: Has Labour Delivered*, London: Bloomsbury.

Truman, D. (1951) *The Governmental Process*, New York: Knopf. under the Welsh Assembly', *Political Studies*, 49 (2), 306–22.

Verney, D. (1991) 'Westminster Model' in V. Bogdanor, (ed.) *Blackwell's Encyclopedia of Political Institutions*, Oxford: Blackwell.

Watkins, S. (2004) 'A Weightless Hegemony', *New Left Review*, 25 (1), 3–29.

Watson, M. (2002) 'Sand in the Wheels, or Oiling the Wheels of International Finance?' *British Journal of Politics and International Relations*, 4(2), 193–221.

Weiner, M. J. (1981) *English Culture and the Decline of the Industrial Spirit, 1850–1980*, Cambridge: Cambridge University Press.

Weir, S. and Beetham, D. (1999), *Political Power and Democratic Control in Britain*, London: Routledge.

Weller, P. (1985) *First Among Equals: Prime Ministers in Westminster Systems*, Winchester: Allen & Unwin.

White, S. (2001) *New Labour : The Progressive Future*, Basingstoke: Palgrave.

Wickham Jones, M. (1995a), 'Recasting Social Democracy: a comment on Hay and Smith', *Political Studies*, 43 (4), 698–702.

Wickham Jones, M. (1995b), Anticipating Social Democracy, Pre-empting Anticipations: Economic Policy-Making in the British Labour Party, 1987–1992', *Politics and Society*, 23 (4), 465–94.

Wickham Jones, M. (1996) *Economic Strategy and the Labour Party: Politics and Policy-Making 1970–1983*, Basingstoke: Macmillan.

Wickham Jones, M. (1997) 'Social Democracy and Structural Dependency: The British Case. A note on Hay', *Politics and Society*, 25 (2), 257–65.

Williams, N. (1999) 'Modernising Government : Policy Making Within Whitehall', *Political Quarterly*, 452–59.

Wilson, D. (2003) 'Unravelling Control Freakery: Redefining Centre-Local Relations', *British Journal of Politics and International Relations*, 5 (3) 317–46.

Wright, T. (2003) *British Politics: A Very Short Introduction*, Oxford: Oxford University Press.

Index